CONTESTED ECONOMIC INSTITUTIONS

This book helps explain two of the most intriguing and politically salient questions in comparative political economy: What are the institutional and macroeconomic policy conditions for full employment and why were these institutions and policies being transformed in some countries during the 1980s and 1990s? It argues that the answers can be found in the intersection of distributive politics, the organization of wage bargaining, and monetary policy-making. Contrary to conventional wisdom, the study shows that monetary economic policies have lasting effects on unemployment whenever wages are bargained above the firm level. Certain combinations of bargaining arrangements and monetary policies produce superior employment performance, but they also entail different distributional outcomes and allocations of political power. Based on this analysis, the book explains how changes in technology and growing capital market integration during the 1980s led to a realignment of partisan governments and cross-class coalitions of unions and employers in some countries. Where this realignment occurred it was associated with a shift in macroeconomic priorities away from full employment, a decentralization of wage bargaining, and rising inequality.

Torben Iversen is Associate Professor of Government and a Faculty Associate at the Center for European Studies at Harvard University. His research and teaching interests include comparative political economy, electoral politics, and applied formal theory. He is the co-editor of *Unions, Employers, and Central Banks: Macroeconomic Coordination and Institutional Change in Social Market Economies* (Cambridge University Press 1999), and his articles have appeared in the *American Journal of Political Science, British Journal of Political Science, Comparative Politics, Comparative Political Studies, International Organization, Oxford Review of Economic Policy, Public Choice, Quarterly Journal of Economics, World Politics*, and numerous edited volumes.

CAMBRIDGE STUDIES IN COMPARATIVE POLITICS

General Editor
PETER LANGE Duke University

Associate Editors
ROBERT H. BATES Harvard University
ELLEN COMISSO University of California, San Diego
PETER HALL Harvard University
JOEL MIGDAL University of Washington
HELEN MILNER Columbia University
RONALD ROGOWSKI University of California, Los Angeles
SIDNEY TARROW Cornell University

OTHER BOOKS IN THE SERIES

List continues on first page following index

CONTESTED ECONOMIC INSTITUTIONS

THE POLITICS OF MACROECONOMICS AND WAGE BARGAINING IN ADVANCED DEMOCRACIES

TORBEN IVERSEN
Department of Government, Harvard University

CAMBRIDGE
UNIVERSITY PRESS

PUBLISHED BY THE PRESS SYNDICATE OF THE UNIVERSITY OF CAMBRIDGE
The Pitt Building, Trumpington Street, Cambridge, United Kingdom

CAMBRIDGE UNIVERSITY PRESS
The Edinburgh Building, Cambridge CB2 2RU, UK   www.cup.cam.ac.uk
40 West 20th Street, New York, NY 10011-4211, USA www.cup.org
10 Stamford Road, Oakleigh, Melbourne 3166, Australia
Ruiz de Alarcón 13, 28014 Madrid, Spain

First published 1999

Printed in the United States of America

Typeface Garamond #3 10.5/12 pt.   *System* DeskTopPro$_{/UX}$® [BV]

*A catalog record for this book is available from
the British Library.*

Library of Congress Cataloging-in-Publication Data
Iversen, Torben.
    Contested economic institutions : the politics of macroeconomics
and wage bargaining in advanced democracies / Torben Iversen.
        p.   cm. – (Cambridge studies in comparative politics)
    Includes bibliographical references.
    ISBN 0-521-64226-4. – ISBN 0-521-64532-8 (pbk.)
    1. Collective bargaining.   2. Monetary policy.   3. Democracy.
4. Macroeconomics.   I. Title.   II. Series.
    HD6971.5.I93   1999
    331.89–dc21   98-53580
                                                        CIP

ISBN 0 521 64226 4 hardback
ISBN 0 521 64532 8 paperback

For Charla

CONTENTS

FIGURES AND TABLES

FIGURES

TABLES

ACKNOWLEDGMENTS

In the course of writing this book I have incurred many debts to both institutions and individuals. I would especially like to thank the Wissenschaftszentrum für Sozialforschung in Berlin and the Institute for Political Science at the University of Aarhus in Denmark for hosting me at various stages of my research. I am also grateful to the Social Science Research Council and the National Science Foundation for providing the financial support without which this project would not have been possible. Some of the ideas and data presented in this book have appeared as "Power, Flexibility and the Breakdown of Centralized Wage Bargaining. The Cases of Denmark and Sweden in Comparative Perspective," *Comparative Politics* 28 (1996), "Wage Bargaining, Central Bank Independence and the Real Effects of Money," *International Organization* 52 (1998), and "Wage Bargaining, Hard Money and Economic Performance: Theory and Evidence for Organized Market Economies," *British Journal of Political Science* 28 (1998).

Three of my teachers, friends, and now colleagues deserve special mention for their invaluable support, advice, and constructive criticism. I owe a particularly great intellectual debt to Peter Lange, whose graduate seminars and intellectual enthusiasm first got me interested in the topic, and who made sure I stuck with it. Always constructive, insightful, and generous with his time, Peter surely must be one of the finest critics, dissertation advisors, and book editors in the field of political science. David Soskice has also been a tremendous source of intellectual inspiration and has taught me much of what I know about economics. I have learned more from my "private lessons" with David than any official course I have ever taken. Finally, Herbert Kitschelt, while less directly involved in this project, has likewise been an invaluable source of inspiration. His exemplary scholarship has been an (unattainable) ideal for my own, and his encouragement and support at critical junctures have been important for the ultimate success of this project.

Two colleagues, Geoff Garrett and Jonas Pontusson, read the entire manuscript and gave me detailed and invaluable comments on every aspect. For many constructive comments on parts of this book, or on related papers, I would also like to thank Neal Beck, William Bernhard, Thomas Cusack, Robert Franzese, Jeffry Frieden, Andrew Glyn, Andrew Graham, Joseph Grieco, Peter Hall, Robert Hancké, Brian Loynd, Andrew Martin, Ronald Rogowski, Michael Shalev, Peter Swenson, Kathleen Thelen, Sigurt Vitols, Stewart Wood, and Anne Wren.

Last, but not least, I wish to express my indebtedness to Charla Rudisill, who made sure that the English is readable and the argument intelligible, and who put up with all the traveling while simultaneously holding a full-time job and attending to a family that multiplied by two during the writing of this book. The book is dedicated to her.

1

INTRODUCTION

How do macroeconomic policies and economic institutions jointly determine economic performance and distribution? This is a classic topic in comparative political economy, and one that preoccupies politicians at a time when high unemployment and rising inequality are tearing apart the social fabric of many societies. Yet it is a topic that has drifted into the background in the scholarly literature as a result of the rational expectations revolution in economics. According to the new orthodoxy, macroeconomic policies in general, and monetary policies in particular, have no long-term effects on the real economy. Consequently, the analysis of macroeconomic policies and institutions has been reduced to a focus on either their short-term effects (e.g., Alesina, Roubini, and Cohen 1997) or their consequences for nominal variables such as inflation (e.g., Cukierman 1992). This book instead argues that even under rational expectations, macroeconomic policies and institutions have long-term effects on unemployment and distribution of income. Hence, it seeks to reunite classic comparative political economy with modern macroeconomic theory.

There are weighty empirical and political reasons for undertaking such a project now. In most advanced industrialized countries the problems of unemployment and inequality are as pressing today as they were in the 1970s. Yet neither traditional comparative political economy nor new classical economics offers credible explanations for these problems, much less proposes credible solutions. For example, in a recent study by the OECD, the neo-corporatist idea that unemployment is determined by the organization of wage bargaining receives no empirical support (OECD 1997a). At the same time, the neoclassical notion that unemployment is caused by labor market rigidities can account for at most a small portion of the variance in employment performance (Nickell 1997). And while rational expectations macroeconomics offers a powerful critique of traditional Keynesian analyses, the theory has next to nothing to say about what governments can do to influence employment and income (Mankiw 1990).

This state of affairs is beginning to change. New classical economists are increasingly concerned with understanding the mechanisms by which macroeconomic policies and institutions affect, not only people's inflation expectations, but also their real behavior. In a new book on the topic by leading macroeconomists, for example, it is acknowledged that "contrary to what many modern macroeconomic models suggest, central bank actions often affect both inflation and measures of real economic activity, such as output, unemployment, and incomes [,] but the nature and magnitude of these effects are not yet understood" (Solow and Taylor 1998). Comparative political economists, with the help of new Keynesian economists, are likewise beginning to explore the consequences of incorporating insights from rational expectations economics into macroinstitutional models of economic performance (see Scharpf 1991; Layard, Nickell, and Jackman 1991; Iversen, Pontusson, and Soskice 1999). This book is written as a contribution to this emerging literature, and it offers a bridge between modern macroeconomic theory and traditional comparative political economy.

The main argument of the book can be briefly outlined as follows. Imagine that unions and employers bargain wages for a large segment of the labor force, with each bargaining area having some effect on aggregate prices. A central question is then whether bargainers will rationally let their behavior be affected by the aggregate price effects of their actions, assuming that they care only about real variables.[1] The answer depends on the extent to which the aggregate price effect will translate into lower demand in each particular bargaining area; or, to put it in the language of monetary economics, whether militancy can rationally be anticipated to reduce the (sectoral) real money supply. In turn, whether this is the case depends on the monetary rule adhered to by the government. If the rule is accommodating (i.e., the monetary authority seeks to avoid a reduction in real demand), the effect on the real money supply of higher wages and prices will be low, and there will consequently be little reason for the wage bargainers to endogenize the macroeconomic effects of their actions. By contrast, if the monetary rule is nonaccommodating (i.e., the monetary authority adheres to a low-inflation target), militancy will reduce the real money supply and bargainers will consequently have an incentive to exercise restraint. With some measure of centralization, a restrictive monetary rule can thus help to alleviate the collective action problem faced by independently bargaining unions and employer associations.

On the other hand, the capacity of unions to act in the collective interest increases with centralization. Hence, the need for a monetary deterrent declines as centralization increases. Indeed, at high levels of centralization restrictive monetary policies can interfere with the solution to another coordination problem, the reconciliation of competing claims within the union (con)federation. Union federations are coalitions of unions, and with centralization comes the need for compromise between increasingly diverse wage groups. Such compromise tends to compress wages (see Figure 1.1), and it produces nominal wage pressure when peak bargainers push up negotiated increases to safeguard against the inequalizing effects of decentralized wage "drift" (unauthorized increases at the local level). When this inflationary pressure runs up against a nonaccommodating monetary policy, the result will be unemployment. There may thus be a point of centralization where the beneficial deterrence effects of nonaccommodation are outweighed by the deleterious effects of its interaction with solidaristic wage policies. The upshot of the argument is that nonaccommodating monetary regimes produce inferior employment performance in highly centralized systems, but superior performance in intermediately centralized systems. Only in completely decentralized systems, where bargainers are too small to affect the macroeconomy, will monetary regimes have no lasting effects on real variables.

This relatively simple argument has remarkably rich implications, theoretically as well as empirically. From the perspective of macroeconomic theory, the most striking implication is that monetary rules and the equilibrium rate of unemployment are causally related, even if we assume complete information and rational expectations. This result collides head on with new classical macroeconomics, which holds that systematic monetary policies are irrelevant for real outcomes. Second, the model shows that the economic effects of bargaining structures are contingent on the macroeconomic regime. Contrary to the view in most of the neo-corporatist literature, there is thus no reason to expect any particular relationship between bargaining centralization and performance (such as the hump-shaped relationship proposed by Calmfors and Driffill 1988). Finally, the theory throws new light on the role of partisan politics for economic outcomes. In given institutional environments certain policies "work better," and governments of all stripes will consequently have an incentive to adopt such policies. But since institutions have different distributional consequences, partisan governments and organized interests diverge in their preferences over equilibria. Who governs therefore becomes important only when the conditions for institutional change are propitious, and part of this book explains how globalization, postindustrialization, and new technology have made such change more likely.

The interaction among monetary regimes, bargaining institutions, and economic performance can usefully be illustrated with some comparative data (see Table 1.1). The monetary regime is here measured as an average of an institutional variable, central bank independence, and a more policy-sensitive variable based on relative exchange rate movements.[2] The centralization variable is divided into three classes: a decentralized category where firm- and plant-level

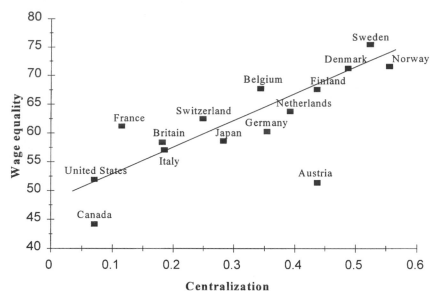

Notes: Wage equality is measured as the ratio of gross earnings (including all employer contributions for pensions, social security, etc.) of a worker at the bottom decile of the earnings distribution relative to the worker at the median (d1/d5 ratios). Figures are averages for the period 1977–93 computed from the *OECD Employment Outlook* (1991, 1996). The measure for bargaining centralization is explained in detail in the text and in Chapter 3.

Figure 1.1. *Centralization of wage bargaining and wage equality.*

bargaining dominate, an intermediately centralized category with most bargaining taking place at the industry or sectoral level, and a centralized category with an important role for peak-level bargaining between encompassing organizations of labor and capital. The monetary regime variable is simply dichotomized.[3]

The most interesting part of the table is the bottom row, which shows the difference in performance between cases with "accommodating" and "nonaccommodating" regimes. Note that for highly centralized systems, there appears to be an employment loss from having a restrictive regime, whereas for intermediately centralized systems the opposite holds true. For decentralized systems – where wage setters are atomistic and therefore not interacting strategically with the central bank – there are no apparent employment effects from the monetary regime. This pattern is contrary to the prediction in both new classical economics and in neo-corporatist theory, but it is consistent with the theory developed and tested in this book.

Table 1.1. *Centralization of Wage Bargaining, Monetary Regime, and Unemployment for 15 OECD Countries, 1973–93.*

		Centralization of Wage Bargaining			
		Low	Intermediate	High	*Low-High*
Monetary regime	Accommodating	8.0	6.9	3.8	4.2
	Non-accommodating	7.9	3.6	7.1	0.8
	Row differences	0.1	3.3	-3.3	N=75

Note: Data were grouped into five four-year intervals for a total of 75 observations. Unemployment refers to standardized rates; the measurement of the independent variables is described in the text. The figures have been corrected for period differences in unemployment.

Sources: For dependent variable: OECD (1992c, 1998); for independent variables: See text and Chapter 2 for details.

INSTITUTIONAL DESIGN

My argument about the economic *effects* of institutions also has consequences for understanding the institutions themselves. There is now a sizable theoretical debate about the role of distribution versus efficiency in institutional design (see Williamson 1985: ch. 9; Tsebelis 1990: ch. 4; Knight 1992), but most of the current literature follows a more or less explicit transaction-cost approach, conceptualizing institutions as efficient solutions to collective action problems or time-inconsistency problems. I do not challenge the idea that efficiency plays a part in institutional design, but since institutions have distributive effects, they are also chosen in part because they favor certain interests over others. This is nicely illustrated by the data presented above. Assuming that collective-action problems could be overcome, we would expect broad support behind one of the two institutional combinations in Table 1.1 that are associated with superior unemployment performance. Yet from Figure 1.1 we know that the distributive consequences of this choice vary. Hence, the choice is ultimately a political one and will therefore be contested by actors with conflicting interests and institutional preferences.

An objection to this argument is that if efficiency varies across institutional "equilibria," which seems likely, people can always devise some side-payment scheme that would leave everybody better off. This is the essence of Coase's Theorem. Efficiency, therefore, would ultimately drive institutional development. Yet such side-payment schemes necessarily entail complicated rules of distribution that must be specified in a comprehensive and enforceable ex ante contract. Transaction-cost economics, despite its claim to account for economic institutions in terms of efficiency, essentially rules out this possibility by demonstrating the insurmountable practical obstacles to such contracts (Williamson 1985). As a result, institutional choices can be understood only if we pay attention to the political struggles between organized, and conflicting, interests whose support is required for a particular institutional outcome ("veto players"). In short, the existence of multiple equilibria with different distributive consequences forces us to adopt a conception of institutional design that pays equal attention to economics and politics.

This does not mean that the existing institutional order is constantly under partisan attack. To break up a national system of collective bargaining, for example, risks jeopardizing a time-tested mechanism to control wages. Likewise, any government will think twice before adopting a new set of economic policies unless it is confident that it can persuade unions and employers to sponsor the necessary institutional mechanisms required to make the policies work. Failure can carry a very high price tag as, for example, the Danish social democrats learned when they lost control of the economy in the late 1970s. Once out of government, it took them over a decade to regain the confidence of voters and centrist parties to return to power. In Britain it took nearly two decades for the Labour Party to do the same after economic reforms had failed in the late 1970s. On the other side of the coin, Sweden in the 1960s and '70s illustrates how partisan politics for a long time can be hidden behind a rhetorical façade of cooperation and common cause – until it suddenly erupts with penned-up intensity, as happened when old political coalitions fell apart in the 1980s and early 1990s.

The idea of politically contested equilibrium institutions puts the analytical spotlight on forces that change the relative power of veto players. Although we cannot measure such power directly (any more than the players can), it is possible to identify the forces of change that are likely to shift the balance one way or the other, and then to link such changes to the timing and cross-national pattern of institutional change. In the following I provide a brief overview of some of the main changes in economic institutions and policies that are subject to this type of explanation in later chapters.

WAGE BARGAINING

Table 1.2 summarizes longitudinal data on the degree of centralization in wage bargaining across 15 OECD countries.[4] The data are averaged across two broad

Table 1.2. *Centralization of Wage Bargaining in 15 OECD Countries*

	Centralization[a]		
	1973-83	1984-93	Δ
Norway	0.52	0.53	0.01
Sweden	0.57	0.41	-0.17
Denmark	0.65	0.58	-0.06
Finland	0.44	0.40	-0.03
Austria	0.42	0.42	-0.00
Netherlands	0.38	0.36	-0.02
Germany	0.35	0.32	-0.03
Belgium	0.36	0.27	-0.09
Japan	0.23	0.29	0.06
Switzerland	0.25	0.25	-0.00
Italy	0.18	0.14	-0.04
Britain	0.21	0.12	-0.09
France	0.13	0.11	-0.02
Canada	0.07	0.07	0.00
United States	0.07	0.07	0.00
Mean	0.32	0.29	-0.03

[a] The index is explained in detail in the text and in Chapter 3.

subperiods: (i) the long recession from the first oil crisis in 1973 to the end of the second oil crisis in 1983, and (ii) the period of slow recovery, but also structural-institutional change, from 1984 to 1993.

Comparing the two periods, no clear patterns of change emerge, but there is some evidence of decentralization. This is quite evident in Denmark and Sweden, where the combination of a devolution of authority away from the peak level and the rise of rivaling union confederations to the dominant blue-collar LOs caused a gradual (and sometimes not so gradual) decentralization of the bargaining system in the 1980s.[5] Several other countries such as Belgium, the Netherlands, Germany, and Italy also experienced some decentralization as corporatist coordination at the national level came to an end in the 1980s. Moreover, while not fully captured by the data, multiemployer bargaining has been on the decline in the already decentralized systems of Britain, Canada, the United States, and France (Katz 1993; Purcell 1995; Howell 1992: ch.8).[6] On the other hand, Austria and Switzerland exhibit remarkable stability, and Japan has seen an increase in centralization with the merger in 1989 of the four largest union confederations. Norway also went through a period of (re)centralization in the late 1980s, although this is not evident in the period averages.[7]

While it is thus difficult to detect any uniform trend in centralization across countries, the data in Table 1.2 hide a lot of interesting cross-time variance that can help unlock the causes of change. Compare in particular the evolution of bargaining centralization in five Northern European countries: Austria, Denmark, Germany, Norway, and Sweden (Figure 1.2a–e). During the 1960s and 1970s, bargaining in the Scandinavian countries (panels a–c) was mainly conducted at the national level by a few dominant blue-collar associations, and the gradual downward trend in centralization is due to the growth in the membership of white-collar confederations, especially in the public sector. This trend is not replicated in Austria and Germany, where the same set of industrial unions have continued to dominate throughout the reference period.

The most striking divergence in the evolution of bargaining institutions across the four countries, however, is not the result of membership deconcentration, but rather the breakdown of peak-level bargaining in Denmark and Sweden in the 1980s. In Denmark, decentralized bargaining between individual unions and their employer counterparts was initiated in 1981, and the relatively centralized bargaining rounds in 1983 and 1985 appear to have been transitory events in a general trend toward a more decentralized equilibrium. In Sweden, the first break with over two decades of centralized bargaining came in 1983, and despite considerable oscillation between centralized and decentralized forms of bargaining since then, the data lend support to the dominant view that the 1980s and early 1990s marked a more radical shift away from centralized bargaining (see Pontusson and Swenson 1996; Elvander 1988).

The Norwegian case (panel b) contrasts to the other Scandinavian experiences. Although subject to the same deconcentration trend, and experiencing a similar decentralization of bargaining authority in the early 1980s (accompanied by considerable volatility), in the second half of the 1980s this trend was reversed, and the late 1980s saw some of the most centralized bargaining rounds in the history of Norwegian industrial relations. Austria likewise contrasts with Denmark and Sweden by the absence of decentralization. The evolution of Austrian institutions, however, differs from all the Scandinavian cases, including Norway, by exhibiting remarkable stability. Germany is likewise very stable if we discount the failed experimentation with a weak form of macrolevel coordination from 1967 to 1977.

Remarkably, the patterns of change observed in these five countries defy virtually all existing conceptual classifications and thus represent intriguing empirical puzzles. First, the data clearly do not fit the hypothesis, proposed by Crouch (1993), that corporatist arrangements collapse only in the countries where they have not been consolidated through a long history of organizational

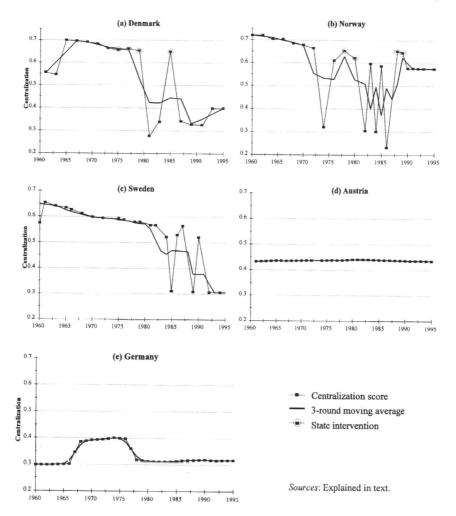

Figure 1.2. *Centralization of wage bargaining in five OECD countries.*

adaptation. With the partial exception of Austria (which is stable), corporatist institutions in all five countries have evolved over a long span of time and enjoyed widespread political support. But the data also do not fit the most comprehensive comparative study of the small corporatist states by Katzenstein (1985). For one thing, the patterns in Denmark and Sweden hardly support Katzenstein's main thesis that "more severe international constraints make the domestic politics of the small European states more cohesive" (1985: 198). Nor does the pattern of change conform to Katzenstein's typology of corporatist countries, which places Denmark, Norway, and Austria in the same subcategory (with Sweden being only marginally different). Likewise, Katzenstein's analysis shows that these countries (Sweden and Germany to a lesser extent) are similarly inserted into the world economy, thus making explanations of the type Gourevitch (1978) calls "second image reversed" unlikely to account for the considerable variation in institutional development. Although technological and economic changes in the world economy have important effects on domestic bargaining institutions, as discussed in later chapters, differences in the institutional consequences of these changes must be mediated by domestic structures and processes.[8] This brings us to the role of macroeconomic policies and institutions.

MACROECONOMIC REGIMES

A frequently used indicator for the "conservatism" of the monetary regime is the independence of the central bank, meaning the autonomy and capacity of central banks to pursue low-inflation targets. In standard models of monetary policy, democratically elected governments are shortsighted and inflation-prone, making delegation of policy-making power to an independent central bank a precondition for low inflation (see, for example, Cukierman 1992; Grilli, Masciandaro, and Tabellini 1991; and Alesina and Summers 1993). This book agrees that central bank independence is one useful measure of the character of the monetary regime, and I will make liberal use of it in later chapters. Yet central bank independence indexes are not very useful to gauge changes in policy regimes over relatively short periods of time, and they simply miss the fundamental changes that took place in many governments' economic policy priorities from the 1970s to the 1980s.

Table 1.3 provides some indicators for this shift, with countries listed in the same order as in Table 1.2. (i.e., by centralization). Note that in most countries real interest rates rose considerably during the 1980s while inflation was everywhere forced down. Inflation remained above average during the 1980s in Britain, Finland, Italy, Norway, and Sweden, but the cross-time trend toward a reduction is universal. Another indicator of monetary policy, which highlights relative changes between countries, is the movement of exchange rates. More than figures for interest rates and inflation, exchange-rate movements reflect policy expectations of currency markets, and therefore indirectly indicate the nature and credibility of monetary policy commitments. The hard currency index summarized in Table 1.3 varies between 0 and 1, with higher numbers implying a more rapidly appreciating currency.[9]

Note that the countries that have extreme scores on the centralization index – Britain, Canada, France, and Italy at the decentralized end, and Sweden, Norway, Denmark, and Finland at the centralized end – have low scores on the hard currency index, while those with high scores all are positioned in the

Table 1.3. *Monetary Policy Indicators for 15 OECD Countries*

	Real interest rates[a]			Inflation[b]			Hard currency index[c]		
	1973-83	1984-93	Δ	1973-83	1984-93	Δ	1973-83	1984-93	Δ
Norway	-0.3	6.1	6.4	9.5	5.1	-4.4	0.43	0.36	-0.07
Sweden	0.5	4.8	3.3	9.9	6.4	-3.5	0.30	0.28	-0.02
Denmark	4.7	6.6	1.9	10.4	3.7	-6.7	0.34	0.49	0.15
Finland	-1.1	5.9	6.4	11.8	4.7	-7.1	0.36	0.41	0.05
Austria	2.9	4.5	1.6	6.2	3.1	-3.1	0.54	0.50	-0.04
Netherlands	2.5	5.6	3.1	6.6	1.8	-4.8	0.54	0.54	0.00
Germany	3.3	4.8	1.5	5.0	2.5	-2.5	0.60	0.59	-0.01
Belgium	2.1	6.0	3.9	8.0	3.0	-5.0	0.42	0.51	0.09
Japan	-0.0	3.7	3.8	8.1	1.7	-6.4	0.66	0.80	0.14
Switzerland	0.2	1.8	1.6	4.7	3.2	-1.5	0.72	0.64	-0.08
Italy	-2.1	5.5	7.6	16.6	6.4	-10.2	0.05	0.29	0.24
Britain	-0.2	4.6	4.8	13.3	5.2	-8.1	0.30	0.28	-0.02
France	0.3	5.8	6.1	10.9	3.6	-7.3	0.30	0.47	0.14
Canada	1.3	6.1	7.4	9.3	4.0	-5.3	0.30	0.39	0.09
United States	1.3	4.8	3.5	8.2	3.8	-4.4	0.49	0.47	-0.02
Mean	1.0	5.1	4.1	9.2	3.9	-5.3	0.42	0.47	
Std.	1.7	1.2		3.1	1.4		0.17	0.14	

[a] Average yearly yield on long-term government bonds minus consumer price inflation (OECD 1992c, 1998).
[b] Average annual change in the consumer price index (OECD 1992c, 1998).
[c] Based on relative changes in nominal effective exchange rates (IMF, *Financial Statistics*).

intermediately centralized category, including Japan, Germany, Switzerland, and the Netherlands. This curvilinear pattern is perhaps more apparent in Figure 1.3, which shows the position of countries in terms of both bargaining centralization and the "conservatism" of the currency regime. Countries with either decentralized or highly centralized bargaining systems exhibit "soft" regimes (fields I and III), whereas countries with intermediately centralized bargaining systems constitute a hard currency block (field II). These clusters of countries are further distinguished by differences in the degree of wage inequality, with reduced levels of inequality as we move from field I to field III.

In terms of change over time, the most unstable cases are found at the extremes. Monetary policies have been tightened in countries with previously lax regimes (using the whole set of monetary regime indicators), with the result that there has been a partial convergence in policies (as seen in Table 1.3 by the decline in the standard deviations of the indicators). There is some agreement that this trend is at least partly due to the liberalization of capital markets.

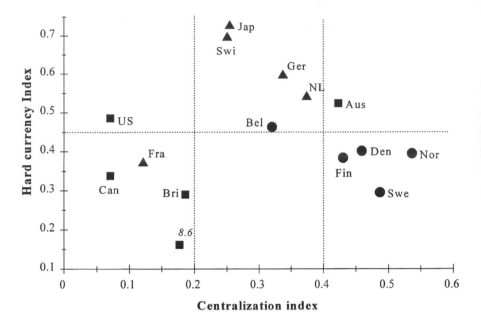

Key: ■ High wage inequality; ▲ medium inequality; ● low inequality.

Sources: See text for centralization indexes. Wage inequality refers to the ratio of gross earnings of a worker at the median in the earnings distribution relative to the worker in bottom decile (d5/d1 ratios) (OECD 1991).

Figure 1.3. *The position of 15 OECD countries on centralization of wage bargaining, hard currency regimes, and wage inequality.*

When exchange rates are fixed, high international financial capital mobility undermines monetary policy autonomy, and hence the ability to pursue expansionary monetary policies (Frieden 1991; Soskice 1999). In semifixed exchange rate systems of the sort currently adhered to by most OECD countries, high capital mobility makes the pursuit of independent and inflationary monetary policies costlier because markets assess an interest rate risk premium against "profligate" governments (see Scharpf 1991; Helleiner 1994; and Andrews 1994). Even governments that are little concerned with inflation are therefore forced to combine macroeconomic stimulation with an offsetting rise in interest rates.

    For most countries the impetus for this liberalization had a strong external or foreign component. As described by Scharpf (1991), Helleiner (1994), and Soskice (1999), once financial market liberalization got underway in important countries like the United Kingdom and the United States, and once the U. S. Federal Reserve embarked on a radically deflationary strategy, the German Bundesbank (given its self-imposed role as the guardian for the international value of the DM) was compelled to follow suit, and this pulled the rest of Europe down a deflationary monetary path. Even Garrett, one of the most skeptical commentators on the globalization literature, concedes that high capital mobility makes expansionary macroeconomic policies more costly (Garrett 1998a: ch. 4; see also Garrett and Lange 1991).

The rise in the costs of accommodating, full-employment policies helps to explain changes in highly centralized bargaining institutions because it shifted the relative political power in favor of those supporting decentralization. Thus the movement in Belgium and especially Denmark away from peak-level bargaining was accompanied by tightening of monetary policies and the adoption of hard currency regimes. In essence a move from field III to field II in Figure 1.3. Sweden also attempted (in 1991) to commit to a hard currency policy after peak-level bargaining had collapsed. But the realignment behind decentralization was clearly also facilitated by changes in technology and by postindustrialization. New technology placed a premium on greater wage flexibility, and the rise of services, which lagged manufacturing in productivity growth, exacerbated sectoral divisions, especially between the private and public sector. In all cases the shift away from centralized bargaining was associated with cutbacks in unemployment benefits, a rise in earnings inequality, and an increase in unemployment among the low-skilled.

These trends and patterns are not well accounted for within the existing literature. For example, neo-corporatist theory emphasizes the benefits of centralized bargaining and Keynesian accommodation and cannot explain why some countries have abandoned both. Likewise, Calmfors and Driffill's (1988) application of Olson's collective action logic cannot explain why the most stable cases are found in the intermediately centralized category, where the conditions for good economic performance are purportedly the worst. In a similar vein, new classical economics fails to explain why countries are not converging on a neoliberal model with decentralized labor markets and a restrictive macroeconomic regime. Finally, none of the emerging arguments about the interaction between bargaining institutions and monetary institutions are consistent with the curvilinear relation between centralization and monetary regimes. Lange and Garrett (1985) imply that nonaccommodation is beneficial only in decentralized systems, whereas intermediately centralized systems are bad for performance.[10] Hall and Franzese (1998) imply that nonaccommodation makes sense only in highly centralized systems, whereas Cukierman and Lippy (1998) argue that especially intermediately and highly centralized bargaining systems would benefit from accommodating regimes. Finally, standard monetary theory simply does not allow the possibility that monetary regimes and centralization are causally related (Bleaney 1996).

The argument in this book deviates from other explanations primarily by emphasizing the multiple-equilibria nature of institutional interaction and by underscoring the political nature of "choosing" between these equilibria. Thus, the comparative analysis will show how exogenous changes in technology, capital market integration, and deindustrialization affect the balance of power between governments and private agents, triggering political realignments that lead to the patterns of change observed in the five cases introduced above.

PLAN OF THE BOOK

The book is divided into two parts. Part I focuses on the economic effects of institutions and policies on outcomes, and Part II focuses on explaining the institutions and policies themselves. Both parts are subdivided into a (mostly) theoretical and a (mostly) empirical chapter. The main text of the theoretical chapters (Chapters 2 and 4) presents the arguments in nontechnical terms, while the accompanying appendixes formalize the arguments and spell out underlying assumptions and nonobvious steps in the logic. It is not necessary to read the technical appendixes to understand the arguments, but for the technically inclined it is possible to read *only* the appendixes (along with the chapter introductions). It is also possible to read either part of the book separately, although Part II cannot be fully appreciated without having read Part I.

Concerning the empirical analysis, Chapter 3 focuses exclusively on the quantitative evidence and is essentially an empirical study of the linkages between macroeconomic institutions and performance. Considerable energy goes into developing good time-sensitive measures of bargaining centralization and monetary regimes, but most of the chapter is devoted to a statistical analysis of economic performance in 15 OECD countries over a 21-year period. Chapter 5 uses a case-oriented method to explain change and stability in wage-bargaining institutions and macroeconomic policy regimes in the five countries discussed above: Austria, Denmark, Germany, Norway, and Sweden. Chapter 6 summarizes the findings and discusses their theoretical and political implications.

PART I

THE REAL
EFFECTS OF
MONETARY
POLICIES

AN INSTITUTIONAL MODEL OF ECONOMIC PERFORMANCE

Since the breakdown of the Keynesian–neoclassical synthesis in the 1970s, the study of the political economy of economic performance has branched into a number of competing approaches. At the most abstract level, the controversy centers around the effect of money and monetary policies on unemployment (Mankiw 1990). Although Keynesian economists have always maintained that money is important for real outcomes, new classical economists, assuming that people have rational expectations, insist that money and monetary policy are "neutral" in the sense that they cannot permanently affect real variables like income or unemployment. Recently, more and more economists are coming to the recognition that rational expectations are not inconsistent with monetary policies having lasting real effects. Still largely ignored by political scientists, this controversy is essential for understanding the political–institutional preconditions for full employment and low inflation.

The rational expectations revolution basically eliminated political economy models that were based on the existence of an exploitable Phillips curve trade-off (most notably Hibbs's 1977 partisan politics model), and analyses that implied real effects of monetary policies largely vanished from the literature. Instead, the study of the causes of unemployment and inflation turned to the role of unions and incomes policies. With the point of departure in Schmitter's revival of the concept of corporatism (1974), and gradually incorporating insights from game theory and especially the work of Olson (1965, 1982), this literature underscored the importance of collective wage bargaining and union–government relations for explaining inflation and unemployment performance (see, for example, Przeworski and Wallerstein 1982; Lange 1984; Cameron 1984; Crouch 1985; Calmfors and Driffill 1988; Alvarez, Garrett, and Lange 1991).

The neo-corporatist literature helped to pinpoint institutional and political mechanisms that could affect real outcomes such as unemployment. The inatten-tion to the rational expectations and central bank independence literature, however, still poses a problem. In particular, it seems inconceivable that large and powerful unions would *not* let their real-wage behavior be influenced by the anticipated effects of such behavior on monetary policies. And if expectations are not allowed to change with changes in monetary policies, then expectations are no longer rational, as explained by Lucas (1976). Yet the problem cuts both ways because if unions adapt their real-wage behavior in anticipation of mone-tary policy responses, such policies must have consequences not only for inflation but also for unemployment. This suggests that monetary policies may be im-portant for real outcomes after all.

Both schools of thought have sidestepped these issues by, simply put, taking everything for granted that is essential to the other. Neo-corporatism does not allow for the possibility that unions change their behavior when monetary policy expectations change, and the rational expectations economic literature ignores the role of unions on macroeconomic aggregates. The theoret-ical model presented in this chapter, by contrast, tries to bring the two litera-tures together and reaches conclusions that are unanticipated by both. Specifi-cally, it is argued that unemployment, inflation, and wage dispersion can, in large measure, be explained as a result of the interaction between wage-bargaining institutions and monetary policy regimes. The argument is formal-ized in Appendix A, which I use to support my main conclusions, as well as to hypothesize and simulate particular functional relationships. The interested reader should consult the formal model to ascertain that particular propositions follow logically from the stated premises (or to see what happens when assump-tions are altered). For the reader who is interested only the basic logic of the argument, however, it is not necessary to work through the formal model.

THE RATIONAL EXPECTATIONS REVOLUTION

Following the onset of the economic crisis in the 1970s, macroeconomic models came under attack for resting on assumptions that were incompatible with accepted notions of individual rationality. In particular, the idea that govern-ments faced a trade-off between inflation and unemployment, the so-called Phillips curve, was seriously challenged in a brilliant and highly influential article by Friedman (1968). In the article Friedman disputes the possibility of any long-run Phillips curve trade-off on grounds that unemployment below a market-clearing rate would bring real-wage expectations and actual wages after inflation out of equilibrium. At the market-clearing rate there is still unemploy-ment because some people will voluntarily search for better paid jobs. To get below this *natural rate of unemployment*, governments would have to raise money wages sufficiently above expected inflation to meet the real-wage expectations of workers searching for better jobs. But since the actual real wage that firms were willing to pay was below that required by some workers to take the jobs, money wages would have to rise faster than people's expectations about inflation so that employment did not fall. If people updated their inflation expectations, the implication would be accelerating inflation. The only way to arrest such accelerating inflation would be to increase unemployment to the natural rate. Hence, over the medium run expansionary policies would simply produce higher inflation.

This conclusion was a serious theoretical challenge to the prevailing Keynesian–neoclassical synthesis, which rested on the notion that governments could permanently trade off lower unemployment for higher inflation. Consequently, Friedman advised that a farsighted government should *refrain* from expansionary macroeconomic interventions that would only lead to rising inflation. However, as Nordhaus (1975) pointed out, if governments were opportunistic and shortsighted, they would try exploit the short-term trade-off before an election to maximize their chances for reelection. Friedman's model therefore implied a gloomy view of politics: At best, policies would have no lasting effects on the economy; at worst, they would create political business cycles with the associated increase in uncertainty and loss in social welfare.

The new classical economists took Friedman's critique of Keynesian theory one step further and denied the possibility for even short-term effects on the real economy. Sargent and Wallace (1975) and Lucas (1972, 1976) arrived at the most radical formulation by showing that even when people were updating their expectations retrospectively, as assumed by Friedman, they could still be "fooled" into making systematic errors by government policies designed to reduce unemployment. To build economic theory on the pervasiveness of such errors was as untenable as relying on the existence of a long-run Phillips curve. Consequently, people should be assumed to have *rational expectations* in the sense that they never make systematic errors when predicting the future. By implication, declared monetary policies (as opposed to random disturbances)[1] would prove ineffective *even in the short run* since prices and wages would instantly be adjusted to reflect a higher expected rate of inflation (Sargent and Wallace 1975).

This *policy neutrality thesis* stood in stark contrast to the Keynesian consensus of the 1960s and implied that the optimal policy plan for any government would be to commit to a zero-inflation policy. The problem was that if economic agents were convinced about such a plan, and expectations were adjusted accordingly, the government would have an incentive to inflate to reduce unemployment. Since price and wage setters would know this, the optimal policy plan would not be credible, and governments concerned with unemployment would inevitably produce socially inefficient levels of inflation (Barro and Gordon

1983). This problem of *time-inconsistent plans* came to play an important role in new classical macroeconomics and laid the foundation for the recent academic enthusiasm for independent central banks.[2]

Over time, new classical economists have retreated from the radical policy neutrality thesis and reaffirmed the possibility for short-term real effects. The reason has to do with various forms of uncertainty that people face in forecasting the effects of government policies. For example, it has been argued by Rogoff and Sibert (1988), Rogoff (1990), and Cukierman and Meltzer (1986) that governments will try to signal to voters their "competency" in producing public goods for a given fiscal revenue by engaging in expansionary preelection fiscal and monetary policies. Because voters do not know the true competency of the government, and because the inflation effects of policies are visible only with a lag, opportunistic governments are prone to engage in inflationary political business cycles. Compared to Nordhaus's political business cycle model, the mechanism creating these cycles is incomplete voter information rather than adaptive expectations, but the conclusions are similar.

Alesina (1987, 1989), Alesina and Roubini (1992), Alesina, Cohen, and Roubini (1992) have likewise argued that if ideologically committed governments pursue distinct monetary policies because their preferences over inflation and unemployment differ, and assuming that there is uncertainty about the outcomes of elections, people's inflation expectations must be some average between the expected inflation under governments with different policy commitments ("left" and "right"). If such expectations are temporarily "locked in" by, say, nominal wage contracts, the result is that left governments will expand output in the beginning of their terms, whereas right governments will create recessions in the beginning of *their* terms. Yet Alesina et al. are quick to add that "systematic [partisan] difference[s] in output and unemployment tends to be short-lived and concentrated primarily in a short period after a change of government" (Alesina et al. 1992: 3–4). At the end of the electoral term, the only difference will be higher inflation under left governments.[3] Monetary policy is thus neutral (has no real effects) except in the very short run, a conclusion that has been supported in a number of empirical studies (Alesina and Sachs 1988; Alesina 1989; Alesina et al. 1992; Alesina and Summers 1993; Cukierman 1992).

Whether we use Friedman's theory of adaptive expectations or rational expectations theory (with or without complete information), the analysis thus leads to the conclusion that democratic governments are best advised to pursue a rule-based macroeconomic policy aimed at controlling inflation while allowing the market to determine the sustainable level of unemployment. None of these theories, however, is sanguine about the willingness of governments to heed the advice because short-term electoral incentives combined with full-employment commitments (especially for left-leaning governments) induce inflationary behavior. A core issue from this perspective is therefore how governments can *credibly* commit to a nonaccommodating monetary target, and the solution that has been proposed is to institutionalize an antiinflationary monetary decision rule through delegation of policy-making power to a "conservative" agency — usually, but not necessarily, an independent central bank (Alesina and Summers 1993; Havrilevski and Granato 1993; Alesina and Grilli 1993; Lohmann 1992; Grilli, Masciandaro, and Tabellini 1991; Burdekin and Willett 1991; Cukierman 1992; Fischer 1977).

Purportedly such an abdication of discretionary power will reduce inflation and perhaps even allow markets to operate more efficiently. Indeed, independent central banks are described as something of a magic bullet in the economic literature. For example Grilli, Masciandaro, and Tabellini (1991) triumphantly conclude that ". . . having an independent central bank is almost like having a free lunch; there are benefits but no apparent costs in terms of macroeconomic performance." Others strike a more cautionary note by arguing that nominal rigidities in the presence of economic business cycles create trade-offs between inflation conservatism (which reduces inflation) and flexibility to respond to exogenous shocks (which reduces employment variability). This trade-off points away from having central banks that are too conservative and independent (see Rogoff 1985; Lohmann 1992; Svensson 1996). Still, the central bank independence literature agrees that institutional design does not affect equilibrium employment. Like money, monetary rules are independent of the equilibrium rate of unemployment.

Some of the strongest prima facie evidence for the new classical model was the inability of OECD governments in the 1970s to sustain the very low rates of unemployment achieved during the 1960s. In addition, the theory can explain (in statistical terms) a substantial portion of the cross-national variation in inflation. For the 15 OECD countries in this study, the correlation between a composite index of central bank independence (explained in the next chapter) and average inflation from 1973 to 1995 is 0.76. This finding is echoed in the empirical central bank independence literature (see, for example, Al-Marhubi and Willett 1995; Cukierman 1992, chs. 20–22; Alesina and Summers 1993), although most evidence is of a rather crude cross-sectional nature and has been criticized for confusing correlation for causation (Posen 1995).

Yet even if we concede that the theory helps to explain inflation performance, it offers few insights into three of the most puzzling macroeconomic "facts" touched upon in the introductory chapter: (i) The cross-national variance in monetary regimes, (ii) the persistent and very considerable cross-national variance in unemployment rates, and (iii) the large differences in wage dispersion across countries and time. Somewhat paradoxically, while the central bank independence literature is committed to a rational expectations framework in which nominal variables are deemed unimportant, the benefits of central bank independence are always appraised in terms of a nominal variable: inflation. Indeed one can question the logical consistency of assuming that policymakers

have inflation preferences while other economic actors do not, and some economists have started to explore the consequences of assuming that *all* economic
actors inherently care about inflation (see Cubitt 1992; Skott 1997; Cukierman
1997; Cukierman and Lippi 1998). But that is in my view to put the cart
before the horse by making a virtue of what is already a poorly justified
assumption. In effect it "smuggles" money illusion into the utility function of
economic agents. The only reasonable justification for politicians and other
actors to care about monetary variables is that these matter for real outcomes.
From this point of view, preferences over monetary variables (including monetary rules) are a function, not a cause, of real economic effects.[4]

This is where the argument in this book fundamentally departs from the
new classical theory. Unlike the central bank independence literature, I insist
that monetary policies have effects on real variables and that they are inherently
political in nature. The difference in the approach does not concern the rationality of expectations, but rather the assumptions that are made about the
formation of wages. For all the theoretical elegance of assuming perfectly competitive labor markets, this is *not* how wages are actually formed – especially
not in Western Europe and Japan. Instead, most wages are subject to *collective*
bargaining between unions and associations of employers who exert market
power within their own bargaining area and often have the capacity to influence
aggregate prices. This fact changes the analysis of macroeconomic policies and
their effects in fundamental ways, and it creates a wedge between rational
expectations and the neutrality of monetary rules thesis.

The link to wage bargaining is provided by the new Keynesian economics.[5]
Unions and employers, through their organized control over wages and prices,
make competing claims on the output of the economy. If these claims exceed
the real value of output, the result will be accelerating inflation. In turn, such
inflation undercuts the real-wage expectations of workers and leads to a wage–
price spiral, similar to that described by Friedman (Carlin and Soskice 1990:
146–57). This vicious circle can be arrested only by raising unemployment and
weakening unions. Because higher unemployment makes the strike threat less
credible, the share of the output claimed by workers will decline. The point at
which the output claims made by workers and by employers are compatible
with real output is called the *competing claims equilibrium rate of unemployment*, or
the *nonaccelerating inflation rate of unemployment* (NAIRU).

Whether there exists one or several NAIRUs in a single economy depends
on its openness to international trade and on the institutionalization of wage
bargaining. In open economies there are numerous NAIRUs because it is possible to combine high real wages in the domestic sectors with low unemployment
and stable inflation by squeezing the costs of imports and the share of profits
and wages going to the export sector.[6] In the medium to long run, however,
macroeconomic policies must be compatible with balance or surplus on the
external balance to prevent an unsustainable outflow of capital (Carlin and

Soskice 1990: ch. 11). More importantly, the location of the NAIRU will differ from country to country depending on the organization of labor markets and the capacity of wage-setting institutions to calibrate claims at a low rate of unemployment. In countries with powerful unions but low institutional capacity for wage restraint, the NAIRU will be relatively high, while in countries with high institutional capacity for restraint, the NAIRU will be relatively low, *even if* unions are organizationally powerful.

New Keynesian economics thus points to the importance of institutional capacity for wage restraint in explaining unemployment, an issue that has been subject to intense analysis in the neo-corporatist literature. In the next section I discuss the contribution of neo-corporatism to the analysis of unemployment, which I argue is incomplete and requires us to revisit the central bank independence literature.

THE NEO-CORPORATIST CHALLENGE

The main problem that bargaining institutions can help to overcome according to neo-corporatist theory is wage competition between unions that are concerned only with the maximization of payoffs for their own members, *not* the payoffs for the collective of workers or the society at large (see, for example, Przeworski and Wallerstein 1982; Lange 1984; Cameron 1984; Crouch 1985; Calmfors and Driffill 1988; Alvarez et al. 1991). Whether the externalities of wage militancy are likely to be internalized by union decision makers, according to this view, depends on the number of salient unions and on the authority of peak associations to bargain wages on behalf of individual unions.

Calmfors and Driffill (1988) provide by far the most influential formulation of the relationship between centralization, militancy, and unemployment. Following Olson (1982), they argue that the costs of wage militancy cannot be externalized by unions in either highly decentralized firm-based bargaining systems or in highly centralized ones. In decentralized systems individual companies face competitive product markets and high elasticity of demand, which create a steep trade-off between wages and employment. Similarly, an economy-wide union confederation cannot hope to pass on the costs of militancy to others, and fear of unemployment therefore gives it a stake in wage moderation. Industry- or sector-level unions, on the other hand, set prices for entire industries that face lower competition and elasticity of demand than individual firms. Consequently they face less of a trade-off between their own wages and unemployment and are therefore more prone to pursue militant strategies. In the aggregate such militancy produces high unemployment. Consequently Calmfors and Driffill posit a curvilinear or hump-shaped relationship between centralization and unemployment.

Some in the neo-corporatist tradition have disputed the conclusion that decentralization leads to moderation and low unemployment, and instead hypothesize a positive linear relationship between centralization and wage restraint (e.g., Crouch 1985; Cameron 1984; Lange 1984). As discussed below, I think there are good reasons to dispute the capacity for decentralized restraint. It is where the neo-corporatist literature agrees – namely, that intermediately centralized bargaining is inferior to centralized bargaining – however, that I most disagree. *The reason is that the possibilities for cost externalization in both intermediately and highly centralized systems are contingent on the monetary rule adhered to by the government.* This is a crucial point that is ignored by both Calmfors and Driffill (1988) and by other neo-corporatist accounts. Let me discuss the different issues as they relate to different points on the centralization continuum.

DECENTRALIZED WAGE PUSHFULNESS

The issue of contention in Calmfors and Driffill's analysis of decentralized bargaining is whether it correctly specifies the effect of unemployment on union behavior. This is most easily seen if we assume that whole industries, as well as individual companies, are price takers – an assumption that is reasonably well satisfied for the traded goods sector (since national industries typically control only a small fraction of the world market). Although Calmfors and Driffill's model is designed to show what happens if the price elasticity of demand falls with the size of unions – a possibility that I consider below – it is useful to keep this variable constant because the model yields simple, yet false, predictions about the behavior of company and industry unions under this assumption.

Because unions in both scenarios (company- and industry-level bargaining) are unable to externalize the costs of militancy, they are forced to bear the costs in the form of rising unemployment among their members. If unemployment benefits are financed through a *profit tax*, then Calmfors and Driffill's model implies that the outcome is identical in the two situations (1988: 34). In either case, the threat of unemployment will deter unions from pursuing overly militant strategies, although they may be willing to accept *some* unemployment among their members in "exchange" for a higher real wage. If unemployment benefits are financed through an *income tax*, the industry union actually has a somewhat greater incentive to observe restraint because militancy now has measurable effects on disposable income. Otherwise the story is identical. The conclusion from this line of argument is that company-level bargaining produces equally good (or only slightly worse) outcomes as industry-level bargaining, *even* when we impose the rather strict assumption about price-taking behavior at the industry level. Since in reality at least some industries or sectors are not pure price takers (whereas individual firms always are), ipso facto the curvilinear result follows.

The model, however, makes a very important assumption that is never explicitly stated: Apart from the taxes necessary to finance unemployment benefits, *there are no externalities of unemployment*. Each union, regardless of size, is affected only by unemployment among its *own* members (see for example equation C5 in appendix C in Calmfors and Driffill 1988). Yet there clearly *are* negative externalities associated with unemployment. With rising unemployment, competition for jobs will increase and thereby magnify the likelihood of prolonged unemployment and raise the search costs for new jobs (Layard et al. 1991: ch. 2). Because these costs of unemployment are *external to individual company unions*, leaders of these unions have no incentives to take them into account when deciding on a wage strategy. It *is* true, of course, that higher average unemployment will raise the costs of being laid off (and hence give unions an incentive to be less militant), but the cost to *other* unions of an additional union member being laid off is completely discounted by individual unions since they cannot affect the economy-wide rate of unemployment. As Layard, Nickell, and Jackman note: "In firm-level bargaining the bargainers take the general level of unemployment as given – ignoring the fact that their own actions will affect the jobs open to other workers" (1991: 130).

As assumed by the linear hypothesis, the situation can thus be understood as a multiplayer Prisoner's Dilemma game in which individually optimal behavior leads to collectively worse outcomes (see Lange 1984). For example, under full employment a company union may very well decide that higher real wages are worth a substantial number of layoffs among its members *so long as* these members can quickly and relatively costlessly find comparable jobs elsewhere. Likewise, any individual member may be quite willing to take some risk of a short spell of unemployment for the prospect of a substantially improved real wage. Yet, of course, since other company unions can reason in a similar fashion, the result will be an overall rise in unemployment. In the formal model in Appendix A this logic is captured through the specification of the unions' utility function. While unions want to maximize real wages and minimize unemployment among their members, as in the Calmfors–Driffill model, the severity of unemployment is made contingent on the overall level of unemployment (by using a multiplicative term, the unemployment rate among members times the general rate of unemployment).

Everything else being equal, as centralization increases, the externalities of unemployment in the fragmented system will become increasingly internalized. An industry union, for example, whose members have skills that cannot easily be redeployed in other industries will have a strong incentive to take account of the increasing costs of growing unemployment and thus to refrain from actions that would bring about these costs. This is particularly the case if centralization leads to collaborations between vertically integrated firms since this increases the size of the wage bill in total costs (Layard et al. 1991: 137). Needless to say, a single national union confederation would have a still greater incentive to internalize these costs since its behavior would have a large and direct effect on the average unemployment rate. The existence of externalities of unemployment therefore undermines the logic that leads to the prediction of low unemployment at the decentralized extreme.

The question remains, however, what happens if industry unions are in *sheltered sectors* of the economy, permitting them to externalize some of the costs of militancy through markup pricing. The unemployment mechanism still functions to some extent because sectoral demand is never completely inelastic, but there is little doubt that the Calmfors and Driffill argument becomes more compelling under this assumption. Unions in the nontraded sectors have less of an incentive to observe real-wage restraint than unions in the traded sectors insofar as they face a downward-sloping demand curve. Not surprisingly, therefore, the division between sheltered and exposed sectors, especially between public services and private manufacturing, has attracted attention in some of the recent debates over wage formation (see Swenson 1991b; Garrett and Way 1999). But the issue has in fact been recognized for a long time. In the Scandinavian context, for example, the problem is central to the so-called EFO model (named after three Swedish economists: Edgren, Faxén, and Odhner), which stipulates that the institutionalization of the bargaining process must be such that the development of prices and productivity in the traded goods sector determine wages both in this sector *and* in the nontraded sectors.[7]

The EFO model implies that peak-level bargaining is an efficient way to tie the wage development in sheltered sectors to that in the exposed. Because wage increases apply unconditionally across all sectors in such a system, it greatly reduces the ability and incentives of unions in the sheltered sectors to try to free-ride on unions in the exposed. This confirms the logic for highly centralized systems proposed by Calmfors and Driffill. Similarly, in the *absence* of peak-level bargaining, the problem of militancy among sheltered sector unions pinpointed in the Calmfors–Driffill model appears to reemerge. To fully explore this possibility let us now assume that all unions are sheltered, that is, operate in a closed economy (as has been done in the formal model in Appendix A). Can it now be concluded that industry- or sector-level bargaining will produce militancy in a manner similar to the collective action problem discussed in the case of decentralized bargaining? The answer, I will argue, is that it cannot.

INTERMEDIATELY CENTRALIZED BARGAINING AND THE POSSIBILITY FOR RESTRAINT

The key to my argument is that the elasticity of sectoral demand is contingent on the monetary rule adhered to by the government or central bank. If unions and employers can anticipate that wage increases will be accommodated through expansionary monetary policies, unions and firms will face relatively elastic demand for the goods produced in their own sector and they will therefore have little incentive to behave in a restrained manner. In the language of Calmfors and Driffill, the inflationary costs of any particular agreement can be external-ized to a high degree, leading to militancy and unemployment. The reason is that the inflationary effect of any particular agreement will not have much of an effect on the real money supply, and hence sectoral demand, when the monetary authority accommodates.

On the other hand, if the government credibly adheres to a nonaccommo-dating macroeconomic policy rule the scope for cost-externalization will be reduced. In this case the aggregate price effects of any particular agreement will translate into a reduction in the sectoral real money supply, thereby creating a tighter linkage between particular wage bargains and unemployment. In effect, the elasticity of sectoral demand goes up when the government adopts a more nonaccommodating monetary policy rule, thereby furnishing unions with a greater incentive to be restrained and giving employers a stronger incentive to resist union demands.[8] This possibility is not considered in the Calmfors and Driffill model.

In the formal model developed in Appendix A, the logic is captured by letting unions play a game with a monetary authority where the latter sets the inflation rate after unions have bargained a particular wage increase.[9] Any discrepancies between the inflation rate implied by economy-wide wage in-creases and the actual rate chosen by the monetary authority leads to a rising real wage and increasing unemployment. This is analogous to the Calmfors–Driffill logic that higher wages in one industry will raise unemployment in that industry when relative prices cannot be increased at the same rate. The model thus amends the Calmfors–Driffill logic – in which unions' wage behavior depends exclusively on their ability to alter relative prices – by casting the wage-formation process in a macroeconomic context that is determined by the "conservatism" of a monetary authority (measured by its relative concerns for inflation and unemployment).[10]

If unions and employers can anticipate with great certainty that militant strategies in their own bargaining area will lead to a deflationary response by the monetary authorities, strategic foresight will dictate self-restraint.[11] Specifi-cally, large sheltered unions whose decisions have nonnegligible effects on the economy will have an incentive to moderate their wage demands to prevent rising unemployment, while employer associations will have an incentive to increase their resolve against excessive wage demands to avoid a reduction in demand and profits.[12] Because of these deterrence effects of a nonaccommodating policy regime, we thus expect unemployment in (semi)decentralized bargaining systems to be *lower* the higher the degree of central bank independence. Keynes-ian policy flexibility will be a liability.

It should be emphasized that while the logic I have spelled out for inter-mediately centralized bargaining systems is *consistent* with the central bank independence literature, it relies on a different micrologic. What makes a nonaccommodating monetary regime effective is the capacity of economic agents to affect aggregate prices and to anticipate the decisions of monetary authorities. Whenever a state of the world exists in which the decisions of rational players have predictable and discernible effects on the welfare and decisions of other players, I will say that these players possess *strategic capacity*.[13] Precisely because beneficial deterrence effects presuppose strategic capacity, the logic does *not* extend to highly fragmented bargaining systems. Regardless of how well publicized and credible a nonaccommodating policy may be in such a system, the only moderating influence on union policies is the actual (as opposed to anticipated) risk and severity of unemployment.[14] Like prices in perfectly competitive markets, even if all unions realize that their collective interest is best served by wage moderation, and even if the government's deflationary policy rule is common knowledge, it is always in the self-interest of unions to push for higher wages to the point where unemployment undermines any incentive to raise wages even further.[15] This is why the new classical assumption of perfectly competitive markets prevents the theory from adequately accounting for cross-country variance in unemployment.

CENTRALIZED WAGE RESTRAINT

The Calmfors–Driffill analysis, as well as much of the neo-corporatist literature, implies that there are no possibilities for free-riding in centralized bargaining systems, and therefore no problem of externalities. The logic dovetails Olson's (1965, 1982) analysis of "encompassing" groups in which free-riding is precluded by the absence of other groups to absorb the costs of such free-riding. The analysis contains a compelling logic, but it is incomplete in two important respects.

First, it overlooks the problem of unions discounting the future in response to uncertainty. As pointed out by Przeworski and Wallerstein (1982), only if workers are reasonably assured that present sacrifices will pay off in the future will they forgo short-term wage maximization and exercise restraint. Uncertainty about developments in the international economy, and about how employers will use increased profits, will prompt more shortsighted union behavior (Lange and Garrett 1985). Since unemployment is a particularly grave concern for unions, state assurances that wage restraint will be "rewarded" with full employment is conducive to farsighted and restrained wage policies. In turn, the ability of the government to make such assurances and to flexibly adjust its policies to a changing economic environment is proportional to the control that the government exercises over macroeconomic policy instruments. Through countercyclical macroeconomic policies and public sector expansion, the government can act as a "guarantor" for full employment and hence reassure labor about its future welfare. Such reassurances encourage cooperative behavior, especially when they are offered as contingent bargains (e.g., Crouch 1985; Katzenstein 1985; Lange and Garrett 1985; Alvarez et al. 1991; Cameron 1984;

Schmidt 1983; Korpi and Shalev 1979). In sharp contrast, commitment to a nonaccommodating policy rule, as advocated in the new classical literature, is premised on the principle that full employment *cannot* be assured. Instead, the threat of unemployment is used as a stick to deter militant behavior (cf. Scharpf 1991).

In assessing the argument it is noteworthy that neither new classical nor new Keynesian economic theory supports the view that the government can, on its own, influence the sustainable level of unemployment (the NAIRU). It is conceivable, however, that the government may reduce deviations of the economy from its equilibrium path through active macroeconomic policies. This is entirely consistent with the new classical economics (Rogoff 1985), although there is actually very little empirical support for this view. For example, the data introduced in the next chapter show that there is no tendency for countries with independent central banks to experience greater variance in unemployment than countries with more dependent banks (with or without control for the movement of the general OECD level of unemployment). Still, the government can undoubtedly influence uncertainty and employment through social and public sector employment, and I will return to a discussion of such policies below. As far as the macroeconomic argument goes, however, there is reason for some skepticism.

There is a second, and in my view much more important, reason that centralization is insufficient for real-wage restraint whereas policy flexibility is necessary. Unlike the Olsonian logic of collective action, in which players are differentiated only by size, a centralized bargaining system is based on a *coalition of diverse and conflicting interests*, and the internal dynamics of such a system depend on the successful reconciliation of these interests (see Calmfors 1993; Hibbs and Locking 1991, 1996). In particular, the confederal leadership has to work out a distributive compromise between high-wage unions and low-wage unions. Such intraorganizational bargaining tends to result in egalitarian wage policies because low-wage unions can veto proposals that do not distribute wage increases "fairly" among members. In the formal model, Nash bargaining theory is used to model this logic. The intuition of the argument is that when unions bargain over the division of collective wage increases, no union can expect to get more than a 50–50 split corresponding to a flat-rate principle (all get the same *absolute* increase), while wage increases that are not subject to inter-union bargaining will conform on average to a market-conforming proportionality principle (all get the same *percentage* increase).[16] This creates a negative relationship between centralization and wage dispersion because solidaristic policies have a greater impact on the wage structure when the diversity of membership is high (i.e., when collective bargaining is encompassing).[17]

The question of wage structure complicates the relationship between centralization and wage restraint because of the way bargained wage solidarism interacts with locally generated "wage drift." Because such drift primarily

benefits high-wage groups, it undermines the distributive terms of the centralized wage bargain. Especially when drift becomes the dominant component in
total wage increases – something that happens as bargained wage increases
approach zero – it poses a real political problem. Under these circumstances,
low-wage unions lose their organizational power over the wage structure. Consequently, the size of wage demands in the collective bargaining process becomes an integral part of the political struggle over the distribution of wages.
To continue to benefit from the politically sanctioned policy of solidarity, low-
wage unions will push for bargained wage increases that may well exceed the
"room" for wage increases in the economy. Solidaristic wage policies, in a
manner of speaking, "spill over" into wage push, and this implies that distributive compromises in the collective bargaining process cannot be separated from
the issue of wage pushfulness. Once again, the logic is tied to the level of
bargaining centralization because the level and size of wage drift will be affected
by the extent of wage compression in the collective bargaining process. The
more wages are compressed, the greater the market pressure to "undo" the
distributive compromise by "rewarding" those whose wages are held back the
most (Hibbs and Locking 1996). In the formal model, centralization increases
the inflationary spillover effect because wage drift increasingly favors high-paid
workers, triggering higher demands in the collective bargaining process, but a
similar effect follows from making the level of drift a positive function of
centralization (or some combination of the two).[18]

The wage-inflationary effects of centralization clearly pose a challenge to
the neo-corporatist emphasis on the dampening effects of centralization on wage
claims. But whether the two logics produce different *real* outcomes depends on
the accommodating or nonaccommodating stance of the monetary authority.
Only if policies are nonaccommodating will nominal wage pressure automatically be translated into higher real-wage pressure and unemployment. Hence, if
the government is able and willing to accommodate higher nominal wages
through an expansion of demand and higher inflation, the confederal leadership
may be able to offer *real-wage restraint* that is compatible with full employment.
Negotiated monetary accommodation, in other words, promotes macroeconomic
efficiency by facilitating the resolution of distributive conflicts within the confederation. On the other hand, if the government lacks such flexibility, higher
nominal wage demands will be equivalent to higher real wages, causing industrial disputes and unemployment to rise.[19] As Walter Korpi notes, "if the
government cannot settle the distributive conflicts, at least temporarily, say, by
increasing the money supply, they will appear in other forms, such as severe
industrial disputes" (1983: 228). Since full employment and labor market
quiescence are important political assets in the electoral arena, the government
has a strong incentive to try to retain policy flexibility; and the higher the
degree of centralization, the greater the need for policy flexibility to maintain
full employment (especially during low-growth periods). The effect of economic

policy regimes in a centralized bargaining system is thus the *opposite* of the relationship in an intermediately centralized system: Economic performance (especially in terms of unemployment) *improves* with the Keynesian flexibility of policies.

This theoretical linkage between solidaristic wage policies and economic policy regimes can be applied to a broader political–institutional "nexus" that includes the welfare state and public sector employment policies. There are two main reasons for this. First, to the extent that publicly provided services and cash benefits are viewed by workers as part of their income – what is sometimes referred to as the *social wage* – the government can influence the behavior of unions by altering the size and composition of this wage, and unions can make their behavior contingent on changes in the social wage. In this fashion the social wage becomes a manipulable component of the bargaining system, and hence subject to the similar political–coalitional constraints that apply to the "private wage." In particular, the government can help to contain the demands from low-wage groups in the collective bargaining process by offering an expansion of solidaristic – that is, decommodifying and egalitarian – welfare benefits. In this fashion, the government can potentially ameliorate the inflationary pressures from solidaristic wage policies.

The role of the state as a "compensator" for wage restraint has long been recognized in the neo-corporatist literature: In return for wage moderation, unions are rewarded by an increase in the social wage (e.g., Cameron 1984; Robertson 1990). Yet the logic of this argument differs from mine, and its explanatory status is in dispute (Lange 1984; Scharpf 1991: ch. 9). The problem is that the "social wage" is a public good from the perspective of unions, and hence cannot rationally forestall free-riding behavior. My argument, however, does not conceptualize the social wage as a compensation mechanism for labor as such, but rather focuses (once again) on its function in facilitating internal distributive compromise between high- and low-wage constituencies. A solidaristic social wage, in other words, alleviates some of the inflationary pressure that emanates from the distributive compromise within the labor confederation, and thus lowers the need for accommodating (and inflationary) monetary policies.

The second main linkage between the character of the welfare state and the industrial relations system is the government's commitment to full employment. As noted above, class cooperation in highly centralized bargaining systems has always been premised on the capacity and willingness of the government to guarantee full employment. By socializing the risks of employment, the government facilitates "responsible" union behavior. In turn, this presupposes that the government has flexible control over monetary policy instruments and that expansion of public sector employment can be used to compensate for private sector redundancies. But, again, the role of public manpower policies in facilitating the pursuit of solidaristic wage policies is a crucial element in the story. Because productivity increases in a variety of services – especially education, health care, personal services, and what Esping-Andersen (1990) calls "food and fun" services – tend to lag behind productivity increases in manufacturing, if wage relativities are to be preserved across sectors, many services will be priced out of the market (Baumol 1967; Baumol and Bowen 1966). As long as the potential for employment growth is high in the most dynamic branches of the economy, this is not necessarily a problem since wage solidarism will keep the cost of labor in these branches down and thus facilitate the transfer of workers from low- to high- productivity firms (especially true accompanied by active labor market policies) – a logic that has been elegantly formulated in the Rehn–Meidner model (Rehn 1985; Martin 1979). But if growth in low-productivity services, rather than high-productivity manufacturing, is the most important source of employment expansion (which has been the case since the mid-1960s), then solidaristic wage policies will have the effect of squeezing out low-productivity jobs in the private services sector without creating the compensating employment growth in high-productivity branches. Barring very high levels of wage restraint (which Rehn and Meidner believed was not possible), the Rehn–Meidner model will therefore not ensure full employment unless the government steps in and generates low-skilled jobs through an expansion of public services (Appelbaum and Schettkat, 1994; Iversen and Wren 1998). [20]

Of course, expansion both in the social wage and in public sector employment ultimately depends on the willingness of better paid workers to exercise wage restraint and foot the rising tax bill for transfers and "overpriced" public services. By raising taxes to finance new benefit programs and services, the state is effectively cutting the relative wages of high-income groups and thus requires that these groups not react with inflationary demands for compensation. A related problem is that precisely because higher taxes have very transparent welfare consequences for the affected constituencies, they may lead to unpleasant electoral responses. An inflation tax is less transparent and hence may be politically more rational, but it obviously defeats the task of controlling wage-push inflation. The point of this discussion is that if the government is unable or unwilling to expand egalitarian (or solidaristic) welfare benefits and public sector employment, distributive conflicts in the centralized bargaining system will intensify for very much the same reasons as they would if monetary policies are nonaccommodating.

ECONOMIC INSTITUTIONS AND PERFORMANCE: SYNTHESIS AND IMPLICATIONS

Figure 2.1 summarizes the unemployment predictions of the theoretical argument, using the formal model in Appendix A to generate the curves. The figure shows the relationship between centralization of wage bargaining and unem-

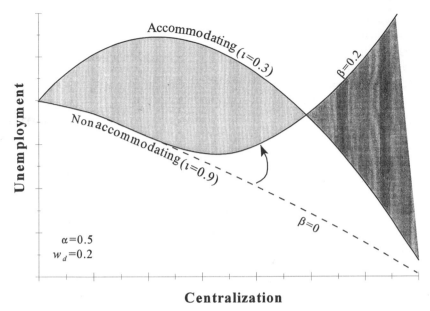

Figure 2.1. *The predicted effect of centralization of bargaining on unemployment depending on the restrictiveness of the monetary regime.*

ployment for both an accommodating and a nonaccommodating monetary regime. For completely decentralized systems, unemployment is unaffected by the monetary regime. It is conceivable that the greater predictability of a nonaccommodating regime may have some beneficial effects on investment and employment, but greater macroeconomic flexibility may, on the other hand, permit a more optimal countercyclical policy mix, which will improve employment performance (although one may be skeptical about governments' capacity for such "fine-tuning"). These possible, and opposite, effects are not part of the main argument, and I leave it to the empirical analysis to sort out the net effect on unemployment. For now I simply affirm the policy neutrality thesis for completely decentralized bargaining systems.

Accommodation in the figure (the top curve) refers to the policy of a monetary authority that is primarily concerned with unemployment (while high values of ι imply greater concern with inflation). Note that when we move away from the decentralized extreme, unions are encouraged to use their indirect power in product markets to push up wages to the detriment of overall employment and welfare. As centralization progresses still further, the externalities of militant (real) wage behavior is gradually internalized, creating the "hump" predicted by Calmfors and Driffill. Note also that unemployment is lower at the centralized end because all employment effects of wage decisions are internalized, whereas in the decentralized case some of these are externalized. The size of the hump also depends on just how much the monetary authority is concerned with unemployment compared to inflation. If inflation is a matter of considerable importance to even relatively "soft" monetary authorities (as is probably a reasonable assumption for most OECD countries in the post-1973 period), the hump will be smaller and the curve will approximate a monotonically declining function. The model thus recognizes the theoretical possibility of a hump-shaped relationship, yet is compatible with arguments that imply a monotonically declining relationship. Ultimately, of course, this is an empirical matter.

When the monetary regime turns in a nonaccommodating direction (the bottom curve), the predicted effect of moving from a decentralized to an intermediately centralized bargaining system is different because the implied aggregate price effect of militancy can no longer be externalized, thereby deterring unions from engaging in such militancy. The result is *lower* unemployment than in the decentralized case. The collective-action problem facing unions in intermediately centralized systems, which can lead to excessive wage demands and unemployment, is thus "solved" (or at least dissipated) by an agent that is deliberately nonaccommodating to union objectives. This crucial (and perhaps surprising) result is completely overlooked in existing models of union behavior (such as Calmfors and Driffill's application of Olson's theory) because they fail to consider the conditioning effects of monetary policies on the strategic calculation of unions.

The beneficial deterrence effects of a nonaccommodating monetary regime dissipate at high levels of centralization because unions progressively internalize the externalities of militancy and thus become increasingly capable of solving their collective action problem on their own. In fact, as I have argued, at high levels of centralization nonaccommodation can turn into a liability if – in addition to real wages and unemployment – unions are concerned with wage distribution (this is indicated by a positive value of β in the formal model). The reason is that nonaccommodating monetary policies now run up against attempts by unions to forge politically acceptable, and often inflationary, compromises between high- and low-paid members. Since the wage-restraining effects of nonaccommodation fall with centralization, whereas the inflationary effects of solidaristic wage policies rise, at some point of centralization monetary accommodation will produce better employment outcomes than nonaccommodation (although the point at which this occurs is theoretically indeterminate). Note that this conclusion is directly dependent on the pursuit of solidaristic policies since if solidarism is of no concern for unions ($\beta = 0$), unemployment will keep falling with centralization.

The implications of the model for *inflation* (Figure 2.2) is likewise hump-

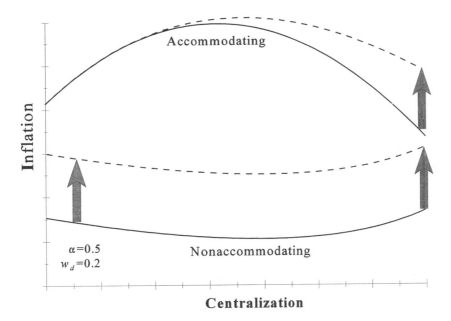

Figure 2.2. *The predicted effect of centralization of bargaining on inflation depending on the restrictiveness of the monetary regime.*

shaped for accommodating regimes, but centralized systems are no longer necessarily better performers than decentralized systems owing to the inflationary consequences of solidaristic wage policies. The more zealous unions are in their pursuit of solidaristic wage norms, and the greater the pressure for wage drift, the worse the inflation performance for centralized systems (indicated by the top dashed line). For accommodating regimes, therefore, expected inflation conforms better to a "symmetric" Calmfors–Driffill pattern than to the predominantly downward-sloping pattern in the case of unemployment. As the monetary authority becomes more "conservative" (i.e., cares less and less about unemployment), the hump-shaped relationship between centralization and inflation "flattens out" and may turn mildly U-shaped as deterrence effects become very effective in intermediately centralized systems, but less so in decentralized systems (due to collective action problems) and in highly centralized systems (due to solidaristic wage policies). The curve for nonaccommodating regimes is "flatter" than in the case of unemployment because most of the effect on inflation is via expectations – which are similarly affected across bargaining systems – whereas for unemployment the effect of nonaccommodation goes through real-wage behavior – which varies a good deal across bargaining systems.

The direct effect of restrictive monetary regimes – that is, the difference between the curves – will be smaller if we allow for uncertainty about the monetary authority's "type" – that is, whether it is "truly" antiinflationary or not (as indicated by the upward-shifted bottom dashed line). Although "soft" monetary authorities have a short-term incentive to inflate, as suggested in the central bank independence literature, when it is easy to alter wage contracts in response to unanticipated monetary policies, the monetary authority can produce only very brief short-term employment effects (if any at all). By the same token, since employment effects are negligible, it would no longer be very costly for the monetary authority to establish a reputation for "toughness" to reduce inflation – quite irrespective of its type. Under these circumstances it would make little difference for outcomes if a nonaccommodating policy rule was institutionalized or not. All monetary policymakers, regardless of their true type, would converge to the same antiinflationary policy.[21]

Type is important only when there are costs associated with developing a reputation for toughness and such costs are rising with the difficulty of changing wages and prices. With sticky wages and prices, only the "tough" type would carry out a threat not to accommodate, and type would again become important (i.e., the two curves should diverge).[22] This contingent role of policy type is important because the degree of wage flexibility is dependent on the character of the bargaining system. Ceteris paribus, decentralized market-based systems tend to be more flexible in the short run than intermediately centralized and centralized systems (where wage contracts are typically synchronized and negotiated for one- or two-year periods). We would therefore predict the monetary authority's type to be less salient for inflation outcomes in completely decentralized systems than in more centralized ones.

Curiously enough, the more we emphasize the assumptions in the new classical theory – rational expectations and perfect market flexibility – the less the theory has to say about *either* employment *or* inflation (as measured by the difference between the curves at the decentralized extreme). All observed variance becomes unexplained variance. The reason is *not* that policies are "neutral" in the case of inflation, but that there is little reason to expect policies to differ. Because the present model expects monetary policies to have unemployment effects, government type will always matter for inflation except in the completely decentralized case where there are no unemployment effects.[23] Hence, if type matters only when monetary policies have real effects (and wages are sticky), the reason for the empirical association between central bank independence and inflation may be that the new classical assumptions about labor markets are in fact poorly met. In any event, the interactive model should give greater explanatory leverage over inflation, compared to using central bank independence alone.

Wage dispersion, finally, is predicted to be monotonically declining with centralization because of the rising effects of wage solidarism on the wage structure (Figure 2.3). It is important to underscore that the model does not

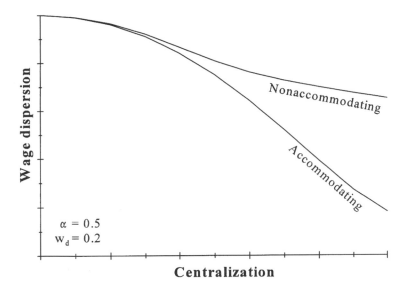

Figure 2.3. *The predicted effect of centralization of bargaining on wage dispersion depending on the restrictiveness of the monetary regime.*

predict this effect because solidarism will become more prevalent with centralization – a misconception that I have frequently encountered – but because solidarism is applied to the wages of progressively more heterogeneous groups of wage earners. In fact, the negative relationship persists even if part of the solidaristic element is being traded for higher employment when centralization is high. As illustrated in Figure 2.3, this may happen when monetary policies become increasingly nonaccommodating because the inflationary effects of solidarism (which are increasing with centralization) will produce growing unemployment (and hence give unions an incentive to relax the solidarity element). Whether nonaccommodation has this conditional effect obviously depends on the weight that unions place on achieving their distributive goals compared to other goals such as low unemployment. In other words, it is an empirical question.

The particular shape of the relationship between centralization and dispersion shown in Figure 2.3 should be taken with a grain of salt because it depends on the wage heterogeneity of unions at different levels of centralization and because the size of wage drift may be positively linked to centralization. If small unions organize people of very different wages, the effect of solidaristic wage policies will be greater at lower levels of centralization, and if drift is increasing with centralization, the relationship will be linear or convex rather than concave. In terms of the downward-sloping character of the relationship, however, the model produces a very robust prediction.

CONCLUSION

The theoretical argument presented in this chapter implies that the covariation in national wage-bargaining institutions, macroeconomic policy regimes, and economic outcomes – described in Chapter 1 – is not coincidental, but reflects a systematic logic whereby macroeconomic efficiency and distribution are a consequence of the interaction between government macroeconomic policies and the price–wage behavior of private actors (unions and employers). Contrary to the new classical economic theory, monetary policies have real effects in all but the most decentralized bargaining systems, but unlike neo-corporatist theory, nonaccommodation can yield beneficial economic effects in intermediately centralized systems. The logic extends to the "social wage" so that solidaristic policies facilitate macroeconomic coordination in centralized systems by diffusing intraconfederal distributive conflict, but exacerbate collective action problems in intermediately centralized systems. At the core of the argument is a series of distinct collective action problems between wage-bargaining agents that can be either exacerbated, reduced, or left unaffected by macroeconomic and social policies. In the next chapter I test the implications of the argument for economic performance on quantitative data for 15 OECD countries across a 21-year period.

Appendix A

A FORMAL MODEL OF THE ECONOMIC EFFECTS OF THE INTERACTION BETWEEN MONETARY REGIMES AND WAGE-BARGAINING INSTITUTIONS

I begin the discussion by defining the players and their objective functions. I then specify the union–monetary authority interaction in a dynamic two-stage game, and finally I discuss the theoretical and empirical implications.

ACTORS AND UTILITY FUNCTIONS

Following the strategy of Calmfors and Driffill (1988), unions are setting nominal wages subject to the constraint that such wages affect the attainment of other union goals, here employment and wage equality.[24] The three main concerns of unions – real wages, unemployment, and wage equality – can be described in the following welfare function for any union i (which may represent a federation of unions):

$$V_i = \alpha(w_i - \pi) - (1 - \alpha)U_i\overline{U} - \beta(r^i - r^e)^2$$

where w_i is the percentage nominal wage increase, π is the percentage increase in consumer prices, U_i is the unemployment rate among union i's members, $\bar{U}$ is the average unemployment rate, r^i is the ideally sought wage ratio between low-wage workers and high-wage workers, and r^e is the actual wage ratio expected from a particular wage settlement. The equation says that welfare increases with real wage increases $(w_i - \pi)$, but falls with unemployment and any discrepancies between ideal and anticipated wage equality. The parameters α and β are the weights unions put on different objectives. In line with the argument about externalities from unemployment, the specification of the effect of unemployment on the welfare of unions is chosen so that the severity of unemployment among union members depends on the overall unemployment rate.

The employment and inflation consequences of wage–price pressure depend on the degree to which such pressure is accommodated by expansive monetary policies. As implied by rational expectations theory, since private wage and price setters can anticipate the monetary authority's policy responses, they will rationally adjust their behavior in the expectation of a particular policy response – in equilibrium fulfilling their expectations. These intentions are incorporated into the present model via the following welfare function (V_m) for the monetary authority:

$$V_m = -\iota\pi^2 - (1 - \iota)\bar{U}^2$$

where π and $\bar{U}$ are the inflation rate and average unemployment rate as before, while $\iota = [0,1]$ is the weight placed on maintaining price stability as opposed to low unemployment. For simplicity, one may think of ι as the authority vested in an independent central bank charged with inflation control, but the equation obviously does not preclude that similar goals can be accomplished through different institutional mechanisms.

A TWO-STAGE GAME OF THE UNION–MONETARY AUTHORITY INTERACTION

Following the strategy of Barro and Gordon, the union–monetary authority interaction can now be modeled as a two-stage game with complete information.[25] First unions choose a nominal wage increase, after which the monetary authority decides on an inflation rate. Because unions know the objective function of the monetary authority, they will rationally take into account the effect of their own wage behavior on the price behavior of the monetary authority. Outcomes are measured in terms of inflation, unemployment, and wage relativities.

In the model, the inflation rate is set by the monetary authority, but the monetary authority will let its choice be influenced by the price effects of unions' wage demands (because these affect unemployment). In particular, it is useful to distinguish between a *relative* and an *absolute* price effect. The relative price effect is *the increase in prices for products made by firms within union i's bargaining area*, and it depends on the market power of firms within that bargaining area to pass on higher wage costs.[26] Assuming (with Calmfors and Driffill) that unions amalgamate within sectors producing close substitutes and that such amalgamation takes place between pairs of unions of equal size, the capacity to externalize wage costs is positively related to the level of centralization since the price elasticity of product demand declines the more firms are subjected to the same wage agreement:

$$\pi_i^r = cw_i \tag{1}$$

where $c = 1/n$ measures the degree of centralization (n representing the number of unions). If the number of unions is very large, c will approximate zero and unions will face nearly perfectly competitive product markets with no possibility for price increases; when c equals one, all wage increases will be completely passed on to prices. Since unions are assumed to be equally sized, if the average wage increase in any other bargaining area is denoted w_o (the subscript o stands for "other") then the relative price effect in any other bargaining area (π_o^r) is similarly

$$\pi_o^r = cw_o.$$

The *aggregate* price effect of a wage increase in a single bargaining area is obviously smaller than the relative price effect since the latter applies only to the segment of the market covered by the agreement in that bargaining area. *Assuming that aggregate price increases are accommodated by the monetary authority*, that is, matched by the chosen rate of inflation, the aggregate effect is a share of the relative effect where the weight is proportional to the degree of centralization:[27]

$$\pi_i^a = ccw_i = c^2w_i. \tag{2}$$

Similarly, the aggregate price effect of wage increases in other bargaining areas is proportional to the share of the labor market covered by unions in these bargaining areas:

$$\pi_o^a = (1 - c)cw_o. \tag{3}$$

In equilibrium it must be the case that the inflation rate chosen by the monetary authority always equals the sum of the aggregate price effects. However, this rate is chosen subject to the constraint that it has consequences for the rate of unemployment, and this is also a matter of concern to the monetary authority. To determine the choice of the monetary authority, we therefore need to look at the consequences for unemployment. The simplest approach is to examine what happens if the inflation rate is set *below* the price increases implied by wage increases. In this *disequilibrium* situation the rise in wage costs will outpace price increases, profits will be squeezed, and layoffs and unemployment will ensue. Analogously, any wage increases *within* a bargaining area that exceed the rate of *relative* price increases will reduce profits and increase unemployment. In both cases, the cause of higher unemployment is rising real wages.

Following this logic, the change in unemployment among the members of union i can be written as a simple additive function of the difference between the aggregate price effect and the actual rate of inflation (the first bracketed term) plus the difference between the union-specific wage increase and the relative price effect (the second bracketed term):

$$\Delta U_i = [\pi_i^a + \pi_o^a - \pi] + [w_i - \pi_i^r].$$

Substituting in the expressions for π_i^a, π_o^a, π_i^r and collecting terms yields:

$$\Delta U_i = w_i(c^2 - c + 1) + w_o c(1 - c) - \pi. \tag{4}$$

Analogously, the increase in *aggregate* unemployment $(\Delta \bar{U})$ is given by the following weighted average:

$$\Delta \bar{U} = [\pi_i^a + \pi_o^a - \pi] + c[w_i - \pi_i^r] + (1 - c)[w_o - \pi_o^r].$$

which (substituting in the values for π_i^a, π_o^a, π_i^r, π_o^r) is equivalent to

$$\Delta \bar{U} = cw_i + (1 - c)w_o - \pi. \tag{5}$$

In *equilibrium* unions will behave identically $(w_i = w_o)$, and the mean increase in unemployment is then simply the difference between equilibrium wage growth (w^*) and price growth (π):

$$\Delta \bar{U} = w^* - \pi. \tag{6}$$

As explained above, real wages (net of productivity increases) can be rising faster than inflation only in a disequilibrium scenario. At some point, unions' demands for higher wages must be equal to the ability of employers to raise prices. When this equilibrium is reached, unemployment is stable $(\Delta \bar{U} = 0)$ and the sum of the aggregate price effects matches the inflation rate chosen by the monetary authority. In the new classical economics this equilibrium is called the natural rate of unemployment, while in new Keynesian economics it is called the competing claims equilibrium rate of unemployment (or NAIRU).

This equilibrium is what we are ultimately interested in knowing, and for that purpose we first solve for the subgame-perfect outcome in the *second* stage of the game by determining the optimal inflation rate chosen by the monetary authority. Specifically, the monetary authority is faced with the following max-imization problem:

$$\max V_m(\pi) = -\iota\pi^2 - (1 - \iota)(\bar{U} + \Delta \bar{U})^2 \tag{7}$$

where $\bar{U}$ is the existing average rate of unemployment.

Substituting the expression for $\Delta \bar{U}$ (equation 5) into equation 7 and setting the partial derivative with respect to π equal to 0 yields the following maximizing condition for π (π^*):

$$\pi^*(w_i) = (1 - \upsilon)[\bar{U} + cw_i + (1 - c)w_o]. \tag{8}$$

Not surprisingly, the monetary authority raises the level of inflation with higher wage increases to reduce the adverse impact on employment, but it is less prone to do so the less it cares about unemployment (as measured by $1 - \upsilon$).

The next question is what wage rate unions will demand given that they anticipate the monetary authority will choose $\pi^*(w_i)$. We find this rate by solving union i's maximization problem in the *first* stage of the game:

$$\max V_i(w_i) = \alpha(w_i - \pi^*) - (1 - \alpha)(U_i + \Delta U_i)(\bar{U} + \Delta\bar{U}) \tag{9}$$
$$- \beta(r^i - r^e)^2.$$

Before we can do this, however, the relationship between wage strategies and wage relativities (the last term in equation 9) must be specified. Since unions organize workers who are similar in terms of industry and skills, different unions tend to differ in terms of the wages of their respective members. Unions therefore have to find a formula to distribute wage increases among members with different incomes, and this will influence their wage behavior (as argued in the main text).

Assuming (as before) that unions amalgamate in pairs and that they represent the interests of the median voter in their membership, the internal bargaining process at any level of centralization can be conceived of as a series of two-player bargaining games between a low- and a high-wage union. If each union seeks to maximize its share of the wage increase, the outcome of these games can be expected to conform to the Nash solution, which is a simple 50–50 split.[28] The Nash solution is theoretically attractive because it is compatible with selfish union behavior (share maximization), yet does not preclude that some unions pay heed to a norm of fairness (equal division). In addition, the solution is realistic since a very common form of bargained wage increases is flat-rate increments.[29] Symbolically, the ideal wage relativity of any union is thus

$$r^i = r_b = 1 \tag{10}$$

where r_b is the bargained wage increase for the median member in the low-wage union relative to the bargained wage increase for the median member in the high-wage union.

As explained in the main text, the distribution of wage increases at the end of a contract period rarely corresponds to what the union desired ex ante due to wage drift. Drift tends to disproportionately benefit those whose wages are held back in the collective agreement, and better paid workers will increase their share of such drift as centralization proceeds because the *effect* of solidaristic policies on the wage structure is rising with the wage spread of workers sub-jected to the same agreement. In symbolic terms, if $c \to 0$ then bargaining is carried out by a large number of unions each of which have members with very similar wages. Solidaristic wage policies will consequently have little effect on overall wage relativities, and drift will be evenly distributed on average (i.e., $r_d \to 1$). As centralization increases, $c \to 1$, the heterogeneity of membership goes up and the effect of solidaristic policies on the wage structure becomes greater. Drift will therefore increasingly benefit high-wage workers – in the limit *only* high-wage workers (i.e., $r_d \to 0$). Although it does not matter much for the results exactly how r_d declines with centralization, a nonlinear function such as $r_d = 1 - c^2$ is a priori preferable since the effect of centralization on wage dispersion becomes more pronounced at higher levels of centralization.[30]

The size of the expected wage relativity, r^e, can now be expressed as a weighted average of the relative distribution of the bargained wage increase (r_b) and the relative distribution of wage drift (r_d):

$$r^e \equiv \frac{w_i r_b + w_d r_d}{w_i + w_d} = \frac{w_i + w_d(1 - c^2)}{w_i + w_d} \qquad (11)$$

Subtracting equation 11 from equation 10 yields the following value for the difference between the ideal and expected wage relativity:

$$r^i - r^e = c^2 \left(1 - \frac{w_i}{w_i + w_d}\right) \approx c^2 \left(1 - \frac{w_i}{\hat{w}_i + w_d}\right) \qquad (12)$$

The approximation substitutes $\hat{w}_i$ for w_i, where the former is the wage increase the union would demand in the absence of solidaristic wage policies ($\beta - 0$). This has no influence on the substantive results, but greatly simplifies the presentation.[31]

The important implication of equation 12 is that equality-oriented union leaders acting with foresight can counteract unwarranted inequalizing effects from wage drift by raising wage claims in the collective bargaining process. Furthermore, the incentive to do so rises with centralization since wage drift will increasingly benefit high-wage workers. This conclusion follows whether wage drift is independent of, or negatively related to, bargained increases.[32] For simplicity, I assume that drift, w_d, only occurs up to a constant threshold above which centralized enforcement mechanisms become effective.[33]

The nominal wage increase that unions will actually demand obviously also depends on the effect of such wages on real wages and unemployment. This (utility-maximizing) wage increase (w_i^*) can be found by substituting the ex-pressions for $r^i - r^e$, ΔU_i, $\Delta \bar{U}$, and π^* into equation 9 and setting the partial derivative equal to zero. The result is the noncooperative equilibrium wage demand by union i. Assuming that all other unions behave identically in equilibrium (i.e., that $w_o^* = w_i^*$), the welfare-maximizing wage increase of any union (w^*) is given by:[34]

$$w^* = \frac{\alpha(1 - c + c\iota) - (1 - \alpha)\iota\bar{U}(c^2 - 2c + 2\iota c + 1) + \beta\dfrac{2c^A}{\hat{w} + w_d}}{(1 - \alpha)\iota(c^2 - 2c + 2\iota c + 1) + \beta\dfrac{2c^A}{(\hat{w} + w_d)^2}} \qquad (13)$$

where $\hat{w}$ is equal to w^* when $\beta = 0$.

Finally, the level of unemployment can be found by using equation 6, which says that the average increase in unemployment is simply the difference between wage growth and price growth. Furthermore, we know that in equilibrium this difference must be equal to zero:

$$\Delta\bar{U}^* = w^* - \pi^* = 0$$

Substituting in the equilibrium values for w^* (equation 13) and π^* (equation 8), and rearranging, yields the following equilibrium rate of unemployment $(\bar{U})^*$:

$$\bar{U}^* = \frac{\alpha(1 - c + c\iota) + \beta\dfrac{2c^A}{\hat{w} + w_d}}{(1 - \alpha)(c^2 - 2c + 2\iota c + 1) + \beta\dfrac{2(1 - \iota)c^A}{\iota(\hat{w} + w_d)^2}} \qquad (14)$$

The predictions of the model are illustrated in Figure 2.1, which is discussed in detail in the main text: When the monetary regime is accommodating, the relationship between centralization and unemployment is hump-shaped, with centralization outperforming decentralization; when the regime is nonaccommodating, the relationship is *reversed* so that unemployment performance is first improving with centralization (as monetary deterrence becomes more effective), and then deteriorating (as the costs of monetary inflexibility outweigh the positive deterrence effects).[35] As can be seen by comparing this pattern to the curve for $\beta = 0$, the upward bend is due to the growing effects of solidaristic wage policies. In contrast to intermediately centralized bargaining systems, at high levels of centralization, monetary nonaccommodation will jeopardize the ability of unions to solve their internal collective-action problem.

The implications of the argument for inflation and wage dispersion can be easily deduced from the model. With respect to inflation, the equilibrium value can be found by substituting equations 13 and 14 into equation 8, which yields:

$$\pi^* = \frac{\alpha(1 - c + c\iota) + \beta\dfrac{2c^A}{\hat{w} + w_d}}{(1 - \alpha)(c^2 - 2c + 2\iota c + 1)\dfrac{\iota}{1 - \iota} + \beta\dfrac{2c^A}{(\hat{w} + w_d)^2}} \qquad (15)$$

The function is illustrated in Figure 2.2 in the main text. Unlike unemployment, inflation is always lower under more conservative monetary authorities, and the gain of nonaccommodation is particularly pronounced when bargaining is intermediately centralized.

The relationship between our explanatory variables, c and ι, and wage dispersion can be examined using the variance of absolute wage increases across the economy. The variance in wages for the whole economy (var W) may be defined as the sum of two random variables:

$$\mathrm{var}W \equiv \mathrm{var}W_b + \mathrm{var}W_d + 2\,\mathrm{cov}(W_b, W_d) \qquad (16)$$

where $\mathrm{var}W_b$ is the *economy-wide* variance in bargained absolute wage increases, $\mathrm{var}W_d$ is the *economy-wide* variance in absolute wage drift, and $\mathrm{cov}(W_b, W_d)$ is the covariance between bargained wage increases and drift.

To simplify matters a bit, assume that the distribution of drift is always proportional to the distribution of wages that would prevail in a completely decentralized system. The logic is that drift is driven by market forces, whereas bargained wages are not. This assumption is consistent with the stipulation made previously that drift will increasingly benefit high-wage workers *within* unions as centralization increases. The reason is simply that the dispersion of member's market wages, and hence also the dispersion of drift among these members according to the just-made assumption, increases as unions become more encompassing. For our present purposes, however, the usefulness of the assumption is that it simplifies the application of equation 16.

To see this, first note that the formula for the covariance, $\mathrm{cov}(W_b, W_d)$, is $1/N \sum (W_b - \overline{W}_b)(W_d - \overline{W}_d)$. In a completely decentralized system, drift is directly proportional to the distribution of bargained wage increases, by definition, and we can use the following formula for calculating the covariance term:

$$\mathrm{cov}(W_i, W_d) = w_d/w \cdot 1/N \sum (W_i - \overline{W}_i)^2 \qquad (17)$$

where N is the number of workers (w_d and w are defined as the growth in wages due to drift and bargaining, respectively, as before). The second term in this equation is simply the variance of W_b, so equation 16 can be reduced to

$$\mathrm{var}W = (2w_d/w + 1)\mathrm{var}W_b + \mathrm{var}W_d \qquad (18)$$

The next step is to note that the variance of bargained increases, $\mathrm{var}W_b$, is dependent on the degree of centralization. For example, in an economy with 16 unions and median wages of 1, 2, 3, ..., and 16, respectively, the variance of a 10 percent bargained wage increase would be 0.85 in a decentralized bargaining system ($c = .06$), 0.64 in an intermediately centralized system ($c = .5$), and 0 in a completely centralized system ($c = 1$) (assuming that all get the same flat-rate increase as implied by the Nash solution).[36] Thus, dispersion decreases more rapidly at higher levels of centralization. To be exact, the functional relationship is given by $\mathrm{var}W_b = \mathrm{var}X\,(1 - c^2)$, where $\mathrm{var}X = w^2/w_d^2\,\mathrm{var}W_d$ is the variance of bargained wage increases in a completely decentralized system. Inserting the expression for $\mathrm{var}W_b$ into equation 18, and rearranging, yields

$$\text{varW} = [(w/w_d +)^2(1 - c^2) + c^2] \text{varW}_d \qquad (19)$$

where w is equal to π^* in equilibrium and given by equation 15.

Finally, to normalize the dispersion measure so that it does not depend on the scale of W, equation 19 can be divided by the variance of W when bargaining is completely decentralized ($c = 0$). Since the distribution of wage increases is assumed to be proportional to existing wage relativities in this case, the magnitude of wage increases should not matter for the distribution of wages. This yields the following standardized dispersion measure:

$$\text{dispW} = [1 - c^2 + c^2/(w/w_d + 1)^2] \qquad (20)$$

Note that disp$W$ is 1 when bargaining is completely decentralized, and that it remains 1 across all levels of centralization unless there is some bargained increase ($w > 0$). Note also that with a given bargained increase, $w = k > 0$, centralization reduces dispersion. Using equation 15 for the equilibrium value of w, this relationship is illustrated in Figure 2.3 for a more or less accommodating monetary regime. It can be seen that the negative relationship between centralization and dispersion is more pronounced the more accommodating the regime. The extent to which the monetary regime matters for the relationship depends on the willingness of unions to trade solidaristic policies for lower unemployment, which is an empirical matter (and influenced by unemployment compensation rates and other social wage components).

3

ECONOMIC INSTITUTIONS AND PERFORMANCE

Quantitative Evidence

The theory presented in the previous chapter has two broad empirical implications. First, it hypothesizes that economic performance is contingent on the particular mix of bargaining institutions and macroeconomic policy regimes. In a centralized bargaining environment we expect a flexible monetary regime to produce the best employment performance, *especially* if international growth is sluggish and centralization is associated with wage compression. Under these circumstances, labor has both the interest and the capacity to adopt a farsighted wage strategy that is compatible with the distributive interests of low-wage groups. If, on the other hand, the government is unable to reassure unions about its ability to sustain full employment (in the event of an unforeseen economic downturn, for example) or, more crucially, if the economic policy regime during low-growth periods leaves no or little scope for nominal wage increases, then solidaristic wage policies are likely to come into conflict with low-inflation targets.

Conversely, in an *intermediately centralized* bargaining system, policy flexibility may tempt sheltered unions to pursue militant strategies in the expectation that the government will, in its own (short-term) political interest, accommodate such wage increases through lax monetary and fiscal policies. In such an institutional environment, there are benefits to be reaped for the government from institutionalizing a commitment to a nonaccommodating policy. If such a commitment is perceived to be credible, it can deter militant union behavior and produce superior employment and inflation performance. When the commitment is not perceived to be credible (even if the government is in fact committed), the government will pay for this lack of credibility in the form of higher levels of unemployment. In decentralized bargaining systems, finally, the model predicts that monetary policy is either neutral or has small real effects.

47

The second broad implication is simultaneously normative and empirical. Normatively the model implies that only certain macroeconomic policies produce desired outcomes in given collective bargaining environments. In the conclusion to this chapter I focus specifically on the implications of the argument for monetary policy in the new Economic and Monetary Union in Europe. Empirically, we expect an association over time between the macroeconomic policy regime and the bargaining system. Except for completely decentralized bargaining systems, monetary policies have real effects and these furnish both governments and organized employers and workers with incentives to adopt efficient institutions. Since the set of efficient institutions is not distributively neutral, however, the choice is subject to political contestation. This part of the argument is further developed and tested in Part II.

The discussion in this chapter is organized into three main sections. The first explains the operationalization of theoretical variables. As is often the case with complex institutional variables, questions of measurement bring to the surface a number of conceptual and theoretical disagreements that must be addressed before a sensible empirical analysis can be conducted. The second section explains the choice of statistical model and presents the main findings for unemployment, inflation, and wage inequality for 15 OELD countries. The analysis focuses on assessing the impact of the institutional variables, but attention is also accorded to the role of partisan policies. The concluding section summarizes and discusses the policy implications of the model.

OPERATIONALIZATION OF VARIABLES

The independent theoretical variables are the centralization of the wage bargaining system and the "conservatism" of the monetary regime. Each is discussed in turn.

CENTRALIZATION

As implied by the theoretical discussion, bargaining institutions can help to solve problems of wage–price competition between unions and employers. Whether the externalities of wage militancy are likely to be internalized depends on the number of bargaining agents and on the authority of higher-level associations to bargain wages on the behalf of their members. For example, the theoretical definition of centralization in the Calmfors–Driffill model, which focuses on the union side, conceptualizes centralization as the number of equally sized unions at any given level. This is also the definition used in the formal model presented in the previous chapter.

In reality, bargaining takes place at several different levels simultaneously, and unions are of very different sizes. Consequently, most discussions of bargaining institutions and union organization incorporate two institutional dimensions: One is *centralization of bargaining authority*, the other is the *concentration of union membership*. Centralization of authority refers to the locus of bargaining power and usually focuses on three dominant levels: the national or confederate level, the branch or industry level, and the local or firm/plant level. Concentration refers to the number and relative size of competing bargaining units at each level of bargaining: the number and relative size of confederations, the number and relative size of industry unions, and so on. Using a slightly different terminology, Visser (1990) distinguishes a *vertical dimension* that corresponds to the centralization of authority variable, and a *horizontal dimension* that includes union concentration as a core variable.[1]

In empirical studies these dimensions are transformed into a composite index of centralization. Thus, Schmitter (1981) constructs an index on the basis of the power and number of union confederations. Calmfors and Driffill (1988) develop an index on the basis of a more differentiated (while brief) assessment of actual bargaining authority and concentration across levels, and the index proposed in Dell'Aringa (1990) is derived in a very similar fashion. In some studies, a third variable is included that measures the degree of coordination between bargaining units at different levels (Crouch 1985; Bruno & Sachs 1985; Soskice 1990a; Layard, Nickell, and Jackman 1991).[2] If such coordination is informal and based purely on reciprocity, however, it is not an *institutional* variable, and it should therefore be excluded from an index of organizational centralization.[3] Another index, proposed by Cameron (1984), is concerned with measuring the "organizational strength" of labor rather than centralization per se, but two of the variables in his index are indicators of centralization.

Even if we focus on the indexes that are narrowly concerned with centralization, they share some key weaknesses. First, as pointed out by Soskice (1990a), with particular reference to the Calmfors–Driffill index, there is no (or only a superficial) attempt to include the organization of employers as an element in the index, even though centralization is necessarily a function of the organization of both labor and capital.[4] The problem is less serious for countries with a strong and well-organized labor movement because here there tends to be a tight relationship between centralization on both sides. Leaving aside the question of causality, whenever unions are strong, if they are organized at the national peak level, so are employers; if they are organized at the industry level, so are employers, and so on. In a few countries where unions are weak and fractionalized, however, it is not uncommon that employers are organized in a centralized fashion to prevent inflationary wage competition between firms and industries. These issues are particularly salient for the coding of Japan and Switzerland, as I will discuss in greater detail below.

The second problem is that the indexes are rather impressionistic, causing obvious problems of intercoder reliability. To a certain extent this is a problem that cannot be avoided, especially in relation to the centralization of bargaining authority variable. The task of determining who decides what requires a rather close monitoring of actual processes of bargaining and intraorganizational decision making, and an element of subjectivity is bound to creep into the assessment of such processes. In a different respect, however, the problem is conceptual. Thus, there is never an attempt in the literature to sort out clearly the conceptual relationship between centralization and concentration, although both are important elements of any composite index. This allows different authors to place greater emphasis on one than the other, resulting in something that is best described by Sartori's (1970) notion of "concept stretching."

Golden (1993) makes an interesting attempt to solve this problem by arguing that the degree of centralization of authority in a union confederation is conceptually subordinate to the degree of concentration. The fundamental justification is that submission to confederal authority "is ultimately voluntary, resting as it does on the ongoing decisions by subordinate union actors to acquiesce to it" (440). According to this argument, because membership in higher-level bargaining units is voluntary, authority at that level is ineffective and therefore conceptually uninteresting. Peak-level authority, in a word, is epiphenomenal to decisions made by constituent unions.

Yet if this is true, then it would seem that the authority of national unions (Golden's units of analysis) is also epiphenomenal to what the regional and local unions do; and their authority, in turn, is a result of what individuals decide. The logical implication of Golden's argument is that we should cease altogether the study of unions as organizational agents and focus instead on individuals.[5] In this conception, organizations are simply collections of people following particular rules of behavior. But Golden is not actually drawing this implication because her justification for treating national unions as the "basic unit" of analysis is that individuals, local unions, and subsections within the union have been de facto stripped of bargaining authority.

If we accepted Golden's methodology, there would be no way to accurately measure decentralization of bargaining authority from, say, a national union to its regional affiliates, or the effects on centralization of the formation of a bargaining cartel between previously independent unions. In either case, should we change our count of unions? The answer to this question must be that numbers have indeed changed, but that the significance of the change in both cases depends on the magnitude of the shift in bargaining authority. But because Golden declines to talk about relations of authority, one would have to decide either that the change was significant enough to now count a new number of unions or that it was sufficiently insignificant to retain the original count. On closer inspection, therefore, it is evident that Golden has simply transformed the measure of authority into a dummy variable: either authority is completely centralized within some organizational entity, or the number of organizational entities has changed. Though this conception would undoubtedly reduce the problem of intercoder stability, it is in my view not a satisfactory solution to the problem of devising a theoretically sound measurement of centralization. There is no way around it: *both* the number/size of bargaining units *and* the vertical distribution of authority matter.

Golden's analysis, however, *does* highlight the conceptual relationship between concentration and centralization. Thus, the measure of concentration presupposes organizational units in which centralization of bargaining authority is complete. Whenever this is *not* the case, we will have to distinguish between different levels of bargaining, and the relative authority that is accorded to each level. At any particular level there should be no hierarchical relationship between the organizational entities located at that level, and we would therefore need to know only the number (and relative size) of bargaining units at that level. Hence, in measuring the structure of bargaining institutions, everything flows from the relationship of authority: Whenever there exists a hierarchical relationship of power, we need to measure the number of levels in this relationship, as well as the power vested in each level; whenever there is no hierarchical relationship of power, the number and relative size of bargaining units are the only relevant variables. By implication, if concentration were to be used as a single satisfactory measure of organizational design, as suggested by Golden, all authority would have to be vested in one level, and we could content ourselves with counting the number and relative size of bargaining agents. In most actual bargaining systems this is too simplistic.

We can formalize and clarify this discussion by creating an index of centralization that pays proper attention to both the number and relative size of bargaining units at each level and to the bargaining authority vested in each level. For illustrative purposes, imagine a bargaining system containing four unions organized into two union federations which, in turn, are members of the same union confederation (Figure 3.1). This system has three bargaining levels with a different number of bargaining units (n) at each level. Dispersion of bargaining power at each level can be expressed by Rae's index of fragmentation, which is defined as $1 - 1/n$ (Rae 1967). Conversely, the concentration of such power can be expressed simply as one minus Rae's index, which is equivalent to $1/n$ (in Figure 3.1 the concentration of power is 1, $\frac{1}{2}$, and $\frac{1}{4}$, at the top, middle, and bottom levels, respectively).

To determine the degree of centralization in this system, we need to combine this information with the bargaining authority vested in each level of the hierarchy. This can be done by attaching weights to each level reflecting the bargaining rights accorded each level. Thus, if *all* authority is vested in one level we can accord it the weight of "1," whereas if a level has no authority it would be given a weight of "0." Levels with real, but limited, authority would be given weights between zero and one. In general, if the number of bargaining units at each bargaining level, j, is denoted n_j, and the weight accorded each level is denoted w_j, then the degree of centralization, C, can be expressed in the following simple formula:

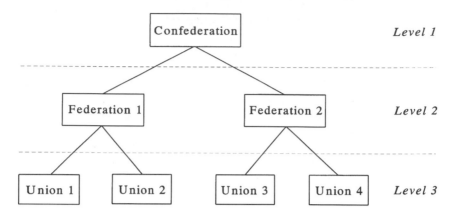

Figure 3.1. *Example of a simple organizational structure.*

$$C = \sum_j \frac{w_j}{n_j} \qquad (1)$$

where J is the number of levels, and $\Sigma w_j = 1$. The index varies between zero (in the limit) and one. In our example, if $w_j = \{.2, .2, .6\}$, then $C = .45$, whereas if $w_j = \{.6, .2, .2\}$, then $C = .75$.

The limitation of this index is that it presupposes that all bargaining units at each level have the same impact on the overall bargaining result. Yet some unions are clearly larger and more important than others, and so we have to somehow adjust the number at each level to reflect these differences in size. Theoretically this is important because size is known to affect the incentives of the decision makers along the lines suggested by Olson (1965, 1982). For example, if all bargaining is taking place at the national level and one confederation bargains wages for 95 percent of the labor force, while five small confederations bargain wages for the remaining 5 percent, we want to be able to distinguish this system from one in which six equally sized confederations control the bargaining process. The first case approximates Olson's concept of a privileged group with no possibilities for the large confederation to free-ride on the restraint of the smaller, while in the latter case there is a much stronger incentive for each union to defect.

Size inequalities are also important because they affect the capacity of particular unions to "lead" the wage setting in other sectors of the economy. Thus, in industrial relations systems where unions are very unequal in size, there is a tendency for wage bargaining in the entire economy to be dominated by bargaining in the area with the largest union. There are two related reasons for such dominance. First, if there is pressure on employers in sectors with fragmented unions to increase wages above the raises that the large union finds compatible with its medium- term interests, these employers are often able to "wait out" the unions until the bargaining results from the dominant area are in. Conversely, if unions in the fragmented sectors are too weak to demand wage increases that would be acceptable for the dominant union, then these unions have an incentive to wait out the employer side.[6]

The "counting problem" created by such inequalities is very similar to the problem of ascertaining the number of parties in a party system, and the common solution in both literatures is to use the so-called Herfindahl index, which weights large unions more than small. In the party literature, the result is called the effective number of parties, but for our purposes it will be called the *effective number of bargaining units*, and denoted N to distinguish it from the actual number, n. N is defined as follows:

$$N = (\textstyle\sum_i p_i^2)^{-1} \tag{2}$$

where p_i is the share of union members organized by union i.[7] The effective number of units is equivalent to *the number of equally sized units that would have the same effect on fractionalization as have the actual differently sized units*.[8] The variable N thus enables us to measure the actual degree of fragmentation by discounting the role of small and relatively insignificant units (achieved by each unit being weighed by itself through squaring). If we now substitute the expression for N in place of n in expression 1, we have the following definition of centralization:

$$C = \textstyle\sum_j \frac{w_j}{N_j} = \textstyle\sum_{ij} w_j p_{ij}^2 \tag{3}$$

This index provides a clear definition of centralization that is theoretically well grounded. Thus, if all bargaining power is concentrated at one level of bargaining, and if there is only one bargaining unit, then $C = 1$. On the other hand, if bargaining authority is concentrated at a low level where fragmentation is great, then C approximates 0.[9] It is also useful to think of $N^* = 1/C$ as a conceptual parallel to the effective number of bargaining units, although one should keep in mind that its calculation involves a judgment of hierarchical authority in addition to adjusting for differences in union size. With this caveat in mind, we may refer to $N^* = 1/C$ as the *implied effective number of bargaining units*, where $N^* = [1,\infty]$.[10] N^* can be interpreted in a straightforward manner as the degree to which a bargaining system approximates Olson's concept of a privileged group (where $N^* = 1 =$ privileged group).

The number N^* can be seen as the operational equivalent to the number of equally-sized unions in the theoretical model, and since $C = 1/N^*$ the operational definition of centralization is directly analogous to the theoretical ($c = 1/n$). I have used this formula to construct time-series data for centralization. For the five countries accorded special attention – Austria, Denmark, Germany,

Norway, and Sweden – this has been done for the period from 1960 to 1995 (as previously presented in Figure 1.2). In the 10 other OECD countries – Belgium, Britain, Canada, Finland, France, Italy, Japan, the Netherlands, Switzerland, and the United States – time series have been constructed for the period 1973 to 1993. The measurement of p_{ij} is based on national data on the distribution of union membership, while w_j is determined through a detailed examination of individual bargaining rounds according to the locus of bargaining authority in each round.[11] I have made no attempt to separately measure the concentration of employer associations (where the comparability of data is more restricted, especially for the public sector), but because fragmentation of unions and employers tends to mirror one another, it would hardly alter the picture much if the data were supplemented with figures for the distribution of employees covered by different employer organizations.[12]

Table 3A.1 in Appendix A to this chapter describes the specific rules I applied in weighting the locus of bargaining power in each country. The coding is facilitated by the fact that only three levels tend to be salient for wage bargaining: the national or peak level, the industry or sector level, and the firm or plant level. Following Visser (1990: 156–65), the assignment of weights depends on the *level of bargaining* and the *degree of enforceability* of agreements at each level.[13] With a few exceptions there is a relatively clear separation between bargaining systems in which peak-level bargaining does or does not play a dominant role, as well as between systems in which the industry or local level is dominant (indicated by a dashed line in the table). Instead of logical completeness, the table is designed to enable a full, mutually exclusive, and reasonably detailed classification of all empirically occurring bargaining rounds in our 15 cases.[14] The degree of enforceability depends on the capacity of bargaining agents to implement their agreements. Enforceable agreements presuppose that bargaining agents control most strike and lockout funds and can impose fines for noncompliance (particularly important on the employer side). Nonenforceable agreements mean that the bargaining agents lack credible threats of sanctions (included here are several instances of "incomes policies" – see Flanagan, Soskice, and Ulman 1983). In some borderline cases, noted in Appendix A, bargaining agents exercised partial control over enforcement.

Austria can serve as a simple illustration of how the final centralization score was calculated. In 1973 Austria had a single labor confederation organizing both blue- and white-collar workers (ÖGB) and 16 industry unions with the following shares of total union membership (in order of magnitude): .183, .180, .129, .095, .092, .074, .046, .045, .041, .031, .018, .017, .016, .013, .011, .009. Substituting this information along with the weights from Table 3A.1, the operational definition of centralization, C, yields the following figure:

$$C = [.1 \cdot 1^2 + .9 \cdot (.183^2 + .180^2 + .129^2 + .095^2 + .092^2 + .074^2$$
$$+ .046^2 + .045^2 + .041^2 + .031^2 + .018^2 + .017^2 + .016^2$$
$$+ .013^2 + .011^2 + .009^2) + .1 \cdot (0.00^2)] = 0.18$$

Note that the share of membership by any single union at the local level is assumed to be negligible – an assumption that is practically always satisfied for plant and firm-level bargaining. The same procedure was used for all countries and periods, which finally allowed the composite index to be constructed.[15]

Countries where the predominant level of bargaining is at the plant and firm level, but with elements of industry-level bargaining (Britain, Canada, France, Italy, and the United States), present a particular problem since data on the number of industry- or sector-level agreements and the number of workers involved are spotty at best (Golden and Wallerstein 1995: 33). Instead, I have simply assigned centralization scores to these countries – *except* for years where national-level bargaining occurred. This implies that the classification of decentralized bargaining systems largely reflects an ordinal scaling. Moreover, the assignment of decentralized values becomes somewhat "truncated" to make a clear distinction from intermediately centralized systems. This "compression" could pose a problem because it has been argued that small differences in otherwise similar industrial relations systems can translate into substantial effects on outcomes (Card and Freeman 1993). The problem may be remedied if we use a square root transformation of C since small differences between decentralized systems will be somewhat magnified, while differences between intermediately centralized and highly centralized systems will remain relatively unchanged. Given these somewhat ambiguous scaling issues, Appendix B contains a sensitivity test for the effect of scaling of centralization on the empirical results. The substantive findings turn out to be robust to scaling.

Table 3.1. shows the average centralization scores for the 15 cases over the 1973–95 period, ranked in order of centralization. For comparison, I have included the widely used rankings by Schmitter (1981), Cameron (1984), and Calmfors and Driffill (1988). As indicated by the correlation coefficients at the bottom of the table, all of these indexes are very similar to the one implied by C. Using the average rank of the three existing indexes, the correlation coefficient is nearly perfect (.95). Assuming that the three indexes are measuring the same underlying attribute – centralization – but disagree due to intercoder instability, C would appear to be a good proxy for the theoretical variable. Where there *is* disagreement, it is mainly over the exact classification of Austrian institutions. In this system, bargaining is exclusively occurring at the industry and local levels, but the authority to initiate bargaining and enforce agreements is concentrated at the peak level. Since the model applies only when actual bargaining is taking place, my coding of Austria reflects the preeminent level of bargaining (the industry level), rather than the preeminent level of authority.[16] In other words, the classification reflects the answers to the following prioritized set of questions: (i) at what level is bargaining taking place? and (ii) how enforceable are the agreements reached at that level?[17]

Compared to the Calmfors–Driffill rankings, Japan and Switzerland come out as being somewhat more centralized than implied by their index. In my scheme these countries are separated from the group of Liberal Market Econo-

Table 3.1. *Centralization of Bargaining, Central Bank Independence, and Currency Regimes, 1973–93*

| | Centralization | | | | Monetary Regime | | | | |
| | | (1) | (2) | (3) | | | (1) | (2) | (3) | |
	Centralization index	Schmitter	Cameron	Calmfors & Driffill	Mean (1)-(3)	*Hard currency index*	Cukierman	Bade and Parkin	Grilli et al.	Mean (1)-(3)
Nor	.569	2	2	2	2	.40	0	.2	-	.10
Swe	.485	4	1	3	2.7	.29	.24	.2	-	.22
Den	.467	4	6	4	4.7	.42	.61	.2	.38	.40
Fin	.445	4	5	5	4.7	.38	.25	-	-	.25
Aus	.437	1	3	1	1.7	.52	.82	-	.50	.66
NL	.392	6	7	7	6.7	.54	.52	.2	.63	.45
Ger	.353	8	8	6	7.3	.60	.96	1	1	.99
Bel	.338	7	4	8	6.3	.47	.09	.2	.25	.18
Jap	.299	-	14	12	13	.74	.07	.6	.13	.27
Swi	.265	9	10	13	10.7	.67	1	1	.88	.96
Ita	.185	15	11	11	12.3	.29	.32	.2	.13	.21
Bri	.182	14	9	10	12.7	.15	.15	0	0	.05
Fra	.114	12	15	9	12	.39	.26	.2	.25	.24
Can	.071	11	12	14	12.3	.35	.59	.2	.75	.51
US	.071	11	13	15	13	.47	.64	.6	.88	.72
r		.88	.86	.88	.95	.41/.71[a] .41/.79[a] .44/.76[a] .60/.80[a]				

[a] Correlation coefficients with and without Japan.

mies (LMEs) where coordinated wage setting above the firm level is at best sporadic. I have here essentially accepted Soskice's (1990a) critique of Calmfors and Driffill's classification on the grounds that it pays insufficient attention to the role of powerful employer organizations at the national and sectoral/industry levels (see also Crouch 1993). The results reported below, however, are *not* sensitive to the inclusion or exclusion of these cases (whether one-by-one or jointly).

MONETARY REGIME

The limitations of existing measures of monetary policies are no less severe than for measures of centralization. Indexes of central bank independence, for example, tend to be rather impressionistic and highly insensitive to changes over time. Conceptually, however, these indexes are very close to the theoretical concern with commitment to a conservative or inflation-averse policy strategy. Thus, Alesina and Summers (1993) conceive of central bank independence as equivalent to "delegating monetary policy to an agent whose preferences are more inflation averse than the society's preferences" (157), a conception they largely attribute to Rogoff (1985) and Barro and Gordon (1983). Similarly, Grilli, Masciandaro, and Tabellini (1991) explain that although "independence to choose the final goals can be defined without reference to the contents of such goals . . . we identify independence with autonomy to pursue the goal of low inflation" (367). Cukierman (1992) has a more elaborate discussion of the issue, but arrives at a very similar conception: "Central banks are more conservative than political authorities in the sense that they attribute relatively more importance to the goal of price stability" (355), and he further notes that "the concept of independence is . . . the ability of the bank to stick to the price stability objective even at the cost of other short-term real objectives" (370).

Cukierman's (1992) index of legal independence is the most detailed and comprehensive that exists, but others are more sensitive to actual as opposed to legal independence. All indexes, however, agree that some attention must be accorded to (i) the policy goals of the central bank, (ii) the institutional insulation of the bank from political influence over policy formulation (or their capacity not to compromise their policy objectives), and (iii) the power that the bank enjoys over monetary policy instruments (or their capacity to implement a certain policy). Thus, a bank that (i) is charged exclusively with maintaining price stability, (ii) is directed by a governor and a board that have a much longer tenure than most governments, and (iii) has exclusive control over monetary policy instruments (including the determination of the amounts and terms for government borrowing) is accorded a high score on the independence index. Conversely, a central bank that (i) must pay attention to several socioeconomic goals simultaneously (e.g., employment and social peace), (ii) is directed by a governor with a short or discretionary tenure and a board with a strong representation of government officials, and (iii) has to share control over monetary policy instruments with the government is accorded a low score.

The Cukierman independence index has been listed for the 15 cases in Table 3.1 along with two other widely used indexes by Bade and Parkin (1982) and Grilli, Masciandaro, and Tabellini (1991). The index presented in Alesina and Summers (1993) is also common in the literature, but it is in fact just an average of the two indexes just mentioned. All three indexes have been standardized to vary between 0 and 1. Since none of these indexes is a priori preferable to any of the others, I have included a *composite CBI index* that is the average of the other three. The logic is that all indexes are seeking to measure the same underlying attribute, but that errors in classification of cases will be reduced through averaging.

One problem that is not solved by this strategy is that central bank independence is neither a necessary, nor a sufficient, condition for commitment to a conservative monetary policy. When the bank is dependent, a credible commitment to a nonaccommodating policy may be achieved through alternative institutional avenues (such as membership in international monetary institutions), or it may come about as a result of persistent policies by governments that are sufficiently secure in power to create a reputation for "toughness" (Barro and Gordon 1983; Backus and Driffill 1985). Conversely, when the bank is independent, policy intentions may be defeated through a combination of expansionary fiscal policies, exhortation, and political threats. It is notable that while policy preferences of the central bank matter for its independence score, the policy preferences of the government do not.

A particularly widely noted disciplinary device in macroeconomic policies is to peg the value of a currency to one or more other currencies generally perceived to be antiinflationary (see, for example, Collins 1988; Fischer 1987; and Goodman 1992: 197–202). The most obvious example is the exchange rate mechanism (ERM) of the European Monetary System (EMS), which has been argued to lend credibility to the price-stabilizing policies of the member countries because of the dominant position of the German mark. Yet such arguments have to be carefully qualified. While membership in the ERM sets a standard against which the success or failure of a government's economic policies can, and often will, be measured, exit or noncompliance is always an option for governments. Besides, the actual operation of the ERM has enabled considerable, though not unconstrained, flexibility in national exchange rate policies.[18]

Membership in the ERM is also not a *prerequisite* for a credible commitment to a hard currency policy. Austria, Switzerland, and Japan have all adhered to strong currency policies (in the case of Austria through the unilateral pegging of the shilling to the German mark) while at the same time remaining outside any formal international institutional arrangements. For all these reasons, neither central bank independence nor international currency arrangements are likely to capture the full range of variation in the underlying theoretical variable (commitment to a nonaccommodating policy rule). Since we are not interested here in the effect of any particular institution, an alternative strategy is to use actual economic history as a guide to the orientation of monetary policies. A particularly sensitive indicator is the relative movement of exchange rates (Dornbusch 1976). The reason is that credible domestic commitments to a nonaccommodating strategy will raise the medium- to long-run confidence in the currency, while the reverse is true if domestic economic policies are perceived to be accommodating. A continuous commitment to antiinflationary policies will therefore reveal itself in the form of a strong and (relatively) appreciating currency.

The drawbacks of using currency movements as a proxy for monetary policy commitments are that (i) they are very sensitive to short-term speculative factors, and (ii) they tend to "exaggerate" monetary policy changes (Dornbusch 1976). The first problem can be remedied by averaging over periods exhibiting relatively stable appreciation or depreciation. Using this logic, a *hard currency index* was created based on the relative growth in nominal effective exchange rates. Like the CBI index, it varies between 0 (reflecting a relatively depreciating currency) and 1 (reflecting a relatively appreciating currency).[19] The index is compared to the three central bank independence indexes (making up the composite CBI index) in Table 3.1. As expected, there is a positive, but by no means perfect, correlation between the currency index and the various measurements of central bank independence. The main disagreement concerns Japan, which, according to the hard currency index and most observers, has followed a monetarist strategy since the mid-1970s, yet scores low on most central bank independence indices.[20] Thus, when Japan is excluded from the sample, the correlation coefficient climbs from .41 to .71 in the case of the Cukierman index, and from .60 to .80 in the case of the composite CBI index. The institutional key to restrictive monetary policies in Japan is the intimate organizational ties between the Bank of Japan and the Ministry of Finance, and the independent, powerful status of the latter. The Ministry, especially the Budget Bureau, holds very strong formal powers in the budgetary and monetary policy process, has a permanent appointee on the board of the central bank, and appoints many of the senior-level vacancies in the Bank (Hutchison, Ito, and Cargil, 1997: ch. 8; Lincoln 1988: 179; Pempel 1982: 61–2). In addition, the Ministry enjoys substantial autonomy in fiscal and monetary policy-making and is widely known to be dominated by fiscal conservatives who believe that inflation is a threat, not only to the Japanese economy and state, but also to their own long-term power within the bureaucracy. When these institutional features are combined with a long reign of single-party rule, farsighted low-inflation policies are to be expected (Hutchison et al. 1997).

The second problem, excessive sensitivity to policy changes, can be addressed by combining the hard currency index with the index for central bank independence. While the first may amplify changes in policy regimes, the latter almost certainly underestimates such changes. Even the Cukierman index, which is supposed to be sensitive to changes in central bank constitutions, shows virtually no change for the 15 countries included in this study. It is simply inconceivable that underlying policy commitments have been equally stable. The combined index, a simple average called I, strikes a more reasonable balance and can be considered a good proxy for a relevant parameter (denoted ι) in the theoretical model.[21] The sensitivity analysis in Appendix B shows that the main results are not dependent on this particular conceptualization, but are basically reproduced if we use the measures for central bank independence and hard currency regimes separately.

EMPIRICAL ANALYSIS

The theoretical model is an equilibrium model, and to limit the impact of short-term situational factors on the dependent variables, the data for the 15 countries was grouped into five four-year intervals from 1973 to 1993.[22] The data for inflation refers to consumer prices and was obtained from the *OECD Economic Outlook* (1992c, 1998). Unemployment data are standardized rates from the same source, except in the cases of Austria, Denmark, and Switzerland, where only data based on national definitions are available.[23] Wage dispersion refers to the gross cash earnings of the worker at the median of the earnings distribution relative to earnings of the worker at the bottom decile and is from the *OECD Employment Outlook* (1991, 1996). The figures focus on the lower half of the earnings distribution because the top decile (for which there are also data) contains a large number of professionals and self-employed, whose wages are generally not determined by collective bargaining.

Table 3.2 is a simple cross-tabulation of the centralization and central bank independence variables using unemployment, inflation, and wage dispersion as the dependent variables.[24] The monetary regime variable was grouped into two categories with an equal number of observations, while the centralization variable was divided into three classes: a decentralized category where firm- and plant-level bargaining dominate, corresponding to what has been referred to as Liberal Market Economies ($C < .2$); an intermediately centralized category with most bargaining taking place at the industry or sectoral level ($.2 \leq C < .45$); and a centralized category with an important role for peak-level bargaining between encompassing organizations of labor and capital ($C > .45$). According to the theory, monetary policies have very different effects in these three types of bargaining systems. The latter category is, not surprisingly, the smallest, and the analysis is hampered by the fact that only three cases (two from Denmark and one from the Netherlands) are above the median in terms of the conservatism of the monetary regime. Still, the table gives a good preview of the econometric results to follow.

Table 3.2. *Centralization of Wage Bargaining, Conservatism of the Monetary Regime, and Economic Outcomes in 15 OECD countries, 1973–93*[a]

			Centralization of Wage Bargaining			Low-High
			Low	Intermediate	High	
	Low	UN	8.0 (12) [a]	6.9 (12)	3.8 (13)	4.2 (37)
		INF	9.2 (12)	8.4 (12)	8.3 (13)	0.9 (37)
Conservatism		DISP	1.7 (11)	1.5 (10)	1.4 (10)	0.3 (31)
of monetary						
regime	High	UN	7.8 (10)	3.6 (25)	7.1 (3)	0.7 (38)
		INF	6.8 (10)	4.2 (25)	6.5 (3)	0.3 (38)
		DISP	2.1 (9)	1.7 (15)	1.4 (1)	0.7 (25)
	Low-High		0.1 (22)	3.3 (37)	-3.3 (16)	
			2.4 (22)	4.2 (37)	1.8 (16)	
			-0.4 (20)	-0.2 (25)	-0.0 (11)	

[a] N in parenthesis.
Note: Data were grouped into five four-year intervals for each country for a total of 73 observations. Unemployment (UN) refers to standardized rates; inflation (INF) is the average annual percentage change in the consumer price index; wage dispersion (DISP) is the gross earnings of the worker at the median of the earnings distribution relative to a worker at the bottom decile. The measurement of independent variables is described in the text and in Appendix A. The figures have been corrected for period differences to avoid time-composition effects.

Sources: For dependent variables: OECD (1991, 1992c, 1996, 1998); for independent variables: see text.

With respect to unemployment, the most interesting part of the table is the bottom row, which shows the difference in unemployment between cases with dependent and independent central banks. Note that for low levels of centralization, the employment gain from having a restrictive regime is negligible, while for intermediately centralized bargaining systems the gain is very substantial (3.3 percent or about 1¼; standard deviations). The magnitude of effect is similar for highly centralized systems, but here a restrictive regime is associated with a net employment *loss*. This is consistent with the hypothesis that at some point of centralization the gains from having an effective monetary deterrent are outweighed by the losses from the inability (or unwillingness) of the monetary authority to facilitate intraconfederal distributive compromises through accommodating policies. In centralized systems where the monetary authorities have been willing to play this role – Norway and Sweden were exemplary cases until recently – employment performance has been very good. Conversely, in centralized systems where monetary authorities have constrained the ability of the government to pursue accommodating policies – Denmark and the Netherlands in the early to mid-1980s are cases in point – intense distributional conflicts and high unemployment have ensued.

In terms of inflation, the data suggest that there is always a gain from having a restrictive monetary regime, but this gain is small at the extremes of the centralization scale. As expected from the theory, even though inflation is ultimately determined by the monetary authority, since private wage–price setters affect the actions of the monetary authority indirectly, effective deterrence can reduce inflation. Fragmented wage bargainers are less likely to be influenced by monetary threats due to collective action problems, and centralized bargainers are unresponsive because nominal wage restraint is difficult to reconcile with wage-distributive objectives. On the latter point, the effect of bargaining centralization on the wage structure is very clear in the data. Centralized bargaining is associated with relative earnings that are on average about 25 percent more compressed than in decentralized systems – a clear and substantial effect. Conservative monetary regimes seem to magnify inequalities slightly, although the effects are too small to allow for clear conclusions.

Taken as a whole, the data presented in Table 3.2 support the neo-corporatist idea that a highly organized labor market is a necessary condition for full employment, and they question the neo-liberal suggestion that a free labor market operating in a stable monetary environment is the most efficient institutional setup. On the other hand, the new classical penchant for independent central banks seems to resonate well with some of the evidence, even if the reasons are insufficiently specified within the new classical framework. Especially for the intermediately centralized category, a restrictive monetary regime seems to be conducive to very good inflation *and* employment performance. Countries such as Switzerland, Austria, and Germany in the 1980s are cases in point, while the abysmal employment performance of countries such as Belgium and Italy (and Sweden after the recent breakdown of peak-level bargaining) warns of the potential costs of accommodating policies. On this background, the preoccupation in the neo-corporatist literature with peak-level solutions to macroeconomic problems appears excessive, although it *is* a necessary condition for combining full employment with high wage equality.

Of course, these conclusions have to be taken with a grain of salt because descriptive statistics, though often suggestive, can mislead. Are the detected differences due to omitted variables? Are they contingent on the particular grouping of values? Are they driven by a few outliers? To answer these questions we need to employ more sophisticated econometric tools.

REGRESSION ANALYSIS

The analysis follows the most recent approach to pooled cross-sectional time-series analysis and uses ordinary least square (OLS) regression with lagged dependent variables and panel-robust standard errors (see Beck and Katz 1995). Thus, the basic regression model for the simple Calmfors–Driffill argument, omitting all controls, is:

$$U_{i,t} = a_i + \overset{+}{b_1}C_{i,t} + \overset{-}{b_2}C_{i,t}^2 + b_5 I_{i,t} + b_6 U_{i,t-1} + e_{it} \qquad (4)$$

where $U_{i,t}$ is the unemployment rate for country i at period t, and $e_{i,t}$ is an error term. The predicted direction of the effect of different variables is indicated with $+/-$ signs above the b-coefficients. Thus, if the Calmfors–Driffill model is correct, b_1 should be positive and b_2 negative since this would imply a hump-shaped relationship.[25] The effect of I (b_5) should be negligible according to the money neutrality thesis.

My theoretical argument, however, gives reason for skepticism about the predictive power of model 4. The reason is that the relationship can be either hump shaped or U-shaped depending on the character of the monetary regime. To allow for this possibility, I use the following transformation of equation 4 into a nonlinear interactive model:

$$U_{i,t} = a_i + (\overset{+}{b_1}C_{i,t} + \overset{-}{b_2}C_{i,t}^2)(k - I_{i,t}) + b_5 I_{i,t} + b_6 U_{i,t-1} + e_{it} \qquad (5)$$

where k is some positive number that depends on the scale of the monetary regime index (I), as well as the particular form of the interaction between central bank independence and bargaining structure. Compared to the simple Calmfors–Driffill model, the idea is that when the monetary regime becomes more restrictive (higher I), the deleterious inflation effects of intermediately centralized bargaining systems (the hump) decreases. Since I varies between 0 and 1, the relationship between C and U is hump-shaped for all $I<k$ (when the parameters for C and C^2 remain positive and negative, respectively), but U-shaped for all $I > k$ (when the parameters for C and C^2 turn negative and positive, respectively). Multiplying through with ($k - I$), and shifting the predicted signs accordingly, yields

$$U_{i,t} = a_i + \overset{+}{b_1}kC_{i,t} + \overset{-}{b_2}kC_{i,t}^2 - \overset{+}{b_1}C_{i,t}I_{i,t} - \overset{-}{b_2}C_{i,t}^2 I_{i,t} + b_5 I_{i,t} + b_6 U_{i,t-1} + e_{it}$$

$$= a_i + \overset{+}{b_1'}C_{i,t} + \overset{-}{b_2'}C_{i,t}^2 + \overset{+}{b_3}C_{i,t}I_{i,t} + b_4 C_{i,t}^2 I_{i,t} + b_5 I_{i,t} + b_6 U_{i,t-1} + e_{it} \qquad (6)$$

The second line of equation 6 simply substitutes b'_1 and b'_2 for $b_1 k$ and $b_2 k$, and b_3 and b_4 for $-b_1$ and $-b_2$. This form of the model can be estimated directly with the predictions given by the $+/-$ signs in the second line.

The analysis includes a number of control variables that have a potentially confounding effect on the results. The variables, including a brief discussion of their predicted effects, are as follows:

Density.

Refers to union density rates measured by the reported membership of all unions as percentage of the total number of wage and salary earners in employment. The source is Visser (1996). There is no clear prediction from the theory (since the important factor is the organization of bargaining), but standard economic theory implies that higher unionization rates cause upward pressures on unemployment and inflation.

Trade.

Defined as exports plus imports as percentage of GDP. The source is IMF, *International Financial Statistics Yearbook* (various years). One argument here is that openness has a dampening effect on unemployment because greater trade shares expose more sectors to the discipline of international competition (Danthine and Hunt 1994; Rama 1994). A contrary argument is that competition from low-wage countries either reduces wages or raises unemployment among low-skilled workers (Wood 1994; Leamer 1996).

Exmar.

Refers to the average annual percentage growth in a country's export markets. The source is OECD, *Economic Outlook* (various years). The simple logic here is that high rates of growth in a country's main export markets will have a dampening effect on unemployment.

LR.

This is an index of the partisan left–right "center of gravity." The index was developed by Thomas Cusack and is calculated using: (i) Castles and Mair's (1984) codings of parties' placement on a left–right scale, weighted by (ii) the decimal share of votes, parliamentary seats, and cabinet portfolios. The index can vary from 1 (extreme left) to 4 (extreme right), although most observations are much closer to the mean. The data are presented in Cusack (1997) and were generously supplied by that author. Following Hibbs (1977), the prediction is that the stronger the left, the lower the level of unemployment.

Fixity.

The variable measuring degree of exchange rate fixity is an index ranging from 0 to 1 based on the square of the rate of growth in the nominal effective exchange rate, with higher values implying that the exchange rate is closer to being invariant or fixed. Higher fixity should imply lower exchange rate risks, and thus lower transaction costs of trade, and possibly lower interest rate risk premiums. Both effects should help reduce unemployment. As suggested by Al-Marhubi and Willett (1995), exchange rate stability may also indicate a greater commitment to price stability and thus lower inflation.

UnOECD.

This is simply the OECD average of the dependent variable for any given time period. It is designed to remove any international diffusion effects from a general change in unemployment. The expectation, of course, is that higher average levels of the dependent variable will be positively related to the level of unemployment.

The results of the regression analysis for unemployment are presented in Table 3.3. The first column shows the result for the simple Calmfors–Driffill model. In this form the effects of centralization on unemployment are not only insignificantly different from zero but carry the wrong signs. If anything, the overall relationship between centralization and unemployment is monotonically declining, although the results are too weak to permit clear conclusions. This "negative" finding corroborates a recent study by the OECD[26] and is entirely consistent with the theoretical argument. There is simply no reason that centralization *by itself* should be related to unemployment, except perhaps in the sense that fragmented systems are more prone to create unemployment (which is what the data suggest).

The picture is very different, and much clearer, when we use the nonlinear interactive model (columns 2 and 3). All parameters on the theoretical variables, including their interactions, are now in the predicted direction, and they are statistically significant at a .05 level or better (with the exception of C and I, for which strong results are not expected). The analysis suffers somewhat from strong collinearity between the independent variables.[27] But there is a simple remedy for the problem since it turns out that I, as expected from the money neutrality thesis, has no (or only a very marginal) direct effect on unemployment. The model is therefore substantively the same if we exclude I, but *not* its interactions, from the regression (see column 3). Note that the coefficients are almost unchanged, but that the standard errors on the theoretical variables are now very small with t-scores in the 3 to 4 range ($p < .002$).

It is also noteworthy that the results are insensitive to the inclusion or exclusion of any particular country. This is especially important in the cases of Austria, Switzerland, and Japan, for which there is some disagreement about their exact classification on the institutional variables (as noted above). In fact, the results do not change much even if we exclude all three countries simulta-

Table 3.3. *OLS Estimates of the Effects of Institutional Variables on Unemployment, 1973–93*

	Predicted sign	Regression estimates and standard errors			
		(1) Calmfors-Driffill Model	Non-linear interaction model		
			(2) Full model	(3) Reduced model	Full model (excl. Austria, Japan, Switzerland)
Intercept		2.65	-0.99	-0.74	-0.86
		(2.14)	(2.38)	(2.23)	(2.51)
$C_{i,t}$	+	-5.92	12.47	9.95	10.78
		(5.87)	(13.21)	(6.81)	(13.39)
$C^2_{i,t}$	-	2.21	-43.73**	-40.17***	-48.92**
		(7.98)	(19.15)	(11.52)	(20.78)
$C_{i,t} \cdot I_{i,t}$	-	-	-57.19***	-51.30***	-59.54**
			(26.94)	(11.87)	(29.37)
$C^2_{i,t} \cdot I_{i,t}$	+	-	142.66***	134.24***	162.40***
			(46.46)	(31.73)	(56.62)
$I_{i,t}$	?	-1.51*	0.94	-	0.74
		(0.88)	(3.97)		(3.90)
$Un_{i,t-1}$		0.70***	0.60***	0.60***	0.40***
		(0.08)	(0.08)	(0.08)	(0.10)
$UnOECD_t$		0.06	0.15	0.15	0.48
		(0.20)	(0.19)	(0.18)	(0.22)
$Exmar_{i,t}$		-0.19	-0.20*	-0.20*	-0.14
		(0.12)	(0.11)	(0.10)	(0.12)
$Trade_{i,t}$		0.01	0.01	0.01	0.02*
		(0.01)	(0.01)	(0.01)	(0.01)
$LR_{i,t}$		0.31	1.28*	1.31**	0.99
		(0.57)	(0.66)	(0.64)	(0.85)
$Density_{i,t}$		0.02	0.02	0.02	0.02
		(0.02)	(0.01)	(0.01)	(0.01)
$Fixity_{i,t}$			-35.14	-35.06	-38.81
			(27.06)	(27.20)	(82.38)
N		75	75	75	60
Adj. R^2		0.75	0.80	0.80	0.79

Note: Variables are defined in text.
*$p < 0.10$; **$p < 0.05$; ***$p < 0.01$ (two-tailed tests based on panel-robust standard errors).

neously (see the last column of the Table 3.3). Clearly, therefore, the findings are not driven by the influence of a few controversial cases. On the other hand, it should be noted that although Austria is not an outlier by conventional statistical standards, unemployment is notably lower in this case than predicted from the statistical model. A dummy variable indicates that the magnitude is about two percentage points, which is substantial, but not enough to throw the model off its feet (consult the sensitivity analysis in Appendix B for details). While it is obviously conceivable that Austria is misclassified on the institutional variables, I shall later argue (in detail in Chapter 5) that the reason has to do instead with the unique combination in Austria of relatively high centralization *without* wage solidarism.

Figure 3.2 graphs the relationship between centralization and unemployment for two "typical" values on the monetary regime variable (defined as a single standard deviation above and below the mean).[28] Note that centralization has a dampening effect on unemployment in the case of an accommodating monetary regime, but that the relationship is U-shaped for a nonaccommodating regime so that both decentralized and peak-level bargaining are associated with high unemployment. The combination of these results implies a net employment gain from central bank independence for intermediately centralized cases (the light-shaded area), but a net loss for highly centralized cases (the dark-shaded area). These findings are exactly as predicted by the model, and the similarity between the predicted and estimated relationships leaves little doubt about the close match between theory and evidence (refer back to Figure 2.1).

The only notable difference is the absence of a "hump" on the curve for accommodating regimes (unless a very low value for I is used), which suggests that even governments with relatively dependent banks are quite concerned with inflation – an implication that is hardly surprising considering the sample of cases (all developed OECD countries) and the time frame (post-1973). The relatively high unemployment figures at the decentralized extreme also suggest that collective action problems are rather severe in fragmented systems. This lends some support to those who have argued that the relationship between centralization and unemployment is linear rather than hump-shaped,[29] but neither relationship generalizes to situations where the macroeconomic regime is restrictive.

The dashed segments of the curves in Figure 3.2 (at the decentralized end) are extrapolations since the most decentralized observation has a value of .07. If the two lines do indeed meet, then the money neutrality thesis is confirmed. However, it may be argued that both the United States and Canada are effectively completely decentralized systems and that the lines therefore should meet when $C = .07$. If this argument is valid, then the reason for the (relatively small) gap may be related to the causes for exceptionally high unemployment in France. Because France is close to the decentralized end, yet has a lower score on the I-index, but higher unemployment, than either the United States or

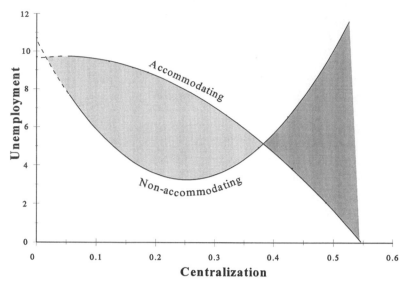

Note: The curves show the predicted level of unemployment for monetary regimes that are one standard deviation above or below the mean degree of conservatism. The predictions are based on the results for the full model in Table 3.3. The light shaded area indicates a net employment *gain* from having a restrictive monetary regime. The dark shaded area indicates a net employment *loss*. The dashed portions of the lines imply extrapolation.

Figure 3.2. *The estimated effect of centralization of bargaining on unemployment depending on the restrictiveness of the monetary regime.*

Canada, France helps to "hold up" the curve for accommodating regimes. Consequently, the lines intersect earlier if a dummy for France is included. Interestingly, the gap also largely disappears if the hard currency index is used instead of the composite monetary regime index. The reason is that the currency index picks up the "Franc Fort" policy since 1983, while the central bank index does not (the French central bank is coded as dependent). Of course, one could also argue that the gap is the result of efficiency gains from (presumably) lower uncertainty about monetary policies. Whatever the explanation, the overall results are clearly consistent with the theoretical predictions.

The estimated relationships in Figure 3.2 assume that all control variables are held at their mean value, but the effects of these variables are interesting in their own right. Referring to the regression results for the full model in Table 3.3, trade turns out to be weakly associated with higher unemployment, whereas growth in export markets is associated with lower unemployment. Since export markets are expanding faster than domestic markets (i.e., trade is growing as a share of GDP), the average net effect from trade (across time and countries) is in fact a small *reduction* in unemployment. Protectionism, in other words, does not appear to be an effective tool in the fight against unemployment.[30] Turning to the role of union density rates, there is a small (though statistically insignificant) unemployment-augmenting effect of unionization. However, the data do not lend much credence to the neo-liberal notion that free (or "flexible") labor markets combined with a conservative monetary regime constitute a recipe for full employment. To the contrary, if union density rates and wage bargaining centralization are both assumed to be zero, while the monetary regime is maximally conservative ($I = 1$), the results imply that unemployment rates are *above* the average – in excess of 3 percent. If in addition we assume a right-wing political environment, we have to add another percentage point.

Overall, the results do not indicate strong partisan effects,[31] but this does not mean that partisanship is unimportant. Rather it implies that partisan governments matter primarily because of the role they play in institutional (re)design. For example, we would expect that left governments are more favorable to centralized bargaining and flexibly accommodating monetary regimes than right governments, and these institutions are crucial for economic outcomes, as we have seen. Yet institutional reform is infrequent and presupposes support from well-organized societal actors, especially in the area of wage bargaining. Most of the time partisan governments will shy away from initiating difficult and risky institutional reforms and will instead adapt their policies to whatever "works" in a given institutional environment. I elaborate this idea further in the next section and in Chapter 4.

Turning to the results for inflation and wage dispersion (Table 3.4), these are equally encouraging for the theoretical argument. In the case of inflation two separate regressions were again run, which included and excluded I as an independent variable. To preempt the criticism that the results are biased because currency movements and prices, and hence I and inflation, are linked through a purchasing power mechanism, the variable I now refers exclusively to the central bank index.[32]

For the institutional variables the results are all in the predicted direction and statistically highly significant.[33] Among the control variables it is notable that trade has a clear negative effect on inflation, suggesting that trade can serve as a helpful disciplinary device in controlling domestic price–wage pressures. Exchange rate fixity also has a negative effect as expected, but the exact interpretation of this variable is unclear, as noted by Al-Marhubi and Willett (1995). Contrary to conventional wisdom, partisanship and union density rates have no independent effects, although both may well exert an indirect influence through the institutional variables as noted above.

Figure 3.3 graphs the estimated relationship between centralization and inflation for two different monetary regimes. For accommodating regimes the relationship between centralization and inflation is hump-shaped (which did not come out clearly in the descriptive analysis in Table 3.2), but the hump is reduced and eventually reversed into a (mild) U-shape when the monetary

Table 3.4. *OLS Estimates of the Effects of Institutional Variables on Inflation and Wage Dispersion, 1973–93*

		Regression estimates and standard errors				
		Inflation [a,b]		Wage dispersion		
	Predicted sign			(3) Non-linear model[c]	Linear model	
		(1) Full model	(2) Robust model		(4) Cross-sectional[d]	(5) Pooled time series[e]
Intercept		-0.90	-0.93	2.67	1.29	0.56
		(2.81)	(2.62)	(0.77)	(0.68)	(0.92)
$C_{i,t}$	+	46.88***	47.13***	-10.04**	-1.43***	-0.19***
		(12.95)	(10.19)	(2.78)	(0.43)	(0.06)
$C^2_{i,t}$	-	-63.70***	-64.05***	10.14**	-	-
		(20.15)	(15.67)	(3.24)		
$C_{i,t} \cdot I_{i,t}$	-	-65.58**	-66.16***	-	-	-
		(25.25)	(13.58)			
$C^2_{i,t} \cdot I_{i,t}$	+	83.29*	84.13**	12.84*	-	-
		(48.23)	(34.51)	(6.07)		
$I_{i,t}$	-	-0.09	-	-0.54	-	-0.08
		(2.85)		(0.56)		(0.08)
$Un_{i,t-1}$		0.02	0.03	-	-	-0.004*
		(0.07)	(0.07)			(0.002)
$UnOECD_t$		1.01***	1.01***	-	-	-
		(0.06)	(0.06)			
$Exmar_{i,t}$		-0.02	-0.02	0.09	-0.04	-
		(0.08)	(0.08)	(0.08)	(0.05)	
$Trade_{i,t}$		-0.04***	-0.04***	0.00*	-	-0.002*
		(0.01)	(0.01)	(0.00)		(0.001)
$LR_{i,t}$		0.39	0.39	-0.15	0.27	-0.005
		(0.68)	(0.68)	(0.24)	(0.22)	(0.009)
$Density_{i,t}$		0.00	0.00	0.00	0.00	-0.001*
		(0.01)	(0.01)	(0.00)	(0.00)	(0.001)
$Fixity_{i,t}$		-163.17***	-163.19***	33.97	-	-
		(44.60)	(44.56)	(29.89)		
LDV[f]		-	-	-	-	-0.51***
						(0.09)
N		73	73	15	14	41
Adj. R^2		0.81	0.81	0.71	0.68	0.73

[a] Pooled cross-sectional time-series regression with panel robust standard errors.
[b] Excludes two observations with high leverage and residuals according to Welsch's Distance test ($W_d > 3 \cdot \sqrt{k}$).
[c] Cross-sectional OLS regression.
[d] Excluding Austria and using forward stepwise regression to determine independent variables (regressors were limited to those with F-statistics above 0.5.).
[e] Dependent variable is change in the log of wage dispersion, and the regression includes a full set of country dummies.
[f] Level of lagged dependent variable.
*$p < 0.10$; **$p < 0.05$; ***$p < 0.01$ (two-tailed tests).

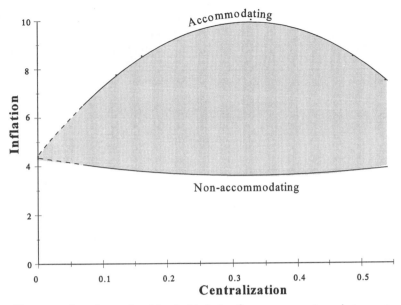

Note: The curves show the predicted level of inflation for monetary regimes that are one standard deviation above or below the mean degree of conservatism. The predictions are based on the results for the full model in Table 3.3. The dashed portions of the lines imply extrapolation.

Figure 3.3. *The estimated effect of centralization of bargaining on inflation depending on the restrictiveness of the monetary regime.*

regime becomes more restrictive. Unlike the pattern for unemployment, the curves never intersect,[34] but the curves are very close to each other for decentralized systems, challenging the notion that decentralized bargaining is an effective means to control inflation and suggesting that uncertainty and short-term wage flexibility cause a convergence in policies across institutional settings. Yet the results also contradict the neo-corporatist thesis that centralized bargaining institutions are superior for controlling inflation. Instead, the results support the hypothesis that distributive compromises within a confederal union structure are inflationary (cf. Calmfors 1993; Hibbs and Locking 1996).

Most notably, the results point to the possibility that intermediately centralized systems outperform all others if combined with an independent central bank. In terms of the theoretical argument, the reason is that unions in intermediately centralized systems can be deterred from engaging in militant behavior (unlike unions in decentralized systems), at the same time as inflationary wage solidarism is kept at modest levels (unlike in centralized systems). On the other hand, intermediately centralized systems can be exceptionally inflationary

when monetary policies are accommodating. Note, incidentally, that this pronounced "hump" is entirely consistent with the finding that only a modest
hump for unemployment exists since even small unemployment effects are
expected to lead to highly inflationary reactions by an unemployment-averse
monetary authority. Conversely, the mild U-shape for the relationship between
centralization and inflation is all that is needed for the U-shape between centralization and unemployment to be very pronounced (compare to Figure 2.2).[35]

The next logical question is whether centralized bargaining is indeed associated with greater wage compression. Unfortunately it is difficult to fully
answer this question through pooled time-series analysis because wage structures
are highly path dependent, whereas there is considerable variance across countries, producing a unit root problem in the basic model. It is, however, possible
to explain the *cross-time* variance through a pooled model, and I will show the
results of such a model in a moment. But since most of the variance is cross-
national, it is obviously important that the regression model can account for
this variance, and the only way to examine this is to rely on whole period means.
Column 3 of Table 3.4 shows the cross-sectional results for a nonlinear interactive model that would be ideally suited to capture the model predictions. This
rather complicated model is obviously a big mouthful for a sample of only 15
cases, but the model actually performs rather well, and it nicely captures the
empirically observed pattern, which is illustrated in Figure 3.4.

Using centralization on the horizontal axis, the figure plots (i) the actually
observed wage ratios (the triangles) and (ii) the predictions of the model for
each country using the actually observed values on all the independent variables
(the ovals). For the accommodating regime, the relationship between centralization and inequality is downward sloping and basically equal to a straight line.
For nonaccommodating regimes, on the other hand, the downward-sloping
function first levels off and then "bends around." This leveling off is anticipated
by the theory, and the overall impression from Figure 3.4 clearly resonates well
with the predictions (refer back to Figure 2.3).

There is, however, an important caveat to this conclusion: One case, Austria,
has a very strong effect on the results (high "leverage" in statistical jargon). The
reason is that Austria, unlike any other case, combines relatively high centralization with a conservative monetary regime and pronounced wage inequality.
In fact, the high level of wage inequality in Austria is what makes the curve for
nonaccommodating regimes bend up. So even if part of the reason for high
inequality in Austria is to be found in monetary policies, as anticipated by the
theory, Austria "drives" the results for the effect of the monetary regime variable
to such an extent that it could easily be some other aspect of Austrian institutions that explains the high level of wage inequality. Indeed, in Chapter 5, I
discuss some unique aspects of Austrian bargaining institutions that are likely
to account for some of the exceptionally inegalitarian wage structure.

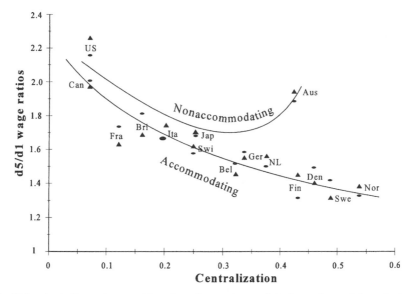

Key: Triangles indicate the actual location of countries; ovals indicate the model prediction.

Figure 3.4. *The estimated effect of centralization of bargaining on wage dispersion depending on the restrictiveness of the monetary regime.*

If we treat Austria as an outlier, the only variable that has a strong effect on inequality is centralization. This is seen in column (4) of Table 3.4, which shows the results for a stepwise regression analysis where only variables with an F-statistic above 0.5 were retained in the regression. Among the three variables that exceeded this threshold, only centralization turns out to have a statistically significant effect. In fact, the simple bivariate correlation between centralization and wage inequality is almost perfect: $r = -.89$. This result is clearly consistent with the argument about solidaristic wage policies, while it leaves unanswered questions about the effect of macroeconomic policies. Without Austria in the analysis, all that really seems to matter is the structure of the bargaining system.[36] Fortunately, this is also all that is required for the theoretical predictions regarding unemployment and inflation to hold.

The importance of centralization is corroborated by a pooled model including a full set of country dummies and changes in dispersion as the dependent variable (the last column of Table 3.4). Data are available only from 1979, but Austria is back in the analysis because the country dummies effectively eliminate the cross-national variance in dispersion. Again, centralization is a strong predictor, a comforting fact because it suggests that the variable is relevant for explaining variance over time in addition to variance across countries. The negative effect of unemployment, which is at first blush surprising, is simply an artifact of measurement since the unemployed are disproportionately drawn from low-income groups, and unemployed are not part of the dispersion data. The negative, though insignificant, result for partisanship is surprising, especially since Reuda and Pontusson (1997) have found a significant positive effect of this variable. However, partisanship is closely related to both union density and centralization, which have the "right" signs; much of the effect of partisanship may therefore be indirect.

ONE CUT CLOSER TO THE BONE: ORGANIZED MARKET ECONOMIES

Both the theory and the evidence presented so far suggest that monetary policy mainly has real effects in intermediately centralized and centralized bargaining systems. What makes a monetary regime effective in terms of unemployment is the capacity of economic agents to anticipate the decisions of monetary authorities and to adjust real-wage demands accordingly. Because beneficial deterrence effects presuppose strategic capacity, this logic does *not* extend to highly fragmented bargaining systems, or what has been referred to as Liberal Market Economies (LMEs). As noted in the previous chapter and discussed at length in the next, this is important to a theory of institutional design because actors are presumed to act on the basis of their preferences over real economic outcomes. Moreover, even if private agents had the incentive to alter the institutionalization of wage bargaining in response to government policies, such change may not be feasible because of pervasive collective action problems. The next chapter on institutional change therefore focuses on countries with highly organized labor markets, what I will here refer to as Organized Market Economies (OMEs), and makes the results for this category of countries particularly important – especially as they relate to unemployment. This section is therefore devoted to a closer look at this subset of cases.

Following David Soskice's classification, there are 10 major OECD countries that can reasonably be viewed as belonging to the group of OMEs: Austria, Belgium, Denmark, Finland, Germany, Japan, Netherlands, Norway, Sweden, and Switzerland.[37] For this subset of countries it is relatively unproblematic to assume strategic capacity, and this in turn leads to very clear predictions about institutionally mediated real effects. Thus, the *best* unemployment performance occurs when *either* the wage bargaining system is centralized and the monetary regime is accommodating, *or* when the bargaining system is (semi)decentralized and the monetary regime is nonaccommodating. The *poorest* employment performance is predicted for situations in which *either* the bargaining system is decentralized while the monetary system is accommodating, *or* in which the bargaining system is centralized while the monetary system is nonaccommodating. This implies a very simple linear interaction model of the following form:

$$U_{i,t} = a_i + \overset{-}{b}_1 C_{i,t} + \overset{-}{b}_2 I_{i,t} + \overset{+}{b}_3 C_{i,t} I_{i,t} + U_{i,t-1} + \text{controls} + e_{it} \qquad (7)$$

where the signs above the parameters are the hypothesized direction of the effect.[38]

The results are shown in the first column of Table 3.5. Note that the parameters are all in the predicted direction and statistically significant at a .01 level or better. Because Austrian unemployment is again somewhat lower than predicted, the results are strengthened if this case is excluded, but the model is well specified even if we keep Austria in the analysis, and the substantive effects are considerable. For example, an accommodating monetary system ($I = .2$) operating in a centralized bargaining system ($C = .5$) would be expected to produce equilibrium unemployment rates about 7 percent below those in a nonaccommodating regime ($I = .7$). Conversely, if the bargaining system were decentralized ($C = .2$), an accommodating monetary system would be associated with 5 percent *more* unemployment than a nonaccommodating regime.

Although the discussion and analysis have focused on the character of the monetary regime, the logic of the theoretical model can also be tested against other public policies that may accommodate union objectives. In particular, expansionary public sector employment policies and social policies that reduce workers' dependence on the market should facilitate union cooperation in highly centralized systems, but encourage militancy in decentralized systems – especially among low-wage workers who are concentrated in the sheltered sectors of the economy. Conversely, restrictive public employment policies and commodifying social policies, by increasing exposure to market forces, should encourage wage moderation in decentralized bargaining systems, but meet with resistance in centralized ones.[39] To test these propositions, I devised an *index of commodification* (COM), which is the average of unemployment compensation rates and total public sector employment (after standardization of both variables).[40] The former is measured as the average unemployment compensation rate over a three-year period for a representative 40-year-old unemployed person, taking into account different family circumstances (single or married with or without working spouse) and previous levels of earnings.[41] The data for public sector employment are based on OECD's standardized measures of government employment as a percentage of total employment. The findings are shown in the second column of Table 3.5.

Again, the results imply that accommodation facilitates full employment in centralized, but *not* in decentralized, bargaining systems. Whichever measure is used, therefore, the results all point in the same direction: the combination of *either* a highly centralized wage bargaining system with an accommodating

Table 3.5. *OLS Estimates of the Unemployment Effects of Institutional and Political Variables on a Subset of 10 Organized Market Economies, 1973–93*

	Predicted sign	Regression estimates and standard errors	
		(1) Using monetary regime variable for I	(2) Using social wage variable for I
Intercept		-0.03	-10.60*
		(4.45)	(5.62)
$C_{i,t}$	-	-22.09***	-17.08**
		(5.02)	(6.67)
$I_{i,t}$	-	-20.34***	-13.41**
		(4.46)	(5.38)
$C_{i,t}*I_{i,t}$	+	59.06***	28.80**
		(12.98)	(12.00)
$LR_{i,t}$		3.02***	2.33***
		(0.90)	(0.83)
$UnOECD_t$		-0.12	-0.08
		(0.21)	(0.25)
$Un_{i,t-1}$		0.58***	0.64***
		(0.10)	(0.11)
$Exmar_{i,t}$		-0.27**	-0.14
		(0.12)	(0.15)
$Trade_{i,t}$		0.02**	0.01
		(0.01)	(0.01)
$Density_{i,t}$		0.04**	0.02
		(0.02)	(0.03)
Fixity		31.94	37.35
		(34.24)	(39.62)
N		50	50
Adj. R^2		0.83	0.74

Note: Variables are defined in text.
*$p < 0.10$; **$p < 0.05$; ***$p < 0.01$ (two-tailed tests based on panel robust standard errors).

policy regime, *or* a decentralized bargaining system with a nonaccommodating policy regime produce low levels of unemployment, whereas "disequilibrium" couplings of the bargaining system and the monetary regime lead to high unemployment.

The next question is whether these institutional couplings are also different with respect to distributive outcomes. Not only should centralization have a dampening effect on wage differentials, but decommodifying unemployment and public employment policies should have similar effects. Such policies cushion workers from the inequalizing effects of unemployment and low-paid private sector employment, and they point to the broader role played by the "social wage" in the interface between the state and the labor market. Thus, to the extent that centralized systems produce coordinated expansions of the social wage (as argued in the neo-corporatist literature), this "wage" should also reflect the underlying structure of power between different occupational groups. Consequently, in centralized accommodating systems, the social wage would be predicted to have a solidaristic or egalitarian structure and the government would be expected to favor policies that reduced workers' dependence on the market. Conversely, in decentralized nonaccommodating systems, we would expect the social wage to be more inegalitarian, and the government to be engaged in policies that created greater exposure to (and less sharing of) the risks of unemployment.

As noted above, comparable data on equality – whether the focus is on wages proper or the social wage – are scarce and typically of a nature that does not permit the application of detailed time-series analysis. With a small number of cases, we instead have to content ourselves with bivariate relationships between the institutional variables and indicators of wage inequality. Table 3.6 shows the result of such an analysis using the OECD data on wage compression and a variety of measures for social wage equality as indicators. Several of these indicators have been developed by Gøsta Esping-Andersen (1990), whose work is intimately tied to issues of labor market stratification. Thus, his measure of decommodification indicates the extent to which benefits reduce people's dependence on the labor market (and hence their exposure to risk), while his measures of benefit equality and universalism are designed to capture the distributive effects of such benefits. The table also includes the previously introduced measure for unemployment replacement rates, which is a particularly salient aspect of Esping-Andersen's decommodification variable.

Note that all correlations are strong and in the expected (positive) direction. Although it is impossible to sort out the independent contributions of centralization and monetary accommodation, let alone their interactive effects, the results clearly suggest that both variables have a dampening effect on inequality. Indeed, the correlations presented in Table 3.6 bring out very clearly the predicted linkages between economic institutions and economic outcomes: *centralization of bargaining is associated with flexible policy accommodation and distributive equality; decentralization is associated with nonaccommodation and distributive inequality.*

PARTISAN POLITICS: HOW IT MATTERS

If we return to the regression results in Table 3.5, it is evident that government partisanship now has a statistically significant effect on unemployment. Thus, a

Table 3.6. *Pearson's Correlation Coefficients between Different Measures of Economic Institutions and Distributional Outcomes*

	Central-ization of wage bargaining[a]	Monetary accom-modation[b]	Wage equality[c]	Decom-modification[d]	Benefit equality/univers-alism[e]	Unemploy-ment replace-ment rate[f]
Central-ization	1					
Accom-modation	0.66	1				
Wage equality	**0.87**	**0.71**	1			
Decom-modification	**0.82**	**0.75**	0.72	1		
Benefit equality	**0.70**	**0.80**	0.85	0.84	1	
Replace-ment rate	**0.81**	**0.84**	0.86	0.94	0.88	1

Measurement and sources:

[a] Based on the mean scores on the index of centralization (1973–93).

[b] Based on the mean scores on the monetary regime index (1973–93).

[c] Wage equality is measured as the (inverse) of the gtoss earnings of a worker at the median of the earnings distribution relative to a worker at the bottom decile. (*Source: OECD* 1991, 1996.) Austria is excluded in the correlations with wage equality.

[d] Decommodification refers to the ease by which a person can opt out of the market, as well as the coverage of the various social security programs that makes this possible. It is based on an assessment of pensions, health care, and unemployment cash benefits and is adapted from Gøsta Esping-Andersen (1990), Table 2.2, p. 52.

[e] Based on an average of universality of sickness benefits, unemployment benefits, and pensions, as well as on the equality of such benefits as measured by the differential between the basic and maximum of such benefits. (*Source*: Esping-Andersen 1990, Table 3.1, p.70.)

[f] Measured as the average unemployment compensation rate over a three-year period for a representative 40-year-old unemployed person, taking into account different family circumstances (single or married with or without working spouse). (*Source*: OECD 1997b.)

one standard deviation shift in the political center of gravity from left to right raises the equilibrium rate of unemployment by about 2.5 percent. The effect falls to a single percentage point if we consider only within-country variation in the index, and the number is roughly the same if we use a more sophisticated conditional model that includes an interaction term for centralization and partisanship (Lange and Garrett 1985). Since macroeconomic policies are predicted to have greater effect in settings with large price and wage setters (OMEs), it makes sense that the results for partisanship are stronger than for the total sample of countries.

Yet the magnitudes of the effects are still dwarfed by the effects of the institutional interactions. When subjected to an exogenously given set of monetary and wage bargaining institutions, left and right governments produce outcomes that are not dramatically different. There are several possible reasons for this: (i) governments may pursue different goals in economic policy, but within a particular institutional environment they adopt similar policies to achieve these goals; (ii) governments pursue different economic policies, but economic forces cause outcomes to converge over the medium term; or (iii) governments pursue similar economic and political goals and hence adopt similar policies with similar results.

The last interpretation can be justified with reference to the Downsian median-voter theorem (Downs 1957). The idea is simply that electoral competition causes policy convergence around the position of the median voter and that outcomes therefore tend to reflect the preferences of the median voter. This idea is prevalent in much of the American literature on political business cycles – originating with Nordhaus (1975) and developed by Cukierman and Meltzer (1986), Rogoff and Sibert (1988) and others – and implies politically undifferentiated time effects (although politicians exploit short-term trade-offs between inflation and unemployment). The median-voter theorem has also been levied as a critique against the Lange–Garrett partisan model by Jackman (1986, 1987, 1989), who maintains that parties seeking to win government power must appeal to the center, and thus produce similar policies and outcomes.

In response to this critique, Lange and Garrett (1987) and Garrett and Lange (1989) have rightly pointed out that when applied to multiparty systems (or to two-party systems with a threat of third-party entry), the convergence argument fails on its own premises. For example, Cox (1987, 1990) and Shepsle and Cohen (1990) have demonstrated that Downsian assumptions do not imply policy convergence in multiparty systems, and alternative theories and evidence predict even greater policy divergence than in a "pure" spatial model (see Rabinowitz and Macdonald 1989; Przeworski and Sprague 1986; Iversen 1994). Furthermore, in multidimensional policy spaces there are no equilibria, and policy can therefore diverge according to ideological preferences.

If the weak partisan effects on employment is not convergence of preferences, then we must attribute it to the constraints under which policies are made. In this category of explanations we find the partisan business cycle theory proposed by Alesina (1989) and Alesina and Sachs (1988), structural Marxist theories of economic policies (e.g., Rowthorn 1977; Block 1977), as well as a more diverse set of case-oriented studies of economic policy failure. The model of contested institutions is consistent with these perspectives, but gives greater scope for partisan politics by positing several distinct institutional equilibria with different distributional effects. To the extent that institutions are the result of partisan politics, the government can affect outcomes *indirectly* through the design of institutions.[42]

This is likely, however, to be a highly mediated causal relationship since the government's direct control over institutional design is severely constrained. This is particularly the case for the structure of the wage bargaining system. Though the government can intervene in the wage formation process through statutory income policies, price controls, tripartite accords, and various less formal methods (including wage guidelines and exhortation), these measures have rarely led to lasting changes in the bargaining system *unless* supported by pivotal sectors of employers and unions (Flanagan, Soskice, and Ulman 1983). The failure of the "social contract" between the British Labour government and the union confederation (TUC), culminating in the "winter of discontent," and the incapacity of the Belgian government in the 1970s to convince employers and unions to resume centralized bargaining are cases in point. On the other hand, governments have occasionally played important *facilitating* roles in the implementation of reforms in the wage bargaining system through extensions of collective agreements to nonsignatory parties, or through the implementation (or subsequent repeal) of supporting legislation, including wage indexation.

The government can affect institutional design more directly through the economic policy regime and associated social policies, provided that it can overcome opposition in the legislature and from organized interests representing valuable resources to the government (in terms of investments, wage restraint, industrial peace, campaign support, etc.).[43] Through the monetary regime the government can place indirect pressure on different groups of employers and workers to accept more centralized forms of bargaining or can facilitate a shift toward decentralization. In the 1980s in Sweden, for example, the government's commitment to full employment made it difficult for different sectors' employers to agree on the desirability of a decentralized bargaining system.

The important point of this discussion is that partisan governments, while influencing economic outcomes indirectly through their power over especially the monetary regime, ultimately depend for their success on their ability to forge alliances with organized private interests. In particular, because the institutionalization of collective bargaining is predominantly an outcome of sectoral coalitions of labor and capital, the capacity of partisan governments to shift the institutional equilibrium in a preferred direction is real but circumscribed. Government economic policies and sectoral coalition formation thus interact in a complex strategic game in which the government shapes the economic environment in which bargaining and coalition formation takes place, while sectoral alliances in support of particular bargaining institutions affect the degree of success in the implementation of government economic policies. Although this approach implies that "who governs" matters for economic outcomes, it does so by adding an important institutional component to our understanding of the mechanisms by which partisan politics gets translated into outcomes. This is the point of departure for the model of institutional design that I develop in the next chapter.

CONCLUSIONS

The results in this chapter are strongly supportive of the theory. Long-term unemployment, inflation, and wage dispersion are largely a function of the institutional interaction between wage bargaining centralization and the accommodating or nonaccommodating nature of the monetary regime. Thus, in intermediately centralized systems, restrictive monetary policies facilitate the solution of collective action problems by reducing the capacity of unions to externalize the costs of militancy. This leads to relatively good employment and inflation performance, but also intermediate levels of wage dispersion. In centralized systems, by contrast, the capacity of unions to exercise self-restraint is jeopardized by a conservative monetary policy that would clash with internal compromises over distribution. Instead, wage solidarism and good unemployment performance are facilitated by accommodating monetary (and social) policies, although such accommodation has an upward effect on inflation. Only in decentralized systems, where unions are too small to influence aggregate prices, does the monetary regime fail to have any real effects.

Most of this evidence concerns differences in performance across countries with different institutional setups. Yet some of the variance in outcomes is also due to changes in institutional design, and in Chapter 5, I will discuss two cases of change – Denmark and Sweden – in some detail. Some institutional change, however, may not be fully uncovered by either the quantitative or case-oriented evidence, yet may explain some of the observed variance. The possibility is raised by the increasing effectiveness of the Exchange Rate Mechanism (ERM) within the European Monetary System during the 1980s. The reason is that a de facto enlargement of a currency area will increase the number of unions, and hence fragmentation, within that area. Since Germany exerted a disproportionate influence on monetary policy in the ERM, unions in the non-German ERM countries would be more prone to behave like unions in a completely decentralized system. This decentralization effect of monetary integration could explain some of the rise in the equilibrium rate of employment in Europe.

The exception is Germany because the Bundesbank was free to target German inflation, and German wage setters could therefore exert the same impact on the real money supply within the ERM as they did outside of it. Empirically the implication of this logic is that German unemployment under ERM should have been lower than in the other ERM countries. This is in fact borne out empirically if we look at the period from 1983 to 1992. Thus German unemployment was below the unemployment levels in *all* other member countries by an average of 3.2 percentage points, and the margin slightly increased from the beginning to the end of the period.

This argument, however, has limitations. Monetary policy continued to matter in non-German ERM countries because their currencies were never *irrevocably* fixed, and because the supply of the national currency continued to be controlled directly by the national central banks. If, for example, the central bank in a small ERM country pursued accommodating policies, the elasticity of demand for labor in each bargaining area would be lower than otherwise, thus inviting wage militancy. To the extent that militancy and accommodation subsequently raised inflation expectations and the probability of a currency devaluation, real interest rates would have to be raised to prevent an outflow of capital. The resulting risk premium on interest rates would translate into higher unemployment. A credible nonaccommodating policy would prevent these problems by reducing union incentives to engage in wage militancy. So national wage bargaining continued to interact, at least to some extent, with nationally specific monetary policy under the ERM.

This is not the case for the European Monetary Union (EMU) because the common currency eliminates all room for nationally specific monetary policies. Ceteris paribus, the number of wage setters should therefore be counted across the EMU area rather than country by country. By implication, the EMU marks a de facto decentralization of wage bargaining in Europe. Moreover, Germany no longer occupies a privileged position in the European monetary system since monetary policy is determined at the European level rather than the German level. Because individual German unions have only a small effect on the price level in the entire EMU area, the result could be an increase in union militancy, and hence unemployment, in Germany.

On the other hand, there are several post-EMU developments that could counteract these effects. I will outline them only very briefly – they are discussed in greater detail in Soskice and Iversen (1998). The first possibility is that wage bargaining becomes coordinated across the EMU with German employers and unions in a wage-leading role across Northern Europe. Unions in both Belgium and the Netherlands seem to be preparing for this possibility, and the crucial question will then be whether German wage setters are able and willing to behave as if they are setting European inflation. The second possibility is that the ECB designs its monetary policy to target German rather than European inflation. Were this to occur, the ECB would essentially be mimicking the Bundesbank, and the German equilibrium rate of unemployment would fall back to what it was under the ERM. The obvious problem here is to produce the necessary consensus behind such a policy within the ECB. Finally, the German government may try to bargain wage moderation against fiscal policy. This possibility is facilitated by the death of the Bundesbank as a macroeconomic actor, but it would require a renegotiation of the stability pact, which Germany itself insisted on. Still, the possibility of a new European fiscal activism embedded in social contracts with unions is an exciting and realistic possibility. It is one that deserves much theoretical and empirical attention in the future.

Appendix A

CALCULATION OF THE INDEX OF CENTRALIZATION OF WAGE BARGAINING

The operational definition of centralization $- C -$ is $(\sum w_j p^2_{ij})^{1/2}$ where w_j is the weight accorded to each bargaining level j $(\sum w_j = 1)$, and p_{ij} is the share of workers covered by union (or federation) i at level j. Information about the concentration of union membership at each level of bargaining (p_{ij}) was obtained from Visser (1989) and (for the most part) national statistical sources (various years): ÖGB, *Tatigkeitsbericht* (Austria), Danmarks Statistik, *Statistisk Årbog* (Denmark), *Statistisches Jahrbuch* (Germany), Statistisk Sentralbyrå, *Statistisk Årbok* (Norway), Statistiska Centralbyrån, *Statistisk Årsbok* (Sweden), *Suomen Tilastollinen Vuosikirja* (Finland), *Japan Labor Bulletin*, *Sociale Maandstatistiek* (continued in *Sociaal-economische Maandstatistiek*) (Netherlands), Bundesamt für Statistik, *Statistisches Jahrbuch* (Switzerland).[44] The weights (w_j) – listed in Table 3A.1 – depend on (i) the predominant level(s) at which bargaining take place, and (ii) the enforceability of bargaining agreements. The weights were assigned to every bargaining round in each country over the 23-year period from 1973 to 1995. Only three levels of bargaining were used in the classification, reflecting the empirical prevalence of peak-level bargaining, sector-/industry-level bargaining, and firm-/plant-level bargaining.

The degree of enforceability depends on the capacity of bargaining agents to implement their agreements. Enforceable agreements presuppose that bargaining agents control most strike and lockout funds and can impose fines for noncompliance (particularly important on the employer side). Nonenforceable agreements mean that the bargaining agents lack credible threats of sanctions (included here are several instances of "incomes policies" – see Flanagan et al. 1983). In some borderline cases, noted in the table, bargaining agents exercised partial control over enforcement.

In carrying out the coding, the monthly monitoring of bargaining in the *European Industrial Relations Review* was an invaluable source for information about particular bargaining rounds. I have also greatly benefited from the data collected for the collaborative NSF project on centralization by Golden, Wallerstein, and Lange (see Golden and Wallerstein 1995); this information has been supplemented with descriptions of particular national bargaining systems in Markovits (1986), Due, Madsen, Jensen, and Petersen (1994), Crouch (1993), Golden and Wallerstein (1995), and chapters in Flanagan, Soskice, and Ulman

Table 3A1. *Classification Scheme for Centralization of Authority*

Weights	Definitions
1, 0, 0	National associations monopolize wage bargaining and agreements are enforceable. Lower level bargaining is banned (Norway 1988-89).
.8, 0, .2	National associations monopolize bargaining and agreements are enforceable. Local bargaining is permitted subject to a peace clause (Belgium 1973-5; Denmark 1965-79, 1985; Norway 1960-73, 1976-80, 1983, 1985, 1990-5; Netherlands 1973; Sweden 1960-82, 1983,[a] 1985,[a] 1986, 1989[a]).
.4, .3, .3 (.4, 0, .6)[b]	National associations negotiate central agreements with some capacity for enforceability, but industry-level organizations retain the right to bargain separate agreements without adherence to a peace clause (Denmark 1961, 1963; Finland, 1974-9, 1981, 1984, 1986,[c] 1987, 1989-92; Netherlands 1982-4; Japan 1973-95[b]).
.1, .7, .2	National associations and/or the government set non-enforceable targets for lower level bargaining, but industry-level organizations retain rights to bargain enforceable agreements. Local bargaining is permitted subject to a peace clause (Austria 1973-95; Belgium 1977, 1981-5, 1989-95; Denmark 1983, 1987, 1989, 1991-5[d]; Finland 1973, 1980, 1983, 1988, 1993-5; Germany 1968-77; Netherlands 1974-81[e,f], 1985-95; Norway 1974, 1982, 1984; Sweden 1984, 1988, 1991-5).
0, .8, .2	Industry-level organizations monopolize bargaining and strike/lockout decisions, and agreements are enforceable. Local bargaining is permitted subject to a peace clause (Belgium 1979, 1987; Denmark 1981; Germany 1960-7; 1978-95; Norway 1986; Switzerland 1973-95).

Centralized (rows 1–2)

Intermediately centralized (rows 3–5)

Table 3A1. (*cont.*)

Decentralized	.1, 0, .9	National associations and the government set non-enforceable targets for plant-level bargaining, but local organizations retain rights to bargain and to call strikes/lockouts (Britain 1974-8; Italy 1976-8, 1993-5; France 1981-4).
	0, .1, .9	Plant- and firm-level bargaining predominates with some elements of industry-level bargaining (United States 1973-93; Canada 1973-95; Italy 1973-5, 1979-92; France 1973-80, 1985-95; Britain 1979-95).

[a] In these instances bargaining is simultaneously carried out by peak-level organizations and by industry organizations depending on the bargaining area. For simplicity all bargaining is considered to take place at the peak level, but the calculation of the centralization score takes into account the coincidence of industry- and peak-level agreements. The exceptional bargaining rounds are for 1983, 1985, and 1989 when separate agreemets were concluded in the metalworking sector.

[b] The Japanese system is unique because the industry/sectoral level plays no role in the bargaining process. The weight for the intermediate level is therefore de facto zero. Note also that in 1987 the four major confederations—Sohyo, Shinsanbetsu, Churitsuroren, and Domei—merged to form a single confederation, Rengo. This greatly increasesd the centralization of the Japanese system.

[c] Early in the year, wage agreements are reached at the sectoral level, but they are superseded by a centralized agreement later in the year.

[d] The figures for the composite index take into account that most bargaining in manufacturing now de facto takes place between a new association of employers (Dansk Industry) and a cartel unions (Industri kartellet).

[e] In 1976 the two main federations, NVV and CNV (and its member unions), merged to form the Dutch Federation of Trade Unions (FNV).

[f] In 1979 the white-collar union MHP was formed.

(1983), Windmuller (1987), Baglioni and Crouch (1991), and Ferner and Hyman (1992). In the case of Japan (which is not covered by the EIRR), the classification is based on Soskice (1990a), Shirai (1987); and news reports in the *Japan Labor Bulletin*.

If some bargaining took place at the local level, $1/N$ is assumed not to be significantly different from 0. With two decimals for the centralization index, and assuming equally sized local unions, this assumption holds whenever $N >$ 200 at the lowest bargaining level (since $1/(N > 200)$ is less than .005). As a practical matter this means that the assumption is always satisfied.

Countries where the predominant level of bargaining is at the plant and firm level, but where elements of industry-level bargaining occur (Britain, Canada, France, Italy and the United States), present a particular problem since data on the number of industry- or sector-level agreements and the number of workers involved are spotty (Golden and Wallerstein 1995: 33). Instead, I have simply assigned centralization (C) scores to these countries – *except* for years where some centralized bargaining does occur – as follows (before square root transformation) .005 (the United States and Canada), .01 (France), .015 (Britain), .02 (Italy). This recognizes that these systems are not completely decentralized, yet codes them as less centralized than any of the systems in which industry (or peak-level) bargaining predominates (the minimum centralization score for the latter is about .05). The empirical results are very robust to changes in this procedure *as long as* the centralization scores for the fragmented bargaining systems are below those in which industry- and/or peak-level bargaining predominates.

A p p e n d i x   B

SENSITIVITY TESTS

Table 3B.1 shows the parameter estimates for the theoretical variables excluding countries and time periods one at a time. All control variables were included in the regressions, but they are not shown in the table. Table 3B.2 shows the regression results when using rank-order numbers for the centralization variable (scaled to have the same range as the original variable in each period). Strictly speaking this is a violation of OLS assumptions, but it gives a good idea of the robustness of the results to scaling. Finally, Table 3B.3 shows the results of using the CBI index and the hard currency index separately (instead of as a mean).

The use of rank-order numbers slightly weakens the results for inflation, but they are by and large identical to the original regression results. The separation of the monetary variable into its component parts also gives similar results, although using central bank independence by itself makes Japan an outlier. As discussed in the main text, the reason is that Japanese monetary

| | | | Regression estimates and standard errors | | | | | | | | | |
| | | Unemployment | | | | | | Inflation | | | | |
		C	C^2	CI	C^2I	I	R^2	C	C^2	CI	C^2I	I	R^2
Excluding countries	Aus	14	-56	-77	193	3	.80	52	-87	-100	170	-2	.81
		(12)	(19)	(29)	(56)	(4)		(13)	(22)	(26)	(53)	(3)	
	Bel	12	-40	-53	132	1.3	.80	50	-79	-87	132	-1	.81
		(13)	(20)	(28)	(49)	(4)		(13)	(22)	(28)	(55)	(3)	
	Bri	12	-42	-52	134	.15	.80	38	-61	-66	106	-2	.81
		(14)	(20)	(27)	(47)	(4)		(14)	(23)	(27)	(52)	(3)	
	Can	15	-47	-58	144	1.3	.79	56	-86	-90	139	0	.82
		(15)	(21)	(27)	(47)	(4)		(14)	(23)	(26)	(52)	(3)	
	Den	11	-44	-63	161	.79	.80	49	-71	-67	85	-1	.81
		(13)	(20)	(29)	(54)	(4)		(13)	(23)	(28)	(57)	(3)	
	Fin	9	-40	-53	138	.23	.82	52	-82	-90	144	-1	.80
		(13)	(19)	(27)	(47)	(4)		(14)	(22)	(26)	(50)	(3)	
	Fra	10	-42	-55	144	.39	.79	48	-73	-79	121	-1	.80
		(14)	(21)	(30)	(51)	(5)		(13)	(22)	(26)	(52)	(3)	
	Ger	16	-48	-71	162	2	.80	58	-93	-116	186	-3	.82
		(13)	(19)	(28)	(48)	(4)		(12)	(20)	(26)	(51)	(3)	
	Ita	16	-50	-65	155	1.7	.79	43	-74	-64	105	-1	.80
		(15)	(22)	(30)	(50)	(4)		(14)	(24)	(28)	(53)	(3)	
	Jap	14	-46	-56	144	-0.0	.78	57	-88	-87	149	-2	.87
		(13)	(19)	(27)	(47)	(4)		(12)	(19)	(24)	(45)	(3)	
	NL	6	-32	-41	106	0.0	.81	54	-82	-89	137	-1	.81
		(13)	(18)	(25)	(39)	(4)		(13)	(21)	(25)	(50)	(3)	
	Nor	15	-45	-59	141	1.3	.80	52	-78	-86	130	0	.81
		(13)	(18)	(25)	(43)	(4)		(16)	(28)	(30)	(60)	(3)	
	Swe	11	-41	-57	137	1.5	.79	36	-50	-53	60	-1	.80
		(14)	(22)	(29)	(54)	(4)		(15)	(25)	(30)	(61)	(3)	
	Swi	10	-40	-48	123	.3	.77	55	-83	-97	154	1	.82
		(14)	(20)	(27)	(48)	(4)		(14)	(23)	(31)	(60)	(3)	
	US	8	-37	-47	129	-.9	.80	61	-90	-111	161	5	.80
		(20)	(27)	(46)	(69)	(8)		(20)	(30)	(44)	(71)	(6)	
Excluding periods	Per1	16	-58	-77	199	.6	.76	26	-38	-44	52	-1	.78
		(15)	(24)	(34)	(66)	(4)		(16)	(26)	(30)	(59)	(3)	
	Per2	4	-31	-45	125	-.7	.79	50	-81	-84	134	1	.83
		(15)	(21)	(30)	(51)	(5)		(16)	(26)	(29)	(56)	(3)	
	Per3	9	-32	-34	88	-.2	.82	53	-114	-115	189	2	.85
		(14)	(20)	(28)	(42)	(5)		(20)	(21)	(38)	(68)	(5)	
	Per4	10	-40	-70	150	0	.70	56	-90	-96	161	1	.76
		(13)	(19)	(26)	(48)	(4)		(14)	(24)	(31)	(59)	(3)	
	Per5	13	-44	-52	135	.5	.82	51	-73	-85	124	0	.81
		(14)	(19)	(28)	(44)	(4)		(14)	(24)	(28)	(56)	(3)	
Full model		12.5	-44	-57	143	.94	0.8	50	-77	-85	131	0	0.8
		(13)	(19)	(27)	(46)	(4)		(13)	(22)	(26)	(52)	(3)	

Table 3B.2. *OLS Estimates of the Effects of Institutional Variables Using an Ordinal-Scale Centralization Variable, 1973–93[a]*

	Predicted sign	Regression estimates and standard errors			
		Unemployment		Inflation	
		Full Model	Reduced model	Full model	Reduced model
Intercept		-0.91	0.22	0.03	-1.08
		(2.84)	(2.35)	(4.38)	(3.17)
$C_{i,t}$	+	13.84	5.09	35.43	43.56***
		(16.35)	(7.21)	(22.09)	(12.24)
$C^2_{i,t}$	-	-44.36*	-31.84***	-51.53	-62.95***
		(23.86)	(11.98)	(31.88)	(19.71)
$C_{i,t}*I_{i,t}$	-	-61.94*	-43.29***	-47.62	-64.76***
		(33.79)	(12.43)	(37.49)	(14.84)
$C^2_{i,t}*I_{i,t}$	+	137.38**	110.64***	67.63	91.90**
		(56.83)	-	(60.72)	(38.40)
$I_{i,t}$	?	2.91		-2.72	-
		(4.91)	(33.60)	(5.56)	
$Un_{i,t-1}$		0.59***	0.59***	0.04	0.04
		(0.08)	(0.08)	(0.08)	(0.08)
$UnOECD_t$		0.20	0.21	0.98***	0.98***
		(0.17)	(0.17)	(0.07)	(0.07)
$Exmar_{i,t}$		-0.18*	-0.18*	-0.01	-0.01
		(0.10)	(0.10)	(0.09)	(0.09)
$Trade_{i,t}$		0.01	0.01	-0.03***	-0.03***
		(0.01)	(0.01)	(0.01)	(0.01)
$LR_{i,t}$		0.95	1.00	0.33	0.28
		(0.62)	(0.61)	(0.69)	(0.71)
$Density_{i,t}$		0.03*	0.03*	0.01	0.01
		(0.01)	(0.01)	(0.01)	(0.01)
Fixity		-45.45	-44.83	-116.65**	-117.11**
		(30.60)	(31.26)	(47.97)	(48.54)
N		75	75	73	73
Adj. R^2		0.79	0.79	0.79	0.79

[a] Pooled cross-sectional time-series.

Note: Variables are defined in text; $*p < 0.10$; $**p < 0.05$; $***p < 0.01$.

Table 3B.3. *OLS Estimates of the Effects of Institutional Variables Using the CBI and Hard Currency Indexes, 1973–93[a]*

	Predicted sign	Regression estimates and standard errors			
		Unemployment		Inflation	
		CBI index	Currency index	CBI index	Currency index
Intercept		-1.42	-1.04	-1.37	-1.90
		(2.18)	(2.58)	(2.48)	(2.44)
$C_{i,t}$	+	5.48	17.90*	43.74***	40.92***
		(11.21)	(11.05)	(12.30)	(11.25)
$C^2_{i,t}$	-	-23.95	-42.93**	-66.02***	-59.27***
		(15.30)	(19.33)	(17.63)	(19.72)
$C_{i,t} \cdot I_{i,t}$	-	-32.78*	-55.86**	-56.79***	-80.30***
		(19.44)	(22.78)	(19.36)	(25.39)
$C^2_{i,t} \cdot I_{i,t}$	+	90.36***	107.86**	93.54***	121.29**
		(33.46)	(45.78)	(34.55)	(47.09)
$I_{i,t}$	?	-1.61	4.44	-0.80	-0.77
		(2.78)	(2.96)	(2.61)	(3.02)
$Un_{i,t-1}$		0.19	0.68***	0.94***	0.82***
		(0.19)	(0.08)	(0.07)	(0.07)
$UnOECD_t$		0.55***	0.08	0.05*	0.17**
		(0.09)	(0.20)	(0.07)	(0.07)
$Exmar_{i,t}$		-0.19	-0.15	-0.10	0.09
		(0.11)	(0.11)	(0.10)	(0.08)
$Trade_{i,t}$		0.01	0.01	-0.05	-0.01
		(0.01)	(0.01)	(0.01)	(0.01)
$LR_{i,t}$		1.84**	0.60	1.38	0.65
		(0.77)	(0.62)	(0.71)	(0.60)
$Density_{i,t}$		0.01	0.02	-0.00	0.00
		(0.02)	(0.02)	(0.01)	(0.01)
Fixity		-24.53	-30.83	1.33	18.03
		(28.05)	(32.22)	(62.96)	(42.11)
Unempl		-		-0.20	-0.11*
				(0.10)	(0.06)
Jap		-2.34**	-	-8.22***	-
		(0.83)		(1.42)	
N		75	75	75	75
Adj. R^2		0.78	0.81	0.78	0.83

[a] Pooled cross-sectional time-series.
*$p < 0.10$; **$p < 0.05$; ***$p < 0.01$.

authorities have pursued a nonaccommodating policy since the early 1970s despite the fact the central bank is dependent. The hard currency index picks this up well. There are no other notable results of the rank-order tests. I therefore focus on the sensitivity to particular periods and countries (Table 3B.1).

Beginning with unemployment, the only country that has a clear effect on the results is Austria (the results are strengthened by exclusion). The reasons for this are discussed in the main text, and the issue will be revisited in Chapter 5. The increase in explanatory power when Finland is excluded is entirely attributable to a single observation that captures the dramatic rise in unemployment following the collapse of the extensive trade with the former Soviet Union. In every scenario where the parameter estimates are borderline significant, the statistical strength of the results are dramatically improved if the monetary variable is omitted from the model (not shown) without altering the remaining parameter estimates. The reasons are, again, the presence of multicollinearity combined with the fact that the monetary regime variable has little independent effect.

The results are more sensitive to periods, which is to be expected given that 20 percent of the observations are omitted with each time period. The exclusion of the 1973–76 period (Per1) strengthens the results and suggests that clear cross-national unemployment patterns were not established until the mid-1970s. Eliminating periods 2 (1977–80) and 3 (1981–84) weakens the results, indicating that the model works particularly well for these periods. Elimination of the last period, however, also leaves the results slightly weaker, indicating that the model does not lose its relevance over time (weakening of results means that the model works well for the excluded period).

In the case of inflation the main results are also robust. The exclusion of Britain somewhat weakens the results whereas the exclusion of Switzerland strengthens them. If both cases are excluded simultaneously (not shown), the results are almost the same (slightly stronger). With respect to periods, the effects are more or less the mirror image of the results for unemployment. Exclusion of the 1973–76 period (Per1) weakens the results, whereas exclusion of the 1981–84 period (Per3) strengthens them. Unlike unemployment, the cross-national variance in inflation performance was greatest in the early to mid-1970s, and the model picks up this variance well. By the early 1980s, most high-inflation countries had undergone considerable macroeconomic retrenchment, while low-inflation countries had more or less stayed put, causing considerable degree of convergence. Nevertheless the results are somewhat weakened when the last period is excluded, implying that the model works well for the early 1990s.

PART II

THE POLITICS OF INSTITUTIONAL DESIGN

4

A THEORY OF CONTESTED INSTITUTIONS

Considering the amount of research on the consequences of central bank independence, it is remarkable how few insights have been generated into causes of cross-national variance in independence. Instead, the new classical literature presents us with a puzzle: If there are benefits to having an independent bank, but no apparent costs, why do we see so much institutional variance?[1] By contrast, if monetary policies have real effects that vary systematically across bargaining systems – as argued in this book – then there is good reason to expect monetary regimes to also vary systematically. In particular, while governments may seek to retain policy autonomy in decentralized systems – where the economic costs are either small or negative if flexibility reduces volatility – in intermediately centralized systems sociotropic voting would furnish governments of all stripes with a strong electoral incentive to adopt nonaccommodating regimes. By the same logic, governments would have a strong incentive to adopt flexibly accommodating regimes in highly centralized bargaining systems.

The institutional design argument also pertains to bargaining centralization. In neo-corporatist theory, centralization is explained as an attempt to control wage costs, but the present analysis highlights the possibility that conservative monetary regimes offer an alternative form of cost control *without* centralization. This is important because bargaining systems are not distributively neutral. Centralized bargaining typically involves intrusive restrictions on employers' discretion over firm-internal wage structures, and it strengthens the bargaining power of low-wage workers relative to high-wage workers. Institutional design is therefore a political game that involves distributive struggles between partisan governments and sectoral interests of employers and workers.

The theory of contested institutions presented in this chapter hypothesizes that, over time, stable coalitions will be formed behind either centralized bargaining with an accommodating regime – *Keynesian centralization* – or interme-diately centralized bargaining with a nonaccommodating regime – *monetarist decentralization*. In its weak form, this thesis simply states that efficiency gains will lead to a convergence around one or the other institutional equilibrium. This is a proposition that is easy to test with quantitative data, and the second section of this chapter presents such a test. That section also illustrates the notion of institutional equilibria with reference to four empirical cases. In the strong form of the institutional argument, outcomes are the result of a political coalition game that presupposes close attention to process and historically spe-cific causal mechanisms. The empirical exploration of this part of the argument is deferred to the next chapter.

THE ARGUMENT

My argument pivots around the concept of *strategic capacity* – that is, the extent to which the actions of economic actors have predictable and discernible effects on the welfare and decisions of other players.[2] I equate empirical cases in which it is reasonable to assume strategic capacity to the previously introduced concept of Organized Market Economies (OMEs), while political economies in which strategic capacity is lacking are equated with Liberal Market Economies (LMEs). As noted in the previous chapter, the first type in practice refers to Northern Europe and Japan and presupposes that a substantial number of employers and workers are organized into industry- or sector-wide organizations and that they bargain wages and working conditions on behalf of their members.

The discussion in this section focuses on OMEs because collective action problems preclude coordinated institutional outcomes in LMEs and because preferences over monetary regimes in these systems are ill defined owing to the relative absence of real economic effects. With these caveats in mind, I make two additional distinctions among Organized Market Economies: (i) between those in which wages (and prices) are determined through *centralized peak-level bargaining* and those in which wages are determined though *decentralized sector- or industry-level bargaining*;[3] and (ii) between those in which macroeconomic policies are subject to *flexible-Keynesian adjustment* to economic circumstances and those in which macroeconomic policies are institutionally constrained by a *non-accommodating* policy rule.[4]

The theory now posits the existence of two macroinstitutional equilibria, both of which facilitate economic adaptation to full employment: *Keynesian centralization* and *monetarist (semi)decentralization*. In the former, adaptation is made possible through a coordinated adjustment between government macro-economic and social policies, and the wage–price behavior of encompassing peak-level organizations of unions and employers. In the latter system, adapta-tion is achieved when industry-level organizations of unions and employers adjust their behavior to the anticipated policy responses by a monetary authority institutionally committed to a nonaccommodating policy rule. Both outcomes are superior, and preferred by all players, to situations in which *either* centralization is coupled with a nonaccommodating policy regime *or* decentralization is coupled with a flexible-Keynesian policy regime. Appendix A is explicit about the assumptions underlying the argument and uses games in extensive form to show that the hypothesized outcomes conform to conventional game-theoretic notions of equilibria. In this section I give a more intuitive presentation of the argument.

In the *weak form* of the thesis, the efficiency gains that can be derived from institutional equilibria are sufficient to bring them about. Based on Coase's theorem, this approach assumes that contracting parties can and will agree on governance structures that maximize the total welfare of the parties, regardless of the bargaining power of these (Milgrom and Roberts 1992: 38). The limitation of this approach is that the empirical predictions about the prevalence of institutional forms tell us little about either the actual processes by which certain equilibria are reached or about how institutional change from one to the other comes about (Kogut, Walker, and Anand 1996). In the *strong form,* institutional outcomes are modeled as the result of deliberate political action by strategically located organized interests and partisan governments. This strategic conception acknowledges that efficient outcomes tend to be stable over time, but seeks to specify the conditions under which a particular equilibrium is arrived at by strategically behaving players (cf. Knight 1992). Efficient outcomes may not be attainable in the short to medium term, and changes in relative power of actors, as well as external constraints on these actors, may lead to the abandonment of one equilibrium for the pursuit of another.

The model assumes that outcomes are linked to institutions in the manner hypothesized in Chapter 2 and documented in Chapter 3 and that control over institutional design is divided between organized private actors and governments. Thus, monetary policy-making is assumed to be the exclusive domain of the government and parliament, which also control institutional commitment mechanisms — especially central bank independence and participation in international exchange rate mechanisms. Conversely, the control over the choice of bargaining institutions is assumed to be primarily in the domain of unions and employer organizations, although the government can play a supporting role in building and maintaining centralized institutions. Unlike the choice of monetary regimes, particular bargaining arrangements come about only as a result of alliances between well-situated sectoral agents of capital and labor.[5]

The first step in this analysis is to identify institutional preferences of the salient actors. As argued by Swenson (1989, 1991a), but in contrast to the suggestion in much of the neo-corporatist literature, such preferences are not simply defined by class divisions but involve a more complex set of sectoral interests that divide workers and employers internally. With respect to workers,

I have previously underscored the distributive conflicts relating to wage solidarism and differences in the capacity for cost externalization. Beginning with the latter, the most important division is between a home-market-oriented, sheltered sector, where costs can potentially be passed on to the consumer, and an export-market-oriented, exposed sector, where prices are exogenously given. The division not only pertains to wage policies but also to macroeconomic policies where employers and workers in the nontraded sector have a common interest in full-employment levels of aggregate demand, while firms (and job-secure workers) in the traded sector will be more concerned with inflationary problems that may negatively affect international cost competitiveness (since they depend primarily on *foreign* demand). With respect to solidaristic wage policies, when bargaining power across different sectors of wage earners is evened out by centralization, weak/low-wage unions will benefit more than strong/high-wage unions from centralized bargaining. This is especially the case where redistribution is coupled with flexible full-employment policies, shielding unskilled workers from structural and cyclical unemployment.

These two dimensions of sectoral cleavages can now be combined into a simple three-sector division of workers, each sector representing a distinct orientation toward wage restraint, leveling, and bargaining institutions (see Figure 4.1). Wage earners who combine the market power to push for higher wages with the ability to externalize the costs of such militancy are referred to as the *sheltered high-skill sector*. The coupling of bargaining power and capacity for cost-externalization among these workers is explosive unless there are centrally enforced limits on militancy or such militancy is systematically "punished" by nonaccommodating economic policies. Organized workers in the *exposed high-skill sector* also enjoy strong market positions but, unlike sheltered unions, these workers have powerful incentives to exercise wage self-restraint to preserve the competitiveness of their companies, and hence the future capacity of these to hire and pay workers. This segment of the labor force shares with the *low-skill, low-wage sector* (i.e., those in weak labor market positions) a vested interest in imposing constraints on the ability of sheltered workers to engage in militant behavior.

One of the primary functions of centralized collective bargaining is precisely to institutionalize such constraints on wage militancy. Institutionalization itself, however, engenders distributional conflicts of interest between low-paid workers and more well-situated segments of the labor force. The reason, discussed previously, is that those who are relatively weak in the market will tend to benefit disproportionately from the organizational bargaining resources that a confederal and centralized union structure confers on its members. In the language of bargaining theory, the "inside options" of low-wage, low-skill groups, measured relative to high-wage, high-skill groups, are superior to their "outside options."

Solidaristic wage restraint also affects the interests of employers differently

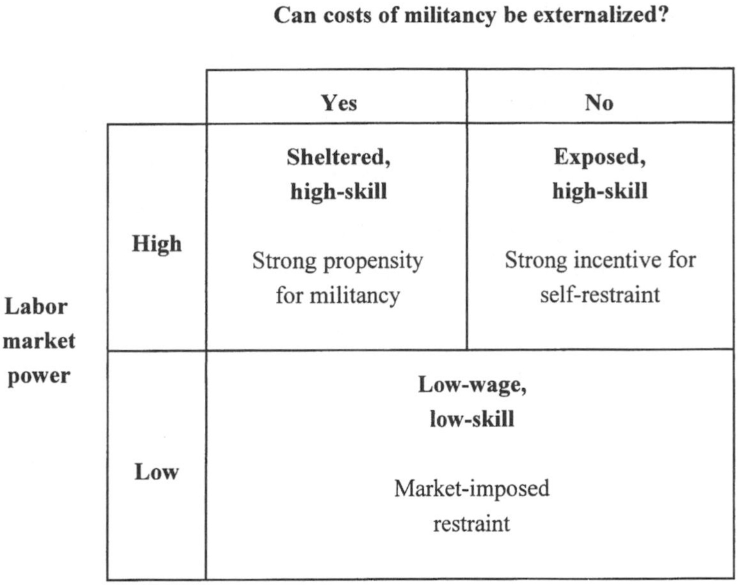

Can costs of militancy be externalized?

		Yes	No
Labor market power	**High**	**Sheltered, high-skill** Strong propensity for militancy	**Exposed, high-skill** Strong incentive for self-restraint
	Low	**Low-wage, low-skill** Market-imposed restraint	

Figure 4.1. *Sectoral cleavages among workers depending on structural constraints on wage pushfulness.*

depending on the relative importance for competitiveness of cost containment as opposed to control over the firm-internal wage structure. The central issue here is how important nonstandard forms of payments are for the efficient operation of different production systems. For producers of standardized products using mostly semiskilled labor, monitoring is relatively cheap and the costs of replacing poorly performing workers are low. Consequently, there is little need for complex wage incentive systems, and uniform wage standards present relatively few problems in terms of achieving satisfactory levels of worker productivity.[6] Costs, by contrast, will figure very prominently in the balance sheets of these employers. For producers of higher-quality products – especially for markets in which there is a high premium on product innovation – monitoring of work effort is more difficult, and the costs of dismissing workers are higher since employees typically represent substantial sunk costs in terms of skills and production-specific knowledge. Hence, nonstandard forms of payment – such as quality bonuses, profit sharing, seniority pay, and pension schemes – become important tools for inducing high work performance and for furnishing workers with incentives to take on more shop-floor responsibilities and company-specific skills.[7] Because centralized, redistributive bargaining systems periodically "iron out" such differentiated rewards in accordance with solidaristic wage norms, the achievement of wage flexibility is undermined. Wage leveling is therefore doubly problematic: It increases the likelihood of dissent among strong groups of labor, and it undermines attempts by employers to design flexible incentive systems.

This discussion leads to a three-sector division of employers similar to that for workers (see Figure 4.2). The first dimension is the dependence on flexibility for competitiveness; the second is the degree to which producers are exposed to competitive world markets (analogous to the division between workers who are more or less capable of externalizing militancy). The sector of *exposed standardized producers* is composed of employers who rely on a mostly unskilled work force and who are exposed to fierce international price competition. This sector is predisposed to support centralized institutions to the extent that such institutions facilitate the containment of wage pressure from unions in sheltered sectors. Only in a highly restrictive macroeconomic environment is this sector of employers likely to favor decentralization. For *sheltered producers*, the need for institutional constraints on wage bargaining is weaker owing to the insulation from international cost competition, while the benefits of decentralized flexibility may often outweigh the cost of reduced wage restraint – especially among firms producing high-priced, high-quality services with a skill-intensive work force. For these employers the optimal system would be one that combined wage flexibility with high and stable levels of domestic demand.

Finally, *exposed quality producers*, like their counterpart among workers, face opposing incentives. On the one hand, they see centralized institutions as a means to keep wage costs under control in a highly price-competitive environment. On the other hand, they depend on wage flexibility for non-price competitiveness, and such flexibility can best be achieved in a relatively decentralized bargaining environment. Their institutional preference is therefore contingent on the possibilities for controlling wage costs in a decentralized system. Since credible, nonaccommodating, low-inflation policies can address the cost-push problem in a decentralized system, such policies will be attractive to these employers.

On the basis of this sectoral classification, we can now hypothesize the likely cross-class coalitions behind different institutional arrangements (see Figure 4.3). The *Keynesian Centralization Coalition* corresponds to the classical cross-class alliance for peak-level bargaining described by Peter Swenson (1991a):[8] In the context of a government committed to full employment, workers who are weak in the market or who cannot externalize the costs of militancy, form an alliance with cost-sensitive employers to oppose "robbers' coalitions" of unions and employers who are able to pass on the bill for higher wages to the rest of the economy. As discussed above, this coupling of accommodating policies and centralized bargaining tends to have most favorable distributive consequences for low-wage workers with a high risk of unemployment.

In contrast, a *Keynesian Decentralization Coalition* combines full-employment policies with decentralized bargaining and would favor only quality producers

Is firm vulnerable to market wage push?

		Yes	No
		Exposed quality producers Constrained by international price *and* quality competition	**Sheltered producers** Unconstrained by international competitive pressure
Is flexibility essential for competitiveness?	Yes		
	No	**Exposed standardized producers** Constrained by international price competition	

Figure 4.2. *Sectoral cleavages among firms depending on their requirements for flexibility and their vulnerability to wage push.*

in the sheltered sectors, while severely undermining the interests of workers and employers in traditional exposed industries. Essentially, such a system would allow the sheltered sector to claim a larger share of total economic output to the detriment of the exposed sector. It needs to be noted, however, that this outcome would be difficult to sustain over time since it is prone to produce a progressive deterioration of international competitiveness, chronic trade deficits, and increasingly costly interest rate policies to fend off currency speculation. Governments with a time horizon that goes beyond the short run would therefore have an incentive to either facilitate centralization or commit to a nonaccommodating policy regime.[9]

The latter possibility is represented by the *Monetarist Decentralization Coalition*, which would find its strongest supporters among diversified quality producers sensitive to both wage flexibility and wage costs as well as among workers who have marketable skills and hence can take advantage of more flexible bargaining, but have only limited capacity to externalize the costs of wage militancy. The dilemma for these pivotal sectors of employers and workers is that, in the absence of a credible nonaccommodating monetary policy commitment, they cannot easily afford to support decentralization because of the likely wage–cost pressure from sheltered sectors. On the other hand, they will be wary of centralized solutions if these imply concessions to low-wage unions resulting

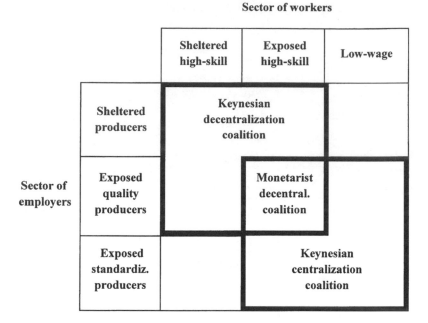

Figure 4.3. *Hypothesized patterns of cross-class coalitions.*

in wage inflexibility and leveling. Because both unions and employers in these sectors face opposing incentives, their coalition behavior is critical for the outcomes as far as bargaining institutions go.

This is particularly clear when we recognize that a centralized bargaining system cannot succeed without the support of the largest and most dynamic firms, which are invariably located in the exposed sector of a modern economy. Specifically, if these firms support decentralization while the government is pursuing Keynesian policies, then the only base of support for centralization will be among cost-sensitive employers and low-wage workers, who can achieve little on their own. In the next chapter I discuss a period in the 1980s when such a situation obtained in Sweden, which proved unstable and short-lived. The upshot is that *no effective coalition can be formed that excludes producers and high-skilled workers in exposed, high-value-added industries* (which is indicated in Figure 4.3 by the inclusion of these sectors of workers and employers in all three coalition scenarios). We may thus think of these sectors of workers and employers as institutional veto players.

Yet it is equally clear that *these veto players cannot ensure their preferred coalition outcome (i.e., a Monetarist Flexibility Coalition) without the cooperation of the government.* Through its control over the macroeconomic policies, the government is therefore also a veto player. Hence, to explain institutional outcomes we need to examine how the economic policy choices of the government interact with the coalition behavior of the strategic sectors of employers and workers. It is this game of strategic interaction that is at the core of the institutional formation process.

In Figure 4.4 I have outlined the structure of this game. The numbers in the top left corners of the matrix are the ordinal payoffs for diversified quality producers and high-skilled workers in the exposed sector, while the numbers in the bottom right corners are the ordinal payoffs for the government. The payoff structure for unions and employers follows the discussion above and is strictly ordinal, with no attempt to *compare* the payoffs for workers and employers.[10] Optimally, this cross-class coalition of workers and employers prefers an institutional arrangement that simultaneously provides for control of costs *and* permits wage flexibility. And such a combination is possible only when the government commits to a nonaccommodating policy regime. If it does not, the only outcome that provides for an acceptable containment of costs, without excessive unemployment, is one where the pivotal sectors of workers and employers ally with low-wage workers and cost-sensitive firms to centralize bargaining.

From the perspective of the government, if the bargaining system is centralized it has a strong incentive to pursue Keynesian full-employment policies since it can depend on the cooperation of unions and employers in maintaining competitiveness, whereas nonaccommodating policies jeopardize the attainment of full employment. If the bargaining system is decentralized, on the other hand, the only way for the government to induce responsible price–wage strategies compatible with full employment would be to commit to a nonaccommodating policy regime. These incentives produce two Nash equilibria corresponding to the institutional equilibria that I have previously referred to as *Keynesian centralization* and *monetarist decentralization*. The "weak" macrologic underlying the concept of institutional equilibria – based on efficiency arguments – has thus been supported by a stronger game-theoretic micrologic – based on the interests of particular sectoral agents of workers and employers (a logic that is spelled out in greater detail in Appendix A).

It is important to underscore that the game is still theoretically indeterminate in the sense that it contains *two* equilibria. Thus, while exposed quality producers would like to see the government adopt a nonaccommodating policy regime, rather than having to support a centralized bargaining system, their options are limited by the ability of the government to sustain political support for full-employment policies. Conversely, even governments that favor redistributive, full-employment policies can be placed under considerable pressure to adopt a nonaccommodating policy regime when the pivotal sectors of workers and employers support decentralization. The interaction between the exposed sector interests and the government therefore take on the character of a battle-

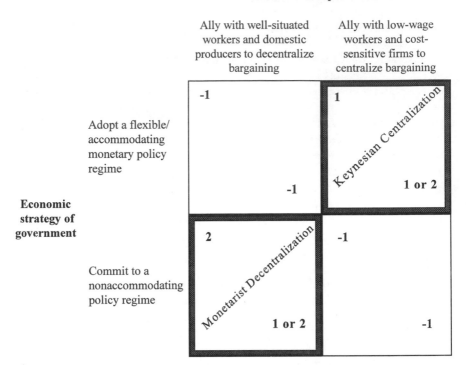

Strategy of quality producers and high-skill unions in the exposed sector

	Ally with well-situated workers and domestic producers to decentralize bargaining	Ally with low-wage workers and cost-sensitive firms to centralize bargaining

Economic strategy of government

Adopt a flexible/accommodating monetary policy regime — top-left cell: -1 / -1; top-right cell: 1 / 1 or 2 (Keynesian Centralization)

Commit to a nonaccommodating policy regime — bottom-left cell: 2 / 1 or 2 (Monetarist Decentralization); bottom-right cell: -1 / -1

Note: Entries are ordinal utility levels for employers and workers (top line) and the government (bottom line); higher numbers indicate higher utility. Highlighted cells are Nash equilibria.

Figure 4.4. *The interaction between government economic strategies and the coalition behavior of high-quality producers and high-skilled workers in the exposed sector.*

of-the-sexes game where the outcome depends on the relative capacity of players to endure the "disequilibrium" outcome (Knight 1992: ch. 5; Alesina and Drazen 1991).

Governments with different partisan objectives will have different preferences over the two equilibria. Thus "right" governments that wish to favor firms in the exposed sector as well as better-paid workers will prefer the decentralized outcome over the centralized. The opposite will be the case for "left" governments primarily concerned with unemployment and wage equality. These partisan differences, however, will be disguised during periods of institutional stability because the median voter, who is likely to have ambiguous distributive interests, will tend to vote on the basis of overall economic performance. In fact, such sociotropic voting is widespread in the electorate (see especially Lewis-Beck 1988), and it furnish governments with an incentive not to institute reforms that will cause a deterioration of the economy, *even when* the government's core supporters stand to gain from the long-run benefits of such reforms.

Consequently, unless the government is very securely in power, any economic strategy that follows a disequilibrium path is unlikely to succeed. Likewise, because electoral preferences for economic policies are "sticky," unions and employers in the exposed sector face an automatic deterrent against abandoning established institutions. Only when the long-term opportunity costs of remaining in one equilibrium compared to another become very high – as a result of changes in the economic and technological environment – and only when the electoral coalition underpinning past economic policies can be expected to break up relatively easily, is it reasonable to expect an institutional transition. In other words, institutional change is possible in the model, but the conditions under which such change is likely to occur are quite restrictive.

Summarizing, the theory of contested institutions implies a tendential correspondence between electoral and sectoral coalitions: when in equilibrium, economic policies and bargaining institutions will be supported by pivotal sectors of workers and employers *and* by a majority electoral coalition; when institutions are changed along a disequilibrium path, as a result of sectoral realignments, we expect either corresponding electoral realignments (as more and more voters become politically dissatisfied with the status quo), *or* a restoration of the original sectoral alignment. Another implication of this argument is that *in equilibrium* we expect partisan differences over economic policies to be relatively subdued, whereas they will "flare up" during transitory periods of institutional change when government policy commitments come to play a crucial role.

THE CAUSES OF INSTITUTIONAL CHANGE

The institutional game between the government and strategic sectors of labor and capital completes the theoretical argument of this book by endogenizing the choices over monetary regimes and wage bargaining institutions. The model implies that, over time, economic institutions will tend to conform to two ideal types (centralization coupled with a flexible and accommodating monetary regime, and decentralization coupled with an independent, nonaccommodating, monetary regime), but it does not predict the *direction of change* in historically specific national and international contexts. Most of this analysis is deferred to Chapter 5, but it is helpful to identify a few broad classes of variables that have played a particularly salient role in the 1980s and 1990s.

These variables are generally associated with the transition from relatively insulated industrial societies characterized by Fordist types of standardized goods, a homogeneous semiskilled labor force, and extensive domestic controls

over the cross-border flow of goods, capital, and people to globalized, postindustrial societies characterized by flexible types of quality production, a heterogeneous work force of low-skilled workers especially in services and high-skilled
workers in especially industry, and integrated markets for goods and capital. All
of these factors have altered the relative salience of cost control, flexibility, and
wage equality, and they have affected the balance of power between governments
and pivotal sectors of workers and employers. Three forces of change merit
particular attention.

First, *capital market integration* is important because it affects the potential
costs for the government of pursuing full-employment policies (Cusack and
Garrett 1993; Scharpf 1991; Helleiner 1994). A number of quantitative studies
have found a pronounced increase in capital market integration during the
1970s and 1980s (see, for example, Feldstein and Horioka 1980; Bayoumi
1990; Frankel 1991; and Simmons 1999).[11] The causes for this increase are
complex and outside the purview of this book. Suffice it to say that once
capital market liberalization got under way in first the United States and then
Britain and Japan, governments in other countries came under competitive
pressure to follow suit (Frankel 1992; Frieden 1991; Andrews 1994; Moses
1994). And once capital controls were lifted, doing so affected macroeconomic
policy-making because full-employment policies without effective means of
wage restraint resulted in capital outflows that either triggered spirals of
inflation and devaluations or raised real interest rates to prevent such spirals
("risk premiums"). Low barriers to capital movement thus reduce the government's ability to control the macroeconomy, while financial investors will find
it easier to escape the costs that policymakers may otherwise impose to facilitate
full employment. In other words, capital market integration makes the government more vulnerable to the exit decisions of financial asset holders, and
it increases the costs of pursuing even mildly inflationary full-employment
policies. This reduction in macroeconomic policy autonomy, or increase in the
costs of such autonomy, is one of the few strong conclusions of the globalization
literature that even its staunchest critics do not dispute (see Garrett and Lange
1995; Garrett 1998a: ch. 4).[12] The significance of growing financial capital
mobility is thus that it weakens the hand of governments committed to full
employment, thereby altering the balance of power in the institutional game
described above.

Second, *change in manufacturing technology* is important because it affects the
parameters for the efficient organization of production and firm-internal incentive structures. A broad consensus now exists that the widespread application of
numerically controlled, multipurpose machinery during the 1970s and 1980s
placed a premium on shop-floor autonomy and intrafirm skill formation (e.g.,
Piore and Sabel 1984; Piore 1986; Sabel 1991, 1993; Windolf 1989; Streeck
1991). These changes have made monitoring of work effort more difficult and
have increased the cost of dismissing workers, who often represent valuable

assets in terms of skills and production-specific knowledge. As a result, higher wages for skilled employees and nonstandard systems of remuneration have become popular managerial tools to achieve higher work performance and longer- term commitments to the firm (Standing 1988; Pontusson and Swenson 1996; Ibsen and Stamhus 1993b: 86–93). To the extent that centrally negotiated wage norms inhibit such wage flexibility, they constrain the pursuit of diversified quality production strategies. Technological change has therefore increased the attraction of leading firms to decentralize bargaining institutions, and simultaneously made wage costs a less crucial (though by no means insignificant) determinant of international competitiveness.

Third, *the rise of low-productivity jobs in the services sectors* has caused severe strains for both wage solidarism and full-employment policies. The root of the problem is, to simplify, that much of the employment growth since the mid-1960s has come in types of services – especially social and personal services – in which the rate of productivity change has lagged that in manufacturing (Baumol 1967; Appelbaum and Schettkat 1994, 1995). If these sectors are subjected to a solidaristic wage policy, the firms and workers that are priced out of low-productivity sectors have to find work elsewhere. So long as employment growth is rapid in high-productivity sectors – possibly spurred by low wages for skilled labor and effective retraining programs – this is not a problem, as elegantly formulated in the Rehn–Meidner model (Rehn 1985; Martin 1979). But if market saturation and shift in demand away from manufacturing toward services, which has been the story for the past three decades, limit the positive employment effects of wage restraint, the Rehn–Meidner logic will be turned on its head: Solidaristic wage policies squeeze out the least productive workers without creating a compensating expansion in the overall level of activity (Iversen and Wren 1998). For full employment to be preserved, this places an increasing burden on the government to provide jobs in the public sector and to raise what is ostensibly a "solidarity tax" on the private sector.[13] Wage restraint is still crucial because such taxes reduce real wages, but restraint is increasingly a redistributive device rather than a collective good. Discontent with solidaristic wage policies may therefore spill over into the electoral arena, where voter discontent with rising taxes can impose tight fiscal constraints on the government's full-employment policy.

The combined effect of capital market integration, technological change, and the rise of services during the 1970s and 1980s has been to increase the capacity, or power, of employers and unions in the exposed, private sector to commit to a decentralized system, while it has weakened the government's hand in holding onto a flexible, full-employment strategy. In terms of the model, these changes in the international economy have made it more difficult for governments to credibly threaten to stick to full-employment policies if the bargaining system is being decentralized, while the changes have made decentralization more attractive to well-positioned employers and unions in the exposed, private sector. In combination, changes in technology and capital market integration have therefore made it more difficult to sustain Keynesian centralized institutions, creating pressures for change primarily in the direction of decentralization and growing central bank independence with tighter fiscal constraints.

PATTERNS OF INSTITUTIONAL LINKAGES: A PRELIMINARY TEST

Whether we focus on its weak or strong form, the theory of contested institutions implies that Organized Market Economies should exhibit either centralized bargaining with an accommodating regime – Keynesian centralization – or intermediately centralized bargaining with a nonaccommodating regime – monetarist decentralization. Predictions about Liberal Market Economies are less clear, but it is at least plausible that if the real effects of flexible monetary policies are small or even mildly beneficial – as I have argued – governments may find it in their political interest to retain autonomy for the short-term advantages that such autonomy can afford around elections.

These correlational hypotheses suggest very simple tests that the institutional theory, at least for the OMEs, must pass. For this purpose, Table 4.1 shows two different measures of how often particular combinations of bargaining systems and currency regimes occurred over the 1973–93 period. I have used the hard currency index introduced in the previous chapter as a measure of the monetary regime because it is particularly sensitive to policy changes and therefore gives the best indication of the extent to which governments seek to maintain macroeconomic policies in "equilibrium" with the bargaining system. The first row of the table lists the number of years that a particular combination is observed (subject to the constraint that at least two consecutive years fall into the same category).[14] Note that among intermediately centralized and highly centralized systems – where the theoretical predictions are clearest – close to 90 percent of the time currency regimes have the predicted orientation (indicated by "bold" numbers).

The second row of the table shows the results when observations are defined in terms of "regimes." A regime here means a string of annual observations that contains more than five consecutive years in the same category (and was not broken by a string lasting more than five years). Half a decade seemed like a reasonable period of time in which to expect the formation of winning coalitions behind particular institutional setups. Stable regimes should therefore be observed only in the "equilibrium" cells. This expectation is clearly confirmed since there are no observations in the off-diagonal cells (for intermediately and highly centralized systems). Sooner or later, it appears, either governments or private collective actors adapt their behavior to one of the "equilibrium" outcomes.

Table 4.1. *The Incidence of Different Economic–Institutional Combinations across 15 OECD Countries, 1973–95*

			Centralization of wage bargaining			
			Low	Intermediate	High	*Sum*
	Low	Years	90	18[a]	70	178
Conservatism		Regimes	5	1	4	10
of monetary						
regime	High	Years	20	138	9[b]	167
		Regimes	1	7	0	8
		Sum	110	156	79	
			6	8	4	

Note: Top entries refer to the number of connected yearly observations in each category (at least two years must be connected); bottom entries refer to the number of instances where a country exhibits a particular institutional combination for more than five consecutive years.
[a]Observations are from Belgium (1981–83), Britain (1975–77), Denmark (1980–82), Italy (1976–78), and Sweden (1990–95).
[b]Observations are from Belgium (1973–75), Denmark (1983–85), and the Netherlands (1982–84).

Sources: Explained in text.

The results underscore the distinction between Liberal Market Economies and Organized Market Economies. In the absence of what I have previously referred to as strategic capacity, governments are under no particular pressure to tie their hands in economic policies and may put a positive value on the flexibility to inflate at politically opportune moments (principally around elections). Certainly this interpretation is consistent with the results. It is for the category of Liberal Market Economies that the new classical approach to central banks is both most applicable and has its greatest force as a normative theory. Even if there are no real improvements to an economy from commitments to a restrictive monetary regime, most would agree that low inflation is a desirable goal. Nothing in my analysis contradicts this view. Indeed, there may in fact be some unemployment gains to be reaped since bargaining is rarely completely decentralized. In this sense Tony Blair and Labour are justified, at least in economic terms, to increase the independence of the Bank of England.

CONCLUSION

The theory of contested institutions presented in this chapter places equal weight on efficiency and distribution as explanations for the design of policy regimes and bargaining institutions. Provided that collective-action problems can be overcome, we expect economic agents to construct wage-setting institutions that will create a prosperous environment for the pursuit of profits, wages, and employment. Likewise, because voters are sociotropic, all governments concerned with staying in power have an incentive to adopt policies and institutions that produce good macroeconomic outcomes. Over longer periods of time, therefore, we expect efficient institutions and policies to prevail, at least in Organized Market Economies, where the number of salient actors is small enough to enable winning coalitions to sooner or later form behind a particular set of institutions. This is borne out empirically since the overwhelming number of observed combinations of wage-bargaining institutions and monetary regimes fall into categories for which we have strong a priori, as well as empirical, reasons to believe that they are conducive to good economic performance.

This type of analysis, however, does not tell us anything about what combination of efficient institutions will be chosen in particular cases, or why institutions may be changing over time. For this task we have to engage in an analysis that focuses on the distributive aspects of institutions, the resources that actors with conflicting interests bring to the struggle over these institutions, and their ability to forge winning coalitions. For this type of analysis the usefulness of quantitative methods is limited because we typically do not have the necessary data and because the relevant actors also lack complete information. Institutional change is fraught with uncertainty, miscalculation, and false starts during which the agents of change only gradually learn who possesses the resources and skills to bring about a desired redesign of institutions and policies.

To uncover the causal mechanisms in these processes, we have to turn to historical cases. This does not mean that we have to give up theoretical rigor. On the contrary, theory prevents us from getting lost in the wealth and complexity of historical detail by directing us to focus on particular variables and by situating experiences from very different contexts within a coherent conceptual typology. Theory, in short, helps us to make sense of particular cases of institutional change, and quite often the cases return the favor by offering nuances and challenging facts that enrich our theories and point to new areas of research. The next chapter is dedicated to such an analysis, using Denmark and Sweden as prominent examples of change toward decentralization (although the transformation has taken different forms). The experience of these countries is contrasted with three other cases that have moved along different institutional trajectories: Norway (which experienced a recentralization of industrial relations), Austria (representing a stable and relatively centralized system), and Germany (representing a stable decentralized system).

Appendix A

A GAME-THEORETIC EQUILIBRIUM
MODEL OF THE CHOICE OVER
ECONOMIC POLICIES AND UNION
WAGE STRATEGIES

In the following it is assumed that unions enjoy *strategic capacity* and that wage setting takes place through *either* peak-level bargaining between a single labor confederation and a single employer association *or* through (semi)decentralized negotiations between unions and employer associations in individual industries or sectors. In each subgame (centralized and decentralized), the government first commits to a macroeconomic strategy, and then the unions in different sectors choose a wage strategy. The government's strategy may be either *nonaccommodating* – implying that inflation is always countered by deflationary policies, regardless of the level of unemployment – or *accommodating* – implying that unemployment is always countered with reflationary policies regardless of the rate of inflation. Unions, in turn, may pursue a strategy of either wage restraint or wage militancy.

Unions are divided into three sectors depending on the occupational composition of their membership: a *sheltered* and an *exposed* sector among relatively *high-paid/high-skilled* workers in strong labor market positions, and a sector of *low-paid/low-skilled* workers in weak labor market positions. The payoff function for the different sectors is a very simple ranking (quasi-ordering, to be exact) of outcomes that is just sufficiently specific to determine the sectoral players' best choices at each decision node. Hence, while the rankings are incomplete across outcomes, they are detailed enough to determine the equilibria in the subgames beginning with choices of the sectoral unions. The orderings of outcomes (summarized in Table 4A.1) are based on very simple assumptions about unions' preferences derived from the analysis of sectoral interests in this chapter (note the ceteris paribus clauses):

For the *exposed sector* these assumptions are:

1. Ceteris paribus, it is always preferable if *all* players (including those in the exposed sector itself) refrain from exploiting their bargaining power (whether in the form of wage militancy or wage leveling). The assumption is a result of firms in the exposed sector being price takers.
2. If *all* unions accept responsibility for wage restraint, then accommodat-

Table 4A.1. *The Structure of Preferences among Different Sectors of Workers*

Sector	Ordering of Preferences
Exposed	ARR > {[(ARM,AMR) > AMM] , [NRR > (NRM,NMR)]} > NMM 4 3 2 3 2 1 ARD > {[(ARL,AMD) > AML] , [NRD > (NRL,NMD)]} > NML 4 3 2 3 2 1
Sheltered	ARM > {[(AMM,NRM) > NMM] , [ARR > (AMM,NRR)]} > NMM 4 3 2 3 2 1 ARD > {[(ARL,AMD) > AML] , [NRD > (NRL,NMD)]} > NML 4 3 2 3 2 1
Low-wage	ARR > {[(ARM,AMR) > AMM] , [NRR > (NRM,NMR)]} > NMM 4 3 2 3 2 1 ARL > {[(AML,ARD) > AMD] , [NRL > (NML,NRD)]} > NMD 4 3 2 3 2 1

Strategies:
A = Accommodating economic policy
N = Nonaccommodating economic policy
R = Wage restraint
M = Wage militancy
D = Wage dispersion
L = Wage leveling

Outcomes:
Line I: Decentralized branch where letters represent government strategy, exposed sector strategy, and sheltered sector strategy, in that order (e.g., ARR means that government is accommodating, that exposed sector is restrained, and that sheltered sector is restrained).

Line II: Centralized branch, where letters represent government strategy, exposed and sheltered sector strategy, and low-wage sector strategy (e.g., ARD means that government is accommodating, that exposed and sheltered sectors are restrained, and that low-wage sector accepts dispersion).

Notes: Top line in each row is for decentralized bargaining; bottom line is for centralized bargaining. Numbers indicate preferences in ascending order (i.e., higher number, higher preference). Equal numbers *do not* necessarily imply indifference. Low wage unions are assumed to lack bargaining power in a decentralized system.

ing economic policies are preferable to nonaccommodating policies. The logic here is that if the government *always* deflates in response to inflation, downward inflexibility in nominal wages (because of solidaristic wage policies, for example) can cause unemployment to unnecessarily rise since real-wage adjustment is always feasible when policies are accommodating and unions are restrained.

For the *sheltered* sector the assumptions are:

1. Ceteris paribus, it is always better if *other* players refrain from exploiting their bargaining power (whether in the form of wage militancy or wage leveling).
2. Wage militancy is always preferable if bargaining is decentralized and economic policies are accommodating. Otherwise it is better to observe restraint. The logic is that sheltered unions will exploit their capacity to externalize the costs of militancy in a decentralized system *unless* they are deterred from doing so by a credible government commitment to a nonaccommodating policy rule. In a centralized system unions have an interest in self-restraint because wage militancy is automatically transmitted to other sectors and hence precludes "free-riding" behavior.

Finally, for the *low-wage* unions the assumptions are:

1. Ceteris paribus, it is always better if *other* players refrain from exploiting their bargaining power.
2. Ceteris paribus, wage leveling is always preferable to wage dispersion. This assumption simply asserts the distributive interests of low-wage unions.
3. If all unions are observing wage restraint, then accommodating economic policies are preferable to nonaccommodating policies. The justification is the same as for the exposed sector.

THE DECENTRALIZED SUBGAME

In the *decentralized* subgame (Figure 4A.1) the government has the first move and can adopt one of three strategies: (i) commit to a nonaccommodating policy rule (N_R); (ii) pursue a nonaccommodating policy (N_P); or (iii) pursue an accommodating policy (A). The former strategy involves an institutional commitment to antiinflationary policies that constrains the ability of the government to flexibly adapt policies to circumstances. Any threat to price stability will trigger nonaccommodating responses with institutionalized certainty. In contrast, the latter two strategies (N_p and A) do not entail any institutional commitment, and in combination they may be referred to as a *flexible Keynesian policy regime*. Hence, a flexible policy regime is one that enables the government to alternate between accommodating and nonaccommodating policies according to economic and political expediency.

In the second stage of the game, unions in each sector simultaneously choose a wage strategy for their sector that may be either militant (M) or restrained (R). The choices of workers in weak market positions (low-wage workers) are eliminated in the decentralized game because, by definition, they

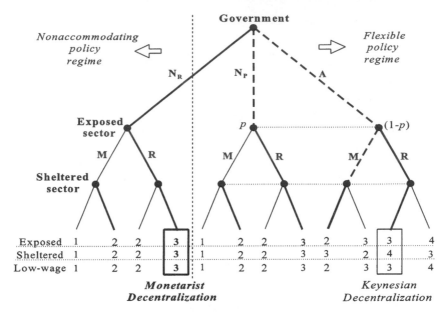

Note: Payoffs are ordinal and defined in Table 4A.1. The subscripts to N (R and P) stand for "regime" and "policy," respectively.

Figure 4A.1. *The interaction between government economic strategies and union wage strategies in a decentralized bargaining system.*

are incapable of pursuing militant strategies (or they would otherwise be classified in either the exposed or sheltered category).

There are different ways to approach the analysis of what will happen if the government retains its policy flexibility, but the most realistic is to assume that unions have imperfect information about the government's intentions. This is indicated in Figure 4A.1 by union information sets that cover both types of government policies (N_P and A). Because unions in the exposed sector are constrained by the imperatives of international competitiveness, they have a strong incentive to observe restraint regardless of policy. However, the dominant strategy of sheltered sector unions is contingent on the policy that the government is actually pursuing. Hence, these unions have to form beliefs about which node in the information set has been reached. It is conventional in game theory to present such beliefs in terms of a probability distribution over the nodes in the information set (Gibbons 1992: 177).

Let p be the probability that the government is adhering to a nonaccommodating policy (N_P) and $(1 - p)$ the probability that it is following an accommodating policy (A). Because the exposed sector has a dominant strategy (R), there are only four outcomes to consider. The payoffs of these outcomes can be denoted (from left to right in the right-hand side of the figure): N_pRM, N_pRR, ARM, and ARR. Given the beliefs of sheltered sector unions, the expected payoff from being militant is $pN_pRM + (1 - p)ARM$ whereas the expected payoff from exercising restraint is $pN_pRR + (1 - p)ARR$. Sheltered unions will thus be restrained whenever the latter payoff is greater than the former, which is equivalent to the following condition for wage restraint:

$$p > \frac{ARM - ARR}{ARM - ARR + (N_pRR - N_pRMR)} \tag{1}$$

The numerator in this equation is the net payoff that a union receives if the government accommodates a militant move, call it T for temptation, while the second term in the denominator is the net cost that the union would incur if it follows a militant strategy while the government is wedded to a nonaccommodating policy, call it P for punishment. Then the inequality in equation 1 can be written simply as

$$p > \frac{T}{T + P} \tag{2}$$

Obviously, when the temptation payoff goes up, and punishment cost goes down, the probability of the government being nonaccommodating must increase in order for restraint to still be the dominant strategy. Knowing this, the government has an interest in manipulating T and P, for example by exhibiting willingness to engage in conflicts with public sector unions over "excessive" pay demands. Since such resolve is difficult to distinguish analytically from a nonaccommodating policy, however, I will focus on the determinants of the size of p.

I begin by noting that the primary government rationale for retaining policy flexibility is that it can use this flexibility to generate favorable economic outcomes. Over the long haul, and in a stable international economic environment, a government that is entrenched in power may be able to develop a *reputation* for fiscal conservatism, but most democratically elected governments are politically too insecure and shortsighted to stick to such a strategy. To see the temptation for deviating from a conservative macroeconomic course, assume for the moment that the N_pRR had actually been reached. With adaptive expectations and/or incomplete information the government would be able to single-handedly produce the superior ARR outcome. Of course, this outcome could be sustained only in the short run until unions and employers updated their inflation expectations and adapted their wage–price policies in an inflationary direction. Even when such an adaptation occurred, however, it would still not be in the interest of the government to reverse its policies because it would now face short-term costs of pursuing restrictive policies in a militant union environment (producing the N_pRM outcome). This is the time-inconsistency problem in monetary policy-making.

For these reasons it would be sensible for unions, at any given point in time, to expect a low probability of nonaccommodating policies, thereby inviting militant behavior corresponding to the outcome called *Keynesian decentralization* in Figure 4A.1. Note, however, that the government could not sustain its policies in this scenario *indefinitely* since they would generate a chronic and rising current account deficit (i.e., $p \neq 0$). Although such deficits could temporarily be redressed through currency devaluations (by improving competitiveness and cutting real domestic consumption), the effect would last only until unions updated their inflation expectations and demanded compensation for rising import prices. In addition, such a devaluation cycle would lead to recurrent speculation against the currency that would put additional pressures on the government for a change in policies. Although economic theory is silent about the timing, at *some* point the government would *have* to address these problems through very severe deflationary policies (see Carlin and Soskice 1990: ch. 11). This constraint was also implied by the formal model introduced in Appendix A to Chapter 2 since the wage equation 13 is undefined if the monetary authority only cares about unemployment (i.e., if $\iota = 0$).

The key rationale for the creation of an independent central bank – or a similar institutional commitment – is to avoid such outcomes by lending credibility to a low-inflation policy commitment, and thereby reducing the time-inconsistency problem. The paradox is that even governments that care deeply about unemployment would be better off with such a commitment (at least beyond the very short term), even though it presupposes abandoning the pursuit of full-employment policies. The key is that the commitment is not easily reversed in response to short-term political expediency. For example, any attempt to take away autonomy from a central bank requires adherence to time-consuming procedures that will exacerbate short-term problems by alerting investors and speculators to the government's future intentions. In addition, as John Goodman notes, "by making the central bank more independent, governments add a new actor to the political system, one that surely seeks to preserve its own autonomy" (1992: 8).

The mechanism linking a credible nonaccommodating policy commitment to positive employment outcomes is the dampening effect that such a commitment has on union militancy. If unions truly believe that the government (and the central bank) is committed to price stability (or a hard currency policy) – that is, that $p = 1$ – and if their wage strategies have non-negligible effects on the economy, strategic behavior would dictate self-restraint. This leads to the equilibrium outcome that is called *monetarist decentralization* in Figure 4A.1. More specifically, as long as the nonaccommodating policy regime is credible, the dominant strategy for unions in *both* exposed and sheltered sectors is to observe wage restraint compatible with a balance of payment equilibrium level of international competitiveness.

THE CENTRALIZED SUBGAME

In the *centralized* subgame (Figure 4A.2), the government again has the first move and commits to a particular economic policy and policy regime. Subsequently, the union confederation decides on a wage strategy that is the outcome of an internal bargaining process between exposed, sheltered, and low-wage unions, each holding a veto over the outcome. We can represent this internal bargaining process, as it relates to our purposes, by distinguishing between the strategy of the exposed and sheltered sectors, on the one hand, and the low-wage sector on the other. In Figure 4A.2 the former makes the first move, but this ordering is not consequential for the analysis. The exposed and sheltered sectors can choose to be more or less militant, as in the decentralized scenario, but they now know that whatever compromise they reach, the resulting wage increase will apply across the entire economy. Another difference from the decentralized case is that low-wage unions now have bargaining power since they can veto proposals that do not accord sufficient attention to their distributive interests. The decision of whether to exploit this power therefore has to be included as separate choice node.

If the government adheres to a *flexible* policy regime (the right-hand side of the figure), the equilibrium outcome corresponds to what I have previously termed *Keynesian centralization*. This is easily seen through backward induction. Thus, it is always in the interest of low-wage unions to exploit their internal bargaining power for distributive gains, regardless of the government's policy choice and the wage strategy of other members of the confederation. Similarly, the exposed and sheltered sectors refrain from pursuing militant strategies because in deciding a *joint* strategy, they realize that real-wage increases that undermine competitiveness will lead to unemployment and lower growth over the medium to long run. Still, the confederation may not be able to guarantee full employment if the scope for nominal wage increases is low and wage drift undermines solidaristic wage policies. Under these circumstances the pursuit of wage leveling by low-wage unions will place upward pressure on total wage increases and thus turn into a form of wage militancy (as explained in the previous chapter). This will be a problem, however, only when monetary policies are nonaccommodating.

Given the willingness and capacity of unions to be restrained in a centralized system, the government should never have to choose a nonaccommodating policy rule. Since the union confederation is always willing and able to calibrate its wage demands to a level that is compatible with equilibrium on the external balance, the government can costlessly pursue macroeconomic policies that

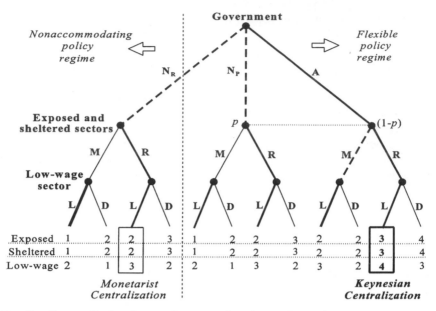

Note: Payoffs are ordinal, and cannot be compared to those in Figure 4A.1.

Figure 4A.2. *The interaction between government economic strategies and union wage strategies in a centralized bargaining system.*

preserve full employment. The resulting equilibrium thus parallels the traditional concept of corporatist concertation characterized by full employment, solidaristic wage policies, and wage restraint.

There is a caveat to the argument that needs to be highlighted. If it is obvious to all players that the dominant government strategy is to play A, then unions should hold the belief that $p = 0$. The problem is that such a belief implies that it would be possible to combine a militant wage strategy with full-employment policies *indefinitely*. We know from the formal model in Chapter 2 that this is not possible ($\iota \neq 0$), and it would lead union leaders (especially in the sheltered sector) to erroneously conclude that they could push up wages without any adverse effects on their future welfare. Consequently, there *has* to be some real possibility that the government will switch from an accommodating to a nonaccommodating policy stand in response to militant union behavior (as indicated by the information set in the second stage of the game). This is the reason that I have refrained here from speaking about accommodating policy *regimes*. Full employment policies presuppose flexibility, but cannot be *unconditionally* accommodating.

I should note that this is what I take to be the main objection in Scharpf's

(1991) critique of neo-corporatist models of union–government cooperation in economic policies (with particular reference to Lange and Garrett 1985). Scharpf argues that "as long as the government's monetary and fiscal policies are in fact able to avoid unemployment, the unions are always tempted to defect from their 'cooperative' strategy of voluntary wage restraint . . . and to improve the distributive position of workers by fully exploiting their bargaining power, which is quite high under full employment" (1991: 170–1). He continues: "A social democratic government committed to the pursuit of full employment is fundamentally defenseless against uncooperative unions. . . . The result is high rates of inflation" (171). Of course, in a centralized system we know that this analysis can be true *only* if unions are either shortsighted or suffer from the illusion that it is possible to sustain full employment and wage militancy in the long run (i.e., that $p = 0$). Nevertheless, it does point to the problem of assuming that the more governments are committed to full employment, the more likely that goal is to be actually achieved. Only governments that are prepared to embark on a deflationary policy in the face of union militancy are likely to generate a sustainable cooperative outcome.

Where the game presented in Figure 4A.2 departs from Scharpf's argument is on the issue of commitment to a nonaccommodating policy. For example, if the government delegates decision-making authority to an independent central bank, then it precludes itself from playing cooperatively, *even* when the unions are cooperative (what has been termed *monetarist centralization* in Figure 4A.2). This makes it impossible for the government to promise an accommodating policy stand in the event of an *unforeseen* change in the international economic environment. Instead, unions must bear the whole risk of future unemployment and form their wage strategies accordingly. Such risk makes it relatively more favorable to maximize present rather than future welfare (Przeworski and Wallerstein 1982). Though it is true that "under pressure of high unemployment the unions will be forced by their own priorities to cooperate with government policies" (Scharpf 1991: 172), unemployment is likely to exceed the level that would be feasible if the government had the flexibility to play (conditionally) cooperative strategies. As argued in this chapter, this is especially true if centralized bargaining is accompanied by solidaristic wage policies, because such policies tend to be associated with nominal wage rigidity that makes inflexible inflation targets particularly harmful.

Because of the advantages of a flexible policy regime, a case can be made for eliminating the uncoordinated centralization outcome as a possible equilibrium. The reason is that it is unclear what incentives the government would ever have for tying its hands in a centralized setting, at least if centralization is associated with solidaristic wage policies. Noncooperative wage strategies, on the other hand, would seem to be deterred by the very possibility of the government switching to a nonaccommodating policy. Therefore, if the structure of the game is common knowledge to all the parties (unions, employers, and the government), the time-inconsistency problem can be "solved" in the centralized setting by simply communicating policy intentions among the actors. Peak-level bargaining systems facilitate such communication, and the government thus has few incentives to abandon its autonomy over economic policy instruments. This has important political implications because regardless of the actual coalition of interests that dominates the government's support base, and regardless of the government's time horizon, we would expect the equilibrium strategy to be (conditionally) accommodating full-employment policies.

FROM KEYNESIAN CENTRALIZATION TO MONETARIST DECENTRALIZATION

Five Northern European Experiences

In this chapter I compare the change and stability in wage-bargaining institutions and macroeconomic policy regimes in five Northern European countries over the past two decades. As argued in the introductory chapter the five
countries – Austria, Denmark, Germany, Norway, and Sweden – pose interesting puzzles for comparative political economy because, despite many institutional, political, and economic similarities, the Scandinavian countries have
experienced profound changes in labor market institutions and economic policy
regimes since the early 1990s while the German-speaking countries have exhibited remarkable stability. One of the primary objectives of this chapter is to
employ the model of contested economic institutions to explain why political
economies that are usually classified as "corporatist" exhibit such divergent
trajectories of change. In particular, I want to challenge the widespread notion
that the five countries represent minor variants of the same "Northern European
Model." Instead, I argue that these cases, at different points in time, exemplify
distinct institutional varieties of organizing labor markets and adjusting to
changing world market conditions. By showing that different combinations of
bargaining institutions, macroeconomic regimes, and welfare states have distinct
distributional outcomes, I also wish to dispel the idea that it is sufficient to
analyze these institutions as collective goods.

Part of the analysis explores how the interaction between wage-bargaining
institutions and macroeconomic policies tends to produce specific economic
outcomes and national patterns of economic policy-making. This analysis is in
broad agreement with the historical institutionalist tradition (e.g., Katzenstein

1985; Zysman 1983; Hall 1986; Thelen 1991), although I place greater emphasis on the rational pursuit of group interests than do most in this tradition. I am not, however, primarily concerned with how institutions *constrain* the strategic choices of economic agents and governments. The main part of the analysis is concerned with how institutions are being reconstructed *as a result* of such choices. Thus, on the one hand, the analysis shows how differences in path-dependent national institutions in the five cases have conditioned their political and economic capacity to adjust to exogenous changes in technology and international economic conditions. On the other hand, it shows how these different institutional capacities have created pressure for institutional change in some cases, but not in others, and how this pressure has triggered sectoral realignments and changes in macroeconomic regimes.

Because of the emphasis on institutional change, I am devoting particular attention to two cases – Denmark and Sweden – in which change has been particularly dramatic. Specifically, I explain the decentralization of wage-bargaining institutions in these countries as the outcome of a cross-class realignment between sectors of employers and wage earners that are responding to changes in the political, economic, and technological environment in which they negotiate wages and work conditions. The government in the two countries has played either an actively supporting role in this process through a monetarist reorientation of macroeconomic policies (Denmark), or delayed the transformation by adhering to full-employment policies (Sweden). I then contrast the experiences of Denmark and Sweden to those of Austria, Norway, and Germany, where similar institutional changes did not take place despite a number of structural, institutional, and political commonalities. I argue that this divergence can be explained by the model of contested economic institutions once we understand the particular political–institutional conditions in each of these countries.

THE BREAKDOWN OF KEYNESIAN CENTRALIZATION IN DENMARK AND SWEDEN

The transition to monetarist decentralization in Denmark and Sweden in the 1980s and 1990s ultimately reflected similar shifts in the relative power of organized groups and partisan governments, but the particular path and timing of the transition were very different in the two countries as a result of path-dependent institutional and political conditions. It is therefore necessary to take a brief historical look back at these conditions before we can understand the changes that took place later.

THE RISE OF THE FULL-EMPLOYMENT ECONOMY

In the decade after World War II, Denmark was a relatively stagnant society with low growth, high unemployment, and an underdeveloped industrial base. Agricultural production and exports dominated the economy, and much of the industrial production was for a protected home market (Hansen 1983: ch. 18). Because international demand for agricultural products was growing more slowly than for other goods ("Engel's law"), and because prices on raw materials for which Danish industry completely depended on imports were increasing, the external balance was in chronic deficit.[1] Unlike the other Scandinavian countries, there was little state regulation of industrial development, and credit markets were comparatively open and left to the oversight of an independent central bank (Nationalbanken). As a result, interest rates were at or above the international level, and they were used by the central bank to induce the private sector to borrow capital abroad to finance the current account deficit (Mjøset 1986: 137; Uusitalo 1984).

In contrast, the Swedish economy in the 1950s had reached a high level of industrialization (greatly facilitated by a large raw material base), and the state was actively engaged in promoting industrial growth – partly through investment funds and active labor market policies, and partly through an extensive set of credit and currency market controls. The aim of the Swedish strategy was to stimulate growth in the manufacturing sector through the provision of low-interest investment capital and to simultaneously facilitate the structural adaptation of the economy to changing international competitive conditions. The central bank (Riksbanken) wielded considerable power over the credit formation in the economy, and the government used its strong influence over the bank to pursue countercyclical monetary policies and to steer investments by means of credit rationing (Mjøset 1986: 131; Scharpf 1991: 205; Huber and Stephens 1998: 364). In turn, the low-interest policy required extensive exchange rate controls to prevent capital flight.

During the 1960s, however, the economic and political–institutional infrastructure of the two economies began to converge. Along with a liberalization of manufacturing trade (through EFTA), small and medium-sized firms in the Danish industrial sector went through a dynamic phase of expansion (especially in the machine tool industry), causing agriculture to lose its position as the main export sector and generating high levels of real growth accompanied by virtually full employment. New credit institutions emerged to provide capital for the booming industrial sector at a rate below the international level, and labor market policies became more active. In addition, the industrial relations systems in the two countries began to converge as wage bargaining was being increasingly centralized in both.

The Danish bargaining system had its origins in the September Compro-

mise in 1899 when a nationwide employer lockout ended in a historic settlement between the employers' association (Dansk Arbejdsgiverforening, or DA)
and the national unions (confederated in Landsorganisationen i Danmark, or
LO). The September Compromise resulted in the signing of a *Basic Agreement,*
which enshrined the fundamental rights of the two parties (especially the management prerogative of employers and workers' right to organize), and created
an orderly system of regular collective bargaining, as well as rules for dispute
initiation and settlement that included the establishment of an industrial court
(cf. Galenson 1952; Swenson 1991a; Due, Madsen, Jensen, and Petersen 1994).

Centralization of bargaining authority to the peak level did not occur until
the 1950s and 1960s and was punctuated by a number of institutional innova-
tions and amendments to the Basic Agreement. A strict peace clause was
introduced by the so-called August Committee in 1908 (policed by the industrial court), which made initiation of conflicts outside the renewal phase of
collective agreements illegal. In addition, the institutionalization of a Conciliation Board and Public Conciliator was very important for the development of
Danish industrial relations system during the 1930s. The crucial innovation,
initiated in 1931, was the acquired right of the public conciliator (a right that
was formalized by an amendment to the Act on the Public Conciliator in 1934)
to *concatenate* agreements from different bargaining areas, and to put the combined compromise proposal to a collective vote among DA and LO members
(Due et al. 1994: 98–9; Galenson 1952: 112–13). The concatenation rule
introduced a centralized element into the bargaining process because if negotiators in one area could not reach agreement, the conciliator could propose a
compromise that would tend to be similar to agreements in other bargaining
areas, and then put the whole package to a collective vote. Knowing this, both
unions and employers had an incentive to try to coordinate their demands
among themselves.

Until the 1950s, however, national unions and employers' associations
retained the right to bargain collective agreements with no or little direct
intervention from LO and DA. This decentralized system proved quite satisfactory in regulating wages and preventing industrial strife during the 1940s and
1950s. But from the late 1950s, the combination of a building boom and a
rapid expansion of public service production created strong pressures on wages
and severely strained the system, threatening the international cost competitiveness of Danish industry (Mjøset 1986: 139–40; Andersen and Åkerholm 1982:
615). On this background, LO and DA began to acquire direct bargaining
competence over all general negotiation issues, *including wage rates and work time,*
while "special issues" applicable to each particular bargaining area, such as piece
rates and safety regulations, were left for the member organizations to negotiate.
In accordance with the rules stipulated in the 1899 Basic Agreement and the
subsequent amendments, member organizations were legally bound by agreements reached between LO and DA.

The history of the centralized Swedish bargaining system begins later than in Denmark, but in some respects the system reached a more completely developed form by the early 1960s. The Basic Agreement signed in the wake of the Saltsjöbaden Compromise of 1938 constituted the institutional backbone of the Swedish system, much as the Basic Agreement did in the Danish case. The agreement laid down the basic rights and obligations of the parties and established a system of rules to govern the bargaining process and the settlement of disputes. Bargaining was left to the labor market organizations, with the government participating only indirectly through mediation and representation on the Industrial Court (Elvander 1988: 31).

The centralization of wage bargaining initiated by the Saltsjöbaden Agreement was furthered through changes in the constitution of LO in 1941. The reforms ensured a greater role for LO's executive committee (*landssekretariatet*) in the wage bargaining of its affiliates, as well as in the management of strike funds (a function that always remained a prerogative of the member unions in Denmark). A very significant change was that member unions could no longer call a strike without the approval of LO. Moreover, the previous practice of members voting on agreements in individual bargaining areas was effectively eliminated by making the executive leadership of the individual unions the only competent bargaining authority below LO (Swenson 1989: 51). The elimination of the membership vote and the subsuming of union authority under LO can be seen as functionally equivalent to the introduction of the concatenation principle in Denmark. Both reforms limited the capacity of unions in individual bargaining areas to pursue their own wage strategy.

At the Swedish LO congress in 1951 another decisive step toward centralization was taken by the adoption of the Rehn–Meidner principle of solidaristic wage policies. The basic idea was that by demanding "equal wages for equal work" across industries and sectors, it would be possible, not only to promote the egalitarian ideals of the union movement, but also to ensure a dynamic modernization of the economy by forcing inefficient companies to either rationalize or close down, while simultaneously assisting the expansion of efficient firms by imposing ceilings on higher incomes (Huber and Stephens 1998: 367). The local and industry-specific unemployment that the policy would generate was to be alleviated through active labor market policies that would ensure retraining and relocation of redundant workers (Martin 1979; Elvander 1988: 32–3; Swenson 1989: 130–3).

The Rehn–Meidner program presupposed a tight top-down coordination of wages across industries, but for lack of support among some unions the call for centralization was never officially endorsed by LO. Instead, the final stages of the centralization process were brought about as the result of pressure from employers (Elvander 1988: 34). This pressure was prompted by concerns among firms, especially those in the exposed metalworking sector, that the combination of full employment and strong unions would lead to wage competition and industrial conflict to the detriment of profits and international competitiveness (Swenson 1989: 53–5, 59). The Swedish employers' association (Svenska Arbetsgivareföreningen, or SAF) succeeded to push the balance of power within the LO in favor of both those unions in the exposed sector, especially the Metalworkers' Union (Metall), who supported centralization for the same reasons as employers, *and* those low-wage unions who stood to gain from the solidaristic wage policy (Swenson 1989: 56; Pontusson 1992b).

By the early 1960s both countries were dominated by highly centralized bargaining systems, and with social democratic parties whose electoral support reached all-time highs of 42 percent in Denmark and 47 percent in Sweden, the stage was set for a "golden period" of social democratic welfare capitalism. The government was expanding employment and educational opportunities for everyone (mainly through public services), while wages and prices were successfully contained through consensual wage agreements between peak associations of labor and capital. The public economy in Denmark almost doubled during the decade of the 1960s, catching up to Sweden in the mid-1970s, when total government spending in both countries reached about half of the gross domestic product. Moreover, rapid economic growth made income redistribution through solidaristic wage policies and increases in the "social wage" (i.e., transfer payments and social services) both a politically viable (indeed, winning) strategy, and a means to facilitate high sectoral transformation and labor mobility.

A prominent example of the Danish politics of class compromise is the 1963 Danish "package solution" (*"Helhedsløsningen"*). Arguably one of the first of its kind in Western Europe, this comprehensive agreement between the social democratic coalition government, the main labor confederation (LO), and the main employers' association (DA) provided for an extension of existing collective agreements with moderate wage increases and low-wage supplements (approved by both LO and DA), combined with legislation that increased various social benefits and instituted a new pension scheme (ATP) whose funds were earmarked for investment in Danish industry. The agreement thus contained all the core elements of the corporatist bargain: wage restraint (to be self-administered by LO and DA), wage solidarity (low-wage supplements), an increase in the social wage, and provisions to reassure workers about their future welfare (the ATP fund) (Esping-Andersen 1990: 171–2).

It is a testimony to the entrenchment of this "bridge-building" policy in Denmark that it was continued and even expanded during the center-right majority government from 1968 to 1971. Despite the obvious signs that the economy was getting "overheated" by decidedly expansionary macroeconomic policies (Nannestad 1991: 137), the bourgeois government did not heed its own advice, when in opposition, to pursue more frugal fiscal policies and curb the growth in incomes. Instead, it embarked on an ambitious "tax-and-spend" program with revenues increasing from 33 to 44 percent of GNP between 1968 and 1971. As if it wanted to beat the Social Democrats at their own game, the government also took steps to improve the capacity of the state to steer the economy through economic planning (Mjøset 1986: 144, 152).[2]

In Sweden economic policies also led to a rapid expansion of public consumption, but "supply-side" policies continued to play a greater role than in Denmark. In particular, the active labor market policy (administered by the Labor Market Board with representatives from both LO and SAF) funneled large resources into training and relocation programs designed to reskill and resettle those made redundant by the solidaristic wage policy (Erixon 1984; Scharpf 1991: 90–4). The policy helped relieve some of the pressure on fiscal policies because it facilitated job growth in the dynamic sectors of the economy without the need for fiscal expansionism (Martin 1979). Although fiscal policies were never restrictive in the sense envisioned by the Rehn–Meidner model, Swedish full-employment policies were not subject to the same "overheating" problems as the Danish. Swings in the Swedish business cycle were counteracted through investment policies that hoarded business surpluses during economic upswings and released them during downturns (Mjøset 1986: 130). Tax and interest rate policies supported this strategy through a combination of high profit taxes and low interest rates which strongly favored investments over consumption (Pontusson 1992b).[3] This expansionary credit policy was further facilitated by exchange rate controls that inserted a "buffer" between the Swedish economy and international capital markets, and by a politically dependent central bank that held a strong hand in the regulation of credit markets and interest rates (Moses 1994: 134, 137–8; Mjøset 1986: 131; Scharpf 1991: 90, 205).

Overall, Swedish policymakers had more monetary policy instruments at their disposal than their Danish counterparts, and they therefore did not have to rely as extensively on expansionary fiscal policies to ensure full employment. However, these differences between the two countries were muted during the 1960s because high growth, public sector expansion, and essentially very similar wage-bargaining institutions overshadowed the differences in macroeconomic steering capacities. Nor should the differences between Danish and Swedish policies and institutions be overemphasized when placed in a broader comparative context. In international comparisons the combination of centralized wage bargaining, solidaristic wage policies, and flexible full-employment policies set the Scandinavian countries clearly apart from most others, and it is not unreasonable to speak of a "Scandinavian model" during this period. The underlying institutional differences, however, *did* contribute to the divergence of economic policies in Denmark and Sweden during the 1970s and 1980s.

THE SCANDINAVIAN MODEL UNDER PRESSURE

One of the core elements of the Scandinavian model that came under attack in both countries during the 1980s was the pronounced compression of wages in the previous two decades. The centralized bargaining system had afforded unions with predominantly low-paid workers influence over the distribution of wages that they would otherwise not have had. In Denmark the central negotiation committee of the LO was composed by the chairpersons of LO and the major national unions – with the Metalworkers' Union (Metall), the General Workers' Union (SID), and later the Union of Commercial and Clerical Employees (HK) as the dominant players. Because any bargaining proposal had to be agreed upon in the negotiation committee, the major unions held an effective veto power, and distributive issues had to be settled through negotiation between the unions. The implication was that "no agreement could be reached without granting raises to low-paid groups," creating a "vigorous element of solidarity" (Due et al. 1994: 189).

The Swedish LO's solidaristic wage policy had a more articulated intellectual and ideological justification, and the organizational foundation for the policy was somewhat different, but the logic of bargaining power being equalized between high- and low-wage workers through centralization was the same. Although the industrial union structure in Sweden is less polarized between high- and low-wage unions than in Denmark, there have always been LO member unions with mostly low-wage workers – such as the large Municipal Workers' Union (SKAF) and the smaller textile and agricultural workers' unions – and these unions have formed a majority in LO's collegiate council, which determines the collective bargaining strategy (Swenson 1989: 59). At the same time, the support for solidaristic wage policies extends deeply into the ranks of even the Metalworkers' Union – itself a coalition of different wage groups – making it problematic for Metall's leadership to go against the LO line without creating internal dissent. In any event, a repudiation of solidaristic wage policies would be vetoed by a coalition of low-wage workers, and in the full-employment economy Metall had no incentive to provoke such a veto (Swenson 1989: 56–60, 130–3).

Solidaristic wage policies, or wage leveling, became official LO policy in the 1950s and has been a recurrent element in wage negotiations ever since.[4] In examining the wage structure of the two countries over time, this policy is clearly reflected in outcomes (see Figures 5.1 and 5.2). Thus, between 1963 and 1977 wage dispersion for Danish manual workers diminished by about 54 percent, while in the period from 1970 to 1982 the decline for salaried private employees in Denmark was 26 percent. In Sweden, wage dispersion in the LO–SAF area decreased by about 54 percent between 1970 and 1980, while the decline for the PTK–SAF area was 26 percent between 1972 and 1980.[5] During the latter part of the 1970s wage compression began to level off, followed by a period in the 1980s of growing dispersion. This trend coincided with a growing importance of wage negotiations at the industry and firm levels and is evident for both occupational categories and for both countries, although the pattern is less pronounced in the case of Danish blue-collar workers.[6]

The obvious consequence of wage leveling during the 1960s and 1970s was

(a) Manual workers

(b) Salaried workers

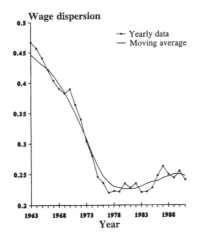

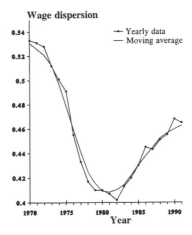

Notes on dispersion measures:

(a)   Dispersion $= \dfrac{W_s - W_{uw}}{W_{um}}$

where W_s is the mean wage of skilled workers, W_{uw} is the mean wage of unskilled women, and W_{um} is the mean wage of unskilled men.

(b)   Dispersion $= \dfrac{P_{75} - P_{25}}{M}$

where P_{75} is the 75th percentile of salaried wage earners, P_{25} is the 25th percentile, and M is the median income.

Sources: Dansk Arbejdsgiverforening, *Lønstatistikken* (Copenhagen, various years).

Figure 5.1. *The evolution of private sector wage dispersion in Denmark.*

that outside options for high-wage groups, ceteris paribus, became more attractive. In fact, there are reasons to expect that outside options – measured in terms of relative labor market scarcities – *improved* for the high-skilled/well-educated segment of the labor force in progression with the greater use of skill-intensive technologies and with the displacement of low-skill jobs that were associated with more standardized forms of production (see for example Piore 1986; Windolf 1989; OECD 1994; Glyn 1993, 1995). In both Denmark and Sweden – as in most other West European nations – unemployment was strongly *negatively* related to training and education, and the association has become more pronounced over time (see Table 5.1). In terms of relative labor market scarcities, therefore, outside options were clearly favoring better educated workers.[7]

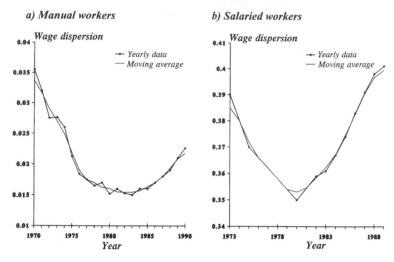

a) Manual workers

Wage dispersion

b) Salaried workers

Wage dispersion

Year

Year

Note on dispersion measures:

(a)   *Dispersion = Variance of log (hourly wages)*

(b) $Dispersion = \dfrac{P_{75} - P_{25}}{M}$

where P_{75} is the 75th percentile of salaried wage earners, P_{25} is the 25th percentile, and M is the median income.

Sources: Statistiska Centralbyrån (1987, 1991); Hibbs and Locking (1991).

Figure 5.2. *The evolution of private sector wage dispersion in Sweden.*

As relative wages grow out of synch with relative market scarcities, some groups of workers are likely to encounter opportunities for additional wage increases at the firm level. Unsurprisingly, therefore, several studies have found a positive relationship between wage compression and wage drift (Flanagan 1990; Andersen and Risager 1990; Hibbs and Locking 1991, 1996).[8] From this perspective, wage drift is a violation of the officially sanctioned distributive norms and contains an element of dissent to centralized bargaining (Schwerin 1980). However, growing wage drift cannot be viewed simply as a form of defection or free-riding by workers with scarce skills. There have *always* been groups of workers with incentives to defect, especially during the full-employment period from the early 1960s to the early 1970s. Indeed, wage drift can be seen as a manifestation of the problems of decentralized wage formation for which centralization is a solution.

Moreover, the intense distributional conflicts that developed within the Danish and Swedish LOs in the late 1970s contrast with the high level of consensus over solidaristic wage policies during the 1960s and early 1970s.

Table 5.1. *Unemployment Rates for Wage Earners with Different Levels of Training and Education for Selected Countries and Years (in Percent)*

Country	Year	No/Short Vocational Training	Long Vocational Training	Short Higher Education	Long Higher Education	Total
Denmark	1983	12	8	5	4	9
	1985	9	5	4	3	8
	1988	11	7	4	3	9
Sweden	1986	7	2	1	1	3
Austria	1987	8	3	2	2	4
West Germany	1975	7	3	2	2	4
	1979	6	2	2	2	3
	1984	16	7	4	5	9
	1989	16	6	3	5	7
Netherlands	1979	4	3		3	4
	1981	9	4		3	8
	1983	16	6		6	14
	1985	15	6		6	13
France	1974	3	2	2	2	3
	1979	8	6	3	3	5
	1984	15	11	7	3	10
	1989	18	10	7	3	13

Note: Some figures are my own calculations based on more detailed educational classifications. In the case of France, the figures assume that men and women are equally represented in each educational category. The data are compiled by OECD from national sources, and educational categories may not be fully comparable across countries.

Sources: OECD (1992d: vol. 1: 26; vol. 2: 71; vol. 3: 77, 343); Walterskirchen (1990: 41).

What differed in the late 1970s and early 1980s was the desire of a growing number of employers to escape the increasingly narrow constraints on their prerogatives to design company-internal incentive structures. In both countries solidaristic wage policies, as well as the system of compensatory mechanisms that underpinned this strategy, came to be viewed by many employers as the principal obstacle to achieving greater production flexibility and international competitiveness (see, for example, Pontusson and Swenson 1996 for Sweden, and Ibsen and Stamhus 1993a: 74–92 for Denmark). As technology became more skill intensive, and as more decision-making power was delegated to the shop floor, many employers felt that it was imperative to improve the wage and employment conditions for their skilled employees and to encourage their continued acquisition of firm-specific skills through appropriately designed incentive systems.

In response to the changing competitive conditions on international markets, many firms therefore began to introduce nonstandard forms of payment systems aimed at increasing labor productivity and long-term company loyalty. Terms such as "qualification wages," "result wages," "productivity bonuses," and "profit sharing" became widespread during the 1980s, especially in the engineering sector, where the exposure to new technology was greatest and where the transition to new flexible modes of production had progressed the farthest (see Standing 1988: 56–63; Pontusson 1992b; Pontusson and Swenson 1996; Kjellberg 1992: 107–12; Ibsen and Stamhus 1993a: 54, 1993b: 86–93; Due et al. 1994: 157, 161). The increasing use of these new forms of remuneration was often supplemented by more traditional wage hikes that primarily benefited well-trained workers with scarce skills. In seeking more flexible wage systems many employers therefore became cooperative partners for those privileged groups of employees who sought to escape the constraints of solidaristic wage policies.

The introduction of more flexible wage systems, however, generated difficult dilemmas within the centralized bargaining structure. When employers placed more emphasis on payment-by-result and on seniority-based wages, they broke the upper limits of centrally negotiated wage standards, which registered as wage drift. In turn, such drift triggered payments of compensation to other employees in both the private and public sectors, either directly, via formal compensation mechanisms ("earnings-development guarantees" in Sweden, and wage indexation schemes in Denmark), or indirectly, via solidaristic wage demands in subsequent bargaining rounds (see Pontusson and Swenson 1996; Ibsen and Stamhus 1993a: 53–8).

One obvious solution to this problem would have been to allow decentralized wage formation to play a greater role within the confines of centrally determined wage ceilings. A bargaining formula along these lines was in fact adopted in the 1985 Swedish bargaining (the so-called Rosenbad talks), and the bourgeois government in Denmark likewise used ceilings in the first few years after coming power. In principle the regulations allowed the distribution of wage increases to be determined at the local level but in practice they served as focal points for all wage groups at the decentralized level and thus effectively became wage *floors* that inhibited the employers' objective to flexibilize the wage structure. Even employers attempt in Denmark to unilaterally use wage ceilings after 1983 had this effect, and the policy was abandoned after 1991 in favor of a more deregulated approach. In the words of Ibsen and Stamhus (1993a: 71), the lesson for the employers was that they could not "have their cake and eat it

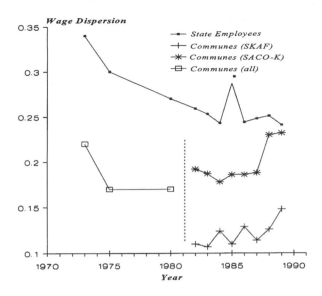

Figure 5.3. *The evolution of public sector wage dispersion in Denmark.*

too" ("*både blæse og ha' mel i munden*"). This still leaves the question of how to achieve effective coordination in a decentralized system open – a topic to which I will return below.

In both countries, the distributional conflict within the labor movement was exacerbated by radical wage leveling in the public sector. Figures 5.3. and 5.4 show the evolution in the dispersion of wages for different groups of public employees. Regardless of which group we look at it is evident that a considerable degree of wage compression has taken place since the beginning of the period and until the early '80s. Thus, between 1970 and 1982 the wage dispersion between civil servants in the Danish state administration decreased nearly 45 percent, while the comparable figure for other Danish state employees is about 38 percent. In Sweden dispersion decreased by 24 percent in the state sector and by 23 percent in the municipal sector between 1973 and 1980. But by the early '80s the trend toward greater wage equality began to level off, and there are now tendencies toward greater dispersion for some groups of employees, most obviously in the Swedish municipal sector.

Although it is difficult to come by wage statistics that are directly comparable to the private sector, there is a broad consensus that leveling progressed further in the public than in the private sector. Thus, high-wage groups in the public sector tend to earn less than their counterparts in the private, while low-wage groups tend to earn more (Smith and Westergård-Nielsen 1988; Zetterberg 1988: 61–2; Elvander 1988: 65, 231–9). Among private sector unions

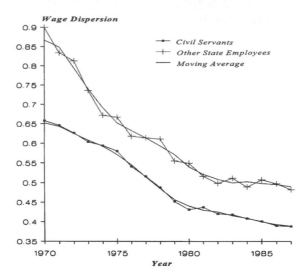

Figure 5.4. *The evolution of public sector wage dispersion in Sweden.*

within LO this situation deepened divisions between, on the one hand, low-wage unions who saw private–public sector wage coordination as a way to defend their relative wages and, on the other hand, high-wage unions who tended to view public unions as both free-riders on productivity increases in private industry and as inflationary wage leaders for low-wage unions. Wage leveling in the public sector, in other words, intensified the conflict over solidaristic wage policies in the private sector.[9]

Internationalization and the Fiscal Crisis of the State

The desire for a more decentralized wage-setting system is always tempered by the risk that decentralization will cause a rise in the overall wage bill and in the cost of living. The original attraction of centralization, after all, was its capacity to contain the inflationary potential of militant unions in sheltered sectors. However, structural-economic changes since 1973, and the policy shifts that accompanied these changes, gradually undermined the cost advantages of centralized bargaining and transformed "ordinary" distributional conflicts into political contests over institutional structure. As domestic markets in Denmark and Sweden grew increasingly exposed to international competitive pressure and as governments adopted more restrictive economic policies to cope with the growing fiscal crisis of the state, the feasibility of controlling wage costs in a decentralized system improved.

    The effect of internationalization corresponds to a "flattening" of the hump in the Calmfors–Driffill model, assuming that monetary policies are accommodating. Recall from Chapter 2 that if entire industries are price takers as a result of international market exposure, there is no difference between centralized, intermediately centralized, and decentralized bargaining, except to the extent that there are externalities from unemployment. In reality, of course, openness is a variable and not a matter of either–or. Thus, the more sectors are exposed to international competition, and the greater the proportion of output being sold on international markets the higher the elasticity of demand and the lower the capacity for cost externalization (Calmfors 1993; Danthine and Hunt 1994). Consequently, the advantages of centralization decline with internationalization. This is especially true if the government is constrained in its pursuit of accommodating full-employment policies, as we know from the theoretical model.

Table 5.2 shows the trends in world market exposure for selected Danish and Swedish industries representing over 95 percent of manufacturing value added. Note that for all industrial categories the share of trade out of total production increased significantly from 1970 to 1985. In some industries, such as textiles and chemicals, the increase in exposure was very substantial, while other industries such as food, paper, and printing remained relatively sheltered. Overall, Danish industries are more exposed to competition than Swedish industries, but the gap narrowed somewhat from 1970 to 1985.

Although to a much lesser extent, traditionally protected sectors such as banking, retail, and insurance have also been subject to somewhat greater international competition along with the liberalization of these trades during the 1980s. With greater European harmonization of rules and regulations in these sectors, and with Danish and Swedish participation in the European Single Market (Sweden as a signatory to the agreement on the European Economic Space, and more recently as a member of the EU), this process will deepen. Equally important, the effect of even moderately growing world market exposure on firms' sensitivity to wage costs has been amplified by increasingly more integrated capital markets, thereby limiting the possibilities for unions to squeeze profits without causing an outflow of capital (Scharpf 1991: 238–55; Streeck 1997). Although one should not exaggerate this mechanism since wage costs are only one out of many considerations that affect investment decisions with outward foreign direct investment increasing nearly ten-fold in Denmark and more than forty-fold in Sweden from 1980 to 1990, it is little wonder that top union officials in the private sector express a keen awareness of the effects of their actions on investment decisions.[10]

But while internationalization has affected large parts of the private sector, this is not so for the public sector, which grew rapidly during the 1960s and 1970s, in part to facilitate centralized bargaining. Scholars within the public choice tradition have argued that public provision of services removes incentives to control costs because the benefits of higher spending are concentrated on producer groups, whereas the costs are dispersed (Buchanan and Tollison 1984; Wildavsky 1986). Some recent work in comparative political economy echoes

Table 5.2. *Export Plus Imports as Percentage of Output in Selected Danish and Swedish Manufacturing Industries (Various Years)*

	Denmark			Sweden		
	1970	1985	Growth in exposure	1970	1985	Growth in exposure
Food etc. (ISIC 31)	28.9	29.1	0.7%	9.2	11.8	28.3%
Textiles etc. (ISIC 32)	52.0	84.7	62.9%	37.5	102.6	173.6%
Wood etc. (ISIC 33)	34.9	49.6	42.1%	16.6	54.5	228.3%
Paper & Printing (ISIC 34)	19.0	28.0	47.4%	20.8	23.6	13.5%
Chemicals (ISIC 35)	59.7	75.6	26.6%	36.1	53.2	39.1%
Basic Metals (ISIC 37)	116.3	173.7	49.4%	43.7	47.5	8.7%
Fabr. Metals (ISIC 381-83)	49.6	64.1	29.2%	48.6	53.7	10.5%
Transport Equip. (ISIC 384)	78.2	91.8	17.4%	39.8	50.3	26.4%

Note: Production in the listed industries accounts for over 95 percent of value added in manufacturing in the two countries. ISIC stands for International Standard Industrial Classification.

Source: Compiled from the *OECD Compatible Trade and Production Data Base* (OECD 1988).

this concern by emphasizing the militant potential of public sector unions unless contained in a centralized bargaining system (Garrett and Way 1999; Franzese 1994). This diagnosis, however, accords too little attention to the employer side and the ability of governments to pass on the bill to voters through larger deficits or higher taxes. At the beginning of the 1980s the debt burden reached unsustainable levels in many countries, and rising international interest rates substantially increased the opportunity costs of deficit financing. Most importantly, soaring levels of taxation met with intensified opposition from business and private sector unions (Swenson 1991b). In Denmark and Sweden, the electoral success of the Danish Progress Party and the Swedish Conservatives – both running on a neo-liberal, antitax political platform – sent a clear message to politicians that there were electoral costs to unconstrained public spending.[11]

The fiscal crisis of the state, and the associated changes in the political cost structure, in both countries led to a search for more effective ways to contain spending, and it soon became clear that public sector unions had few friends outside their own ranks. A series of budgetary and administrative reforms linked to a controlled decentralization and sectoralization of public wage bargaining simultaneously improved control over wage costs and facilitated a more market-conforming wage structure (see Elvander 1988: 314–16; Due and Madsen 1988; Kjellberg 1992; Pontusson 1992a: 119; Schwartz 1994). As shown in Table 5.3, public sector wages have in fact fallen quite noticeably relative to private sector wages. The data are not adjusted for the possible effects of uneven changes in the composition of qualifications and type of employment contracts, but more controlled statistical studies show a similar trend (see Zetterberg 1988: 43–62; Smith and Westergård-Nielsen 1988).

The shift is supported by the evolution of relative prices (see Table 5.3). Thus, when we compare government consumption price index to the general consumer price index, it is evident that there has been a marked slowdown in the rise in relative prices of government services from 1970s to the 1980s. Since almost all government expenditures go to paying wages, and since the productivity gap in public service production is hardly diminishing, the slowdown in relative price increases is clearly indicative of a reduction in public sector wage pressures. With this taming of public sector wage costs, the old bargaining system's mechanisms to coordinate wages across the private–public sector divide became increasingly dispensable and even counterproductive. *The need to contain public sector wage militancy was not a barrier to decentralization in Denmark and Sweden.*

Full-Employment Policies Under Attack

In addition to its direct control over wage formation in the public sector, the government can indirectly affect the wage-push potential in the economy through its use of macroeconomic policy instruments. The transition in both countries from a Keynesian full-employment regime to a monetarist low-inflation regime marked a fundamental reorientation of macroeconomic policy priorities that cemented the transition to a decentralized bargaining system. The transition was encouraged by the growing constraints of a deflationary international economy, but it was ultimately the result of deliberate political choices mediated by the capacity of existing political-economic institutions to cope with external pressures. Overall, such capacity was lower in Denmark than in Sweden, and as the global economic crisis wore on, macroeconomic policies started to diverge in the two countries. While a social democratic government in Sweden practiced its own homegrown variety of Keynesianism, full-

Table 5.3. *Relative Wages and Prices in the Public Sector (Various Years)*

		1963-70	1971-80	1981-90
Denmark	Wages	124.5	109.2	97.6
		n.a.	113.6	100.8
	Prices	87	100	103
Sweden	Wages	112.5	96.7	88.9
		n.a.	92.9	86.2
	Prices	85	100	103

Notes: Wages refer to the average level of gross wages for public and private employees; prices refer to the government consumption price index relative to the GDP price deflator when the figure for the 1971–80 period is set equal to 100.

Sources: Cusack (1991) and (for the second line of entry for wages) OECD, *International Sectoral Data Base* (1993).

employment policies collapsed in Denmark and led to a monetarist solution under a bourgeois coalition government. Eventually, however, Sweden followed Denmark down the same monetarist path, and the purpose of this section is to explain how and why this happened.

From Convergence to Divergence. Since the end of Bretton Woods, especially in the small countries, the issue of choosing a monetary regime has been tightly related to the issue of choosing an exchange rate regime. Under conditions of capital mobility, if the value of the national currency is credibly pegged to another noninflationary currency (or basket of currencies), it is equivalent to following a monetarist policy rule: Any growth in domestic costs or inflation that threatens the government's ability to maintain the peg must be met by restrictive monetary and fiscal policy responses. Doubts about the capacity and determination of the government to defend the value of the currency will manifest itself in a higher level of interest rates (the "risk premium") and a growing debt burden. The latter is exacerbated by the need for the central bank to increase foreign currency holdings to deter speculative runs on the currency.

Until recently Sweden has refrained from using the hard currency option because of the desire to defend its monetary policy autonomy. The value of the currency has been determined by a "basket" of the currencies of major trading partners, subject to "technical" adjustments and occasional devaluations. Sweden briefly joined the so-called European currency "snake" in 1973, a system to limit and manage exchange rate movements, but when the soft currency policy came into conflict with the aim of maintaining exchange rate stability in the system, Sweden resolutely withdrew (in 1977). Subsequent to this withdrawal, the Swedish currency was devalued by 10 percent, even though it had just been granted a 6 percent devaluation within the snake (Gylfason 1990: 186).[12] The result was an immediate improvement in the international competitiveness as expected from standard economic theory. Yet a key to the medium-term success of the Swedish policy was the collective wage agreement following the devaluation, which produced across-the-board wage restraint (Mjøset 1986: 258–9). In fact, real wages *fell* in the 1977–79 period, thereby contributing to a substantial improvement of the current account and the maintenance of full employment (Martin 1985).[13] But the success of the policy was also facilitated by Sweden's elaborate set of exchange controls and related financial regulations, which ensured that Sweden would not pay an interest rate premium for its exchange rate flexibility.

The Danish experience in the mid- to late-1970s differs in important respects from the Swedish. Denmark had joined the "snake" when it was formed in 1973, and it subsequently became a member of the EMS (in 1979). Participation in these organizations was strongly favored by the central bank, by the financial community, and by the Radical Party, on whose support the government depended for legislative majorities. Representing farmer interests, the Radicals were anxious to maintain an alignment between the value of the "Green krone" – which was used by the European Community to compensate Danish agricultural producers for goods sold under the auspices of the Common Agricultural Policy – and the main exchange rate. If the value of the krone devalued more rapidly than the Green krone, Danish farmers would in effect be selling their goods in an overvalued currency and lose purchasing power in terms of the price on foreign goods determined by the normal exchange rate.[14]

The restrictions on Danish monetary policies had important, and undoubtedly partly unintended, consequences for the functioning of the domestic economy and especially the relationship between the social democratic party and the unions. The problem for the Danish government was double. On the one hand, because Danish inflation was above the German level, there existed a persistent expectation that the krone could not, over time, retain its value against the German mark (DM). Since Danish capital markets have always been relatively open, a feature guarded by a strong financial sector and a relatively independent central bank, this expectation required Danish interest rates to be raised to compensate for the risk that foreign investors faced in the event of a devaluation. Thus, real long-term interest rates in Denmark in the 1973–82 period exceeded those in Germany by an average of 2.7 percent, whereas a fully committed hard currency country like Austria kept interest rates at roughly the same level as in Germany.

Of course, the Danish government could have solved its problem by convincing the parties on the labor market to contain wage increases at a level consistent with German inflation and external balance. But to the recurrent frustration and embarrassment of the government, LO defiantly refused to accept the limits for wage increases that the government – heeding advice from its own economists – tried to impose on the social partners. Although there were extensive consultations between the government and LO over wage policies, they could not come to any consensus and clashed again and again, sometimes in very public ways. More than any other political problem during the 1970s, this growing gulf between the "restrained" impulse in the government's macroeconomic policies and the escalating wage demands of LO became symptomatic for the structural imbalances in the Danish economy.

From the perspective of LO, the core dilemma was that the government could no longer credibly promise full employment as a quid pro quo for "responsible" wage policies by the unions. This became particularly clear to the LO during the 1975 and 1977 bargaining rounds, when the Social Democratic government, hard pressed by a negotiation deadlock and a deteriorating economy, felt compelled to legislate statutory settlements. With real effective exchange rates appreciating by 18 percent in the first three years of membership in the "snake", the government desperately needed to improve competitiveness. But although the settlements were below the wage increases LO had been willing to accept voluntarily, and although they secured lower unit cost increases than in Sweden, they failed to achieve any improvement either in the current account or in unemployment. Between 1976 and 1978 Danish price competitiveness remained unchanged while Sweden, aided by the devaluations, achieved a significant 12 percent improvement (Gros and Thygesen 1992: 19).

With unemployment rising, the Danish government tried to use expansionary fiscal policies but again ran up against the currency constraint and the antiinflationary policies of the Nationalbank, which openly criticized the government in its annual reports.[15] Notwithstanding the political objectives and ideological commitment of the government, Danish economic institutions were not well suited to facilitate an accommodating full-employment strategy during a severe and prolonged international recession. The only area in which the government could claim some success was the introduction of a flat-rate cost of living (CoL) compensation mechanism in 1975, and a minimum wage guarantee in 1977, both of which greatly assisted LO in its pursuit of solidaristic wage policies.

Nothing the government did, however, helped shore up support for either its economic cure or the centralized bargaining system. High-wage groups resented the fact that their relative wages were falling as a result of the solidaristic wage policies, while their sacrifices had no discernible positive effects on the economy. Employers, especially in the export-oriented engineering sector, complained loudly that the centralized bargaining system had led to an inflexible wage system that undermined work motivation, inhibited adjustment to new technology, and did nothing to improve price competitiveness. Even low-wage unions were discontented because the government failed to honor what was perceived to be its historical obligation to maintain full employment. By the late 1970s, therefore, the centralized collective bargaining system and the economic policy program of the government were in a deep crisis. In the words of Due et al.: "The Danish collective bargaining model had reached its peak level of centralization, which at the same time led to a crisis in which the collapse of the system seemed imminent" (1994: 188).

From Divergence to Convergence. Events in the early 1980s solidified the opposition to the centralized bargaining system in Denmark. After yet another government-mandated incomes policy settlement in 1979, the Liberal–Social Democratic coalition government (which had come to power in August 1978) enacted an antiinflationary economic package in response to the second oil shock. Having ignored its previous pledges to coordinate its policies with the parties on the labor market, the government defended its unilateral measures by reference to the unanticipated deterioration of the economy. But the government received no sympathy from LO, whose chairman, Thomas Nielsen, engaged in increasingly more public confrontations with Prime Minister Jørgensen. The unions argued that it was precisely during times of economic hardship that close consultations and policy coordination between the two segments of the labor movement were most needed, and they felt betrayed by the decision of the Social Democrats to enter into a government with the Liberal party.

As an EC member, Denmark had by this time joined the European Monetary System. From the beginning the Danish krone showed weakness, and it was devalued twice in 1979. Additional relief against non-EMS currencies came when the effects of the German "locomotive strategy" caused the DM to depreciate in 1980. Even when the Bundesbank put on the monetary brakes in early 1981, flexibility in the system was maintained by permitting Italian and French devaluations, and by revaluing the DM against all the other currencies. Clearly, the participation of large non-DM zone countries in the EMS initially had the effect of making exchange rate policies, and hence monetary policies, less dependent on Germany (Gros and Thygesen 1992). This allowed a substantial depreciation of the Danish currency and produced a considerable (while temporary) improvement in Danish competitiveness.[16]

The greater scope for exchange rate maneuvering in the early turbulent phase of the EMS suddenly and unexpectedly opened the prospect that the Social Democratic government could embark on a Swedish-type strategy of devaluations followed by negotiated wage restraint. But is was too little too late. The institutional conditions for such a strategy had begun to erode in 1981, when wage bargaining was decentralized to the industry level. The employer's association (DA) was opposed to a resumption of centralized bargaining, especially in the political context of a social democratic government desperate to improve its relations with LO, and stronger employee groups such as those represented by the Metalworkers' Union were in no hurry to resume solidaristic wage policies.

In the absence of any institutional mechanisms to link devaluations to wage restraint, one leg was missing in the government's incomes policy. Besides, with the steep rise in international interest rates following the reversal of U.S. monetary policies in 1979, domestic real interest rates had now reached a level (close to 10 percent) where housing construction had come to almost a complete halt. Public debt, domestic and foreign, was rising exponentially. The government was losing control of the economy, and new solutions were desperately needed. In a dramatic TV appearance Finance Minister Heinesen – an otherwise restrained and cautious man – told the nation that Denmark was "standing on the edge of an economic abyss" and that the only way to prevent the economy from free-falling was through an all-out assault on the problems of rising wage costs, inflation, and public debt. Although this was meant primarily as a wake-up call to the unions, it was also a serious indictment of the government's economic policies, and the bourgeois opposition parties lined up to declare their unqualified agreement with the minister.

As if to acknowledge its complete lack of a credible strategy, a tired Social Democratic party in 1982 turned over the reins to a reform-minded bourgeois coalition government without calling an election.[17] The new center-right government quickly initiated four fundamental economic reforms: (i) a firm pegging of the krone to the DM, (ii) a complete liberalization of capital markets, (iii) elimination of the fiscal budget deficit, and (iv) suspension of all cost-of-living indexation.[18] After a relatively short transitory period, the lifting of capital controls and especially the initiation of dramatically restrictive fiscal policies (an 8 percent deficit was converted into a 4.5 percent surplus in the course of five years!) convinced markets that the government meant business and that the new hard currency policy was credible. In addition, by suspending the automatic CoL indexation, and by repealing the mechanism compensating public employees for private sector wage increases, the government reduced the inflationary contagion from wage drift.

The new economic policies had the simultaneous effects of lowering the inflationary costs of decentralized wage increases, while deterring unions from pursuing militant strategies. By abandoning full employment as a policy goal and by pegging the currency to the DM, the government had created an unambiguous bottom line for the economic policy: Any wage–price behavior that was incompatible with the fixed exchange rate policy would be met by a tightening of monetary policies, and hence with a rise in unemployment. Once this commitment was made, all domestic economic policy instruments were relegated to the sole objective of maintaining confidence in the currency, which essentially meant that the government adopted the monetarist line of the German Bundesbank.

The policies were accompanied by some social cutbacks (described below) and initially greeted with massive political demonstrations. Spearheaded by SID and public sector unions, the protests culminated in a general strike in the spring of 1985 aimed at toppling the government. But the government stood firm, and the protests gradually faded away. In fact, the government's policies enjoyed broad support in the electorate, which could not help but notice the improvements of the economy and had the image of "standing at the edge of an abyss" in fresh memory. Between 1983 and 1988 Denmark experienced a nearly 10 percent increase in the number of employed, an improvement that was unparalleled in other European countries and took even the government by surprise. "The Danish economy is doing unbelievably well" (*"det går ufatteligt godt for dansk økonomi"*) became the motto of an ever optimistic Prime Minister Schlütter.

This remarkable recovery was driven by improvements in competitiveness and lower interest rates. Although the trade-weighted exchange rate went from depreciation to appreciation, unit labor costs and inflation decelerated even faster, and the trade balance started to improve. In addition, nominal interest rates were more than halved between 1982 and 1986, from 21 to 10 percent, and real rates fell by nearly as much (from 11 to 5.5 percent).[19] The expansionary effect of this decline, leading to massive wealth gains in securities and one-family houses, was stronger than the contractionary effects of the government's freeze on public consumption and simultaneous tax increase, and the result was a simultaneous rise in investment and consumption.

But the road to recovery was not without bumps, and these bumps directly concerned the relationship between economic policies and wage restraint. With access to abundant and cheap credit, the economy started to overheat,[20] and the question became whether unions would act with sufficient restraint to be compatible with the government's hard currency policy and commitment to low inflation. The answer turned out to be a resounding "no," and wages soared by over 10 percent in the 1987 bargaining round. One of the causes for the increase was the construction sector, which went from bust to boom in a few years and had substantially outpaced other sectors in terms of wage improvements (Finansredegørelse 1994: 149).[21] Yet the government itself opened the floodgates by granting large "compensatory" wage demands to public sector unions in January 1987 (Due and Madsen 1988). This sellout was the result of simple pragmatism in a difficult election year, but it severely undermined the image of a principled commitment to a nonaccommodating strategy. With doubts about the credibility of the economic policy, unions in the private sector closed the gap to construction in one single stroke, causing substantial inflationary pressure.

The government had clearly invited this challenge, but the unions misjudged the government's resolve to stick to its monetarist guns once the damage was done, and unemployment consequently rose markedly. Further speculation about the government's commitment to a nonaccommodating regime was put to rest with the adoption of a new package of restrictive economic policies (called the "potato cure"). The measures included a tax on interest payments and a notable tightening of the conditions for getting credit and house loans. The consequences were a drop in new construction, a tightening of the fiscal stance, and a decline in private consumption. At the same time, the government reaffirmed its commitment to a tight monetary policy by replacing the current peg to the ECU with an anchoring of the krone to the core EMS currencies, which were determined by the deutschmark. Although clearly not without blame for the problems, the government's firm response was a clear lesson to wage bargainers that excessive wage increases would be punished by economic contraction and rising unemployment.

All indications are that bargainers learned this lesson. Wage growth quickly returned to the pre-1987 trend, and both competitiveness and the external balance went through a substantial improvement. This set the stage for the second period of economic growth and declining unemployment in the 1990s. Although much of this improvement came under a new Social Democratic coalition government, it happened within the parameters of the macroeconomic principles laid down by the outgoing government. Committed to satisfy the Maastricht convergence criteria (despite the Danish opt-up of the final phase of EMU), the new government made low inflation and fixed exchange rates the baseline targets for the economic policy, and while it promised more active fiscal policies, the government also warned that it would use such policies as a "linebacker" ("bagstopper") against inflation should adverse developments on the labor market require it (Finansredegørelse 1994: 9). In hindsight it is thus clear that 1982 marked a fundamental regime shift in Danish macroeconomic policy, which now enjoys bipartisan support. If monetarism used to be a policy of the political Right, as well as of an overzealous central bank, today it is considered an indispensable component of any sound economic policy.

For a brief moment around 1980, it looked like Swedish macroeconomic policies might also convert to a monetarist regime under the center-right government.[22] However, a more compromise-oriented policy prevailed as the two center parties (Centern and Folkpartiet) agreed with the Social Democrats on a tax reform, as well as on a 10 percent currency devaluation. When the Conservative party – more firmly committed to a neo-liberal strategy – subsequently left the government, the path was paved for the Social Democratic "Third Way" strategy of devaluation-led reflation after the 1982 election.[23] The policy was masterminded by Finance Minister Feldt and involved a large 16 percent devaluation to restore Swedish competitiveness and to address the emerging signs of unemployment.[24] Crucial to the immediate success of the devaluation was that the LO in advance had agreed *not* to demand compensation for the cost of living increases expected from higher prices on imports (Elvander 1988: 291; Pontusson 1992a: 116–17). Hence, the economic causes and effects of the 1982 devaluation followed a very similar pattern to devaluations in 1976–77: declining international competitiveness and currency devaluation followed by negotiated wage restraint, real-wage decline, and a restoration of competitiveness compatible with full employment. At the time, it therefore looked like the Swedish government had pulled it off once more: maintain full employment and cost competitiveness inside a stagnant world economy.

A closer look at the mechanisms linking centralized bargaining, solidaristic wage policies, and the soft currency option reveals a great deal about how monetary–exchange rate policies interacted with the centralized Swedish bargaining system. Because collective bargains were inevitably followed by some wage drift, and because such drift undermined the redistributive terms of the centralized bargain, low-wage unions had an incentive to keep the ratio of wage drift to bargained wage increases low by maintaining the latter as the dominant element of total wage increases. During a recession like the one in the early 1980s, this created inflationary pressures that the soft currency policy helped alleviate. The logic is nicely illustrated with the data in Figure 5.5, which shows the relationship between bargained wage increases, wage drift, and wage compression in Swedish industry during the 1971–85 period.

Begin by noting the very high predictability of the different wage components from the perspective of the peak negotiators.[25] Thus, LO negotiators were in a position to clearly anticipate the effects of different wage demands on both overall wage increases and the wage structure. In particular, they knew that the higher the level of bargained wage increases, the lower the proportional size of wage drift (left axis), and the higher the increase in wage compression and total wage increases (the right axis). Because the wage demands by LO were the result of a delicate compromise between different groups of wage earners, it was difficult for LO to accept wage restraint at a level necessary to maintain competitiveness during the severe recessions in the mid-1970s and early 1980s. Instead, the restoration of Swedish competitiveness was achieved through large, but infrequent, currency devaluations followed by negotiated restraint. The strategy permitted Swedish nominal wage costs to grow at a rate compatible with the LO's solidaristic wage strategy, and generally at a faster rate than in most of its competitor countries,[26] while simultaneously achieving a real-wage adjustment sufficient to maintain full employment.

On its own institutional premises, the Swedish Third Way strategy was thus coherent. Yet one of the institutional pillars was starting to crumble, with the decision of the Engineering Employers' Association (VF) and the Metalworkers' Union (Metall) to conduct separate negotiations in 1983. The attempt by the government to salvage centralized wage setting through the Rosenbad talks and subsequently the Rehnberg Commission, which set broad wage guidelines in consultation with the main organizations, generated little support and smacked of traditional incomes policies – not unlike those attempted in Denmark in the late 1970s. Nor did the government succeed in controlling wage

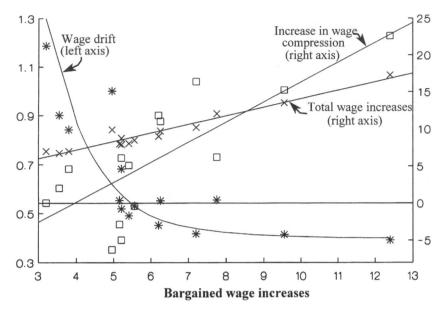

Notes: (1) *Wage drift* is the proportion of noncontractual wage increases to bargained wage increases. (2) *Increase in wage compression* is the percentage increase in the log of the variance of industry earnings. (3) *Total wage increases* is the percentage increase in nominal wages.

Sources: Statistiska Centralbyrån (1987); Hibbs and Locking (1991).

Figure 5.5. *The relationship between bargained wage increases, wage drift, wage compression, and total wage increases in Sweden, 1971–85.*

costs. In the absence of effective peak-level control and in the context of tight labor markets, it simply proved impossible to prevent unions in sheltered and booming sectors from exploiting their bargaining power and "leapfrogging" other unions during wage negotiations.[27] The result was a rapid deterioration of Swedish competitiveness.[28]

For more traditional exporters of standardized goods, especially in the forest and paper and pulp industries, this was sufficient evidence that decentralization did not work,[29] but for the most powerful Swedish companies – organized primarily in the Metal Employers' Federation – the failure of the Rehnberg commission was another reason to push for a more radical transformation of both industrial relations and economic policies. Having experienced a profit boom in the wake of the devaluations in the early 1980s, their coffers were full and, more significantly, macroeconomic developments suggested that time was on their side. When the current account drifted into deficit, confidence in the Swedish krona slipped, and eventually the Social Democratic government was faced with the choice of either making another devaluation or adopting a "Danish" solution of committing to a hard currency regime.[30]

A crucial difference between this choice and the one that led to the devaluations in the early 1980s was that the krona had become much more vulnerable to international currency speculations. With the expansion of world capital markets and the liberalization of capital controls in most OECD countries during the 1980s, Swedish currency markets were increasingly embroiled in the global market place, and efforts to regulate these markets were impeded by the rapid expansion of gray markets (Moses 1994: 140–2; Huber and Stephens 1998: 373–4). Instead of trying to go against this tide of change, the Swedish government decided in the mid-1980s to follow the examples of Norway and Denmark and liberalize capital markets. The result had been an enormous expansion in credit and consumption, which had fueled inflation and undermined the confidence in the Swedish currency.

But the more fundamental problem was that the government now needed to convince currency markets that it was able to effectively control inflation in the wake of a devaluation, or face rising interest rates and the prospect of another run on the currency. Yet the government could guarantee such an outcome only if it was able to elicit the support among unions and employers for a resumption of centralized wage bargaining, and so far it had failed to do so. Besides, even if the government was able to persuade unions and employers to return to the bargaining table, the Third Way strategy had a proven record of inflation that would almost ensure that a risk premium would be assessed against interest rates. With the abolishment of exchange rate controls, another leg in the Keynesian centralized model was thus missing. The Third Way had come to a dead end, and the government decided in late 1990 to peg the value of the krona to the ECU (taking effect in early 1991).

Like the Danish policy reversal in 1982, this was arguably the most important change in Swedish macroeconomic policies since the 1950s because it signaled a de facto abandonment of the post–World War II commitment to full employment. This interpretation is supported by the restrictive fiscal policy measures accompanying the peg and by the government's decision to apply for EC membership and participation in the EMS. The policy was supported on the political right, which adopted it when a new center-right government came to power in the fall of 1991. The timing of the peg, however, could not have been more unfortunate, as the EMS went through its worst crisis since its launching in 1979. As happened for most other EMS countries, the Swedish currency came under pressure when German interest rates soared in the wake of the deficit-financed German unification. Although cutbacks were immediately initiated to defend the peg (supported by the Social Democrats), the floating of the Finnish markka caused a run on the Swedish krona and quickly overwhelmed monetary authorities.[31]

The forced decision to float, however, did not mean that other elements of the new policy would be dropped. Although Social Democratic support for cutbacks fell away with the floating, the low-inflation policy was accompanied by a substantial discretionary tightening of fiscal policies, more restrictive monetary policies, and reductions in unemployment benefits. The aims were to eliminate a substantial interest rate premium that now burdened the Swedish economy (as it had the Danish in the early 1980s), balance the budget and the current account, and restore the competitiveness of the Swedish economy. In the eyes of the government, the causes for the current economic malaise were clear: "The root to the evil of," wrote the government, had been "an exaggerated belief in devaluations and employment expansion in a monopoly-dominated public sector" (Regeringens Budgetförslag 1994: 4; my translation). What is perhaps more remarkable is that the Social Democrats fundamentally agreed after they returned to power in 1994:

> The inflation route for Swedish economy is blocked. Historically it has resulted in devaluations that interfere with the necessary structural adjustments in the economy. Price stability is the precondition for a sustained reduction in unemployment. (Regeringens Budgetförslag 1996: 11; my translation)

The budget proposal went on to underscore the need for a surplus on both the internal and external balances and that growth in employment should come in the private, not in the public, sector. As far as these fundamental goals in the economic policy were concerned, the Social Democrats were now in complete agreement with the neo-liberal Conservatives and their determination to pursue these goals were bolstered by a government alliance with the fiscully Conservative Center Party.

The continued floating of the krona, however, does leave some unanswered questions about the Swedish economy. Although more power over policies has been de facto delegated to the central bank, there is still no firm *institutional* commitment to low inflation, and the close consultation established between the government and the unions, as well as the threat to impose mandated incomes policies, has done little to reassure the private sector of a final break with the past. In some respects it therefore seems more accurate to compare the Swedish situation in the mid-1990s to that in Denmark *before* the 1982 policy turnaround, when policies were suspended between a tight monetary constraint and a commitment to centralized wage bargaining. Indeed, relative unemployment performance in the two countries has been exactly reversed since the early 1980s. At that time unemployment in Denmark was in double digits whereas Sweden enjoyed close to full employment. In 1996 standardized unemployment figures were in double digits in Sweden but below 6 percent in Denmark. Likewise, the Swedish 1980 GDP per capita, measured in purchasing power parities, exceeded the Danish figure by 7 percent; by 1996 the Danish numbers exceeded Swedish by 18 percent. A quite remarkable reversal of fortunes!

Summarizing, the restrictive monetarist regime initiated by the Danish government in 1982 facilitated the transition to a more decentralized system, while the Swedish full-employment strategy complicated such a transition. Despite common pressures toward more decentralized bargaining institutions, Swedish macroeconomic policies led to countervailing pressures that help to explain the pattern of oscillation between centralization and decentralization in the 1980s. This tension seemed to have been resolved in favor of monetarist decentralization with the 1991 reversal of Swedish macroeconomic policies.

Adjusting the Social Wage

Institutional commitment to a nonaccommodating economic policy induces responsible price–wage behavior in a decentralized system to the extent that it creates credible threats of demand constraints and unemployment in response to militant price–wage behavior. Reversing the logic of the centralized system, the more concentrated the costs of such behavior on individual unions and employers, the more likely these are to behave in a collectively responsible manner. This suggests that a coherent, nonaccommodating strategy would produce a system of unemployment compensation and financing that concentrated the costs and risks of unemployment on the collective price–wage setters.

Over the past decade, limited reforms of this nature have been initiated in both Denmark and Sweden. By the 1980s the Social Democrats had created an extremely generous state-financed unemployment benefit system in Denmark, with average replacement rates of about 80 percent of previous earnings and a maximum of 90 percent. Eligibility rules were liberal, and benefit duration was practically unlimited.[32] The system was targeted for reform by the new Conservative government, but it proved politically difficult in a situation where many feared that austerity measures would lead to even higher unemployment. Instead, the government settled for a seemingly minor adjustment of the system that removed the indexation of the upper limit for benefits. As a result the average compensation rate fell markedly over the course of a few years to less than 60 percent in 1985.

Nevertheless, public financing continued to make up the lion's share of the unemployment bill, and the erosion of the benefit ceiling had no effect on the compensation rates for the lowest paid. Because low-paid workers were predominantly semiskilled with a high incidence of unemployment, the wage-disciplining effects of a less generous benefit system were the weakest where they were most needed. This problem, which strikes at the heart of the solidaristic wage system during the 1960s and '70s, is widely recognized by Danish economists and is a main reason for the lack of wage flexibility at the low end of the pay scale, where unemployment hovers around two to three times the national average.[33] But the problem is also one of financing because, despite a major reform in 1993 that shifted the burden away from the state, the financing of mandated benefits is still through a national and pooled system that gives few incentives for *individual* employers or unions to internalize the costs of unemployment.

As in Denmark, most of the cutbacks in the Swedish welfare state were initiated in support of the hard currency policy introduced by the bourgeois government in 1991 (Huber and Stephens 1998: 378–9). Similar to the situation in Denmark in 1982, the government deemed it necessary to commit to a fiscal austerity package to convince capital markets that the pegging of the krona to the ECU was credible. Cuts in the compensation for sick leave, the introduction of a waiting day, reductions in pensions, and a general political resolve to scale back the public sector were measures that the government (with the *support* of the Social Democrats) announced to communicate its commitment to the new economic policy.[34]

The most intensively contested reform in Sweden has been in the area of labor laws and unemployment insurance. The conservative government introduced two amendments to the 1974 Security of Employment Act that made it easier for firms (especially small ones) to hire and fire workers, and it initiated reforms to increase the unemployment contributions of employees, restrict the maximum duration of benefits to two periods of 300 days (previously there were no limits on the number of periods), tighten eligibility, and reduce the rate of compensation from 90 percent to 80 percent of previous earnings (subject to a ceiling). When entering government, the Social Democrats vowed to reverse these changes, but while the (relatively minor) labor law reforms have been repealed, unemployment replacement rates have been further cut so that the average compensation rate now is 74 percent.

On balance, real but limited reforms have occurred to the unemployment benefit systems of the two countries. These reforms raise one of the most fundamental dilemmas currently facing social democracy: If the concentration of risks and greater earnings equality is necessary to secure full employment in a monetarist decentralized economy, is equality or employment the more important goal? Or are there ways to circumvent this trade-off that do not presuppose a return to Keynesian centralization? In the concluding chapter I discuss these issues in greater detail based on the overall theory and evidence presented in this study.

Institutional Accommodation to Decentralization

The shift toward a decentralized equilibrium reflects a new balance of power between organized interests in the labor market and between these and the government. The organized representatives of the better educated segments of the labor force and employers in the exposed sector of the economy are in many ways in charge in the new system, and there are no signs this will change. SAF shut down its central bargaining unit in 1991, and DA is only occasionally involved in direct bargaining through the public conciliation institution. The transition, however, has given rise to a variety of new issues and problems, which have required continuous institutional adjustment and development.

In Sweden, sectoral bargaining cartels have been forming in the engineering sector that bring white- and blue-collar workers together in the same bargaining units.[35] The cartels may help ameliorate the schism that developed between blue- and white-collar workers in the old system, where many blue-collar workers were doing essentially the same work as white-collar workers but were paid on a very different scale (Mahon 1991: 295–325). On the employer side, the Engineering Industry Association (VI) has been created through a merger between the two powerful employer organizations in the metalworking sector – the Engineering Employers' Association (VF) and the Metalworking Industrial Association (Mekanforbundet) – with the explicit aim of creating a stable bargaining system where collective wage agreements concluded in the exposed sector set the pattern for the rest of the economy (cf. *EIRR*, September 1992).

Yet such a system has not yet been accomplished. In the 1995 bargaining round, for example, strikes (or strike threats) were rampant, and wage agreements were strongly influenced by a generous settlement in the paper and pulp industry, which was concluded while the engineering area was still in mediation. Engineering employers were enraged, and some of the largest firms have called for a greater role for firm-level bargaining, which they feel will limit "targeted" strike action and facilitate a further flexibilization of the wage structure. It seems implausible, however, that the problems created by decentralization in 1995 could be addressed by further decentralization, and many employers would prefer instead to see a strengthening of the industry-based system. In particular, proposals have been made for legislative changes that would limit the use of strikes (including the use of cooling-off periods), strengthen the role of mediators, and establish a fixed calendar for bargaining (initial demands, negotiation, mediation, industrial action and agreement) as in the Danish system. Though these reforms are being debated, it is noteworthy that the 1998 bargaining round was peaceful and characterized by restrained union demands that led to moderate wage increases. Industry bargaining clearly *can* be made to work in Sweden.

The main issue for Danish employers has also been how to effectuate a decentralization without endangering an effective coordination of wages. In the words of Due et al.: "If the Structure of Danish industry (and commerce), still characterized by the high percentage of small and medium-sized firms, were not to cause a certain measure of chaos when bargaining competence was decentralized, the organizations would have to be centralized to form entities capable of coordinating and controlling developments" (1994: 190). These concerns led to a spate of mergers and reorganizations in the 1980s. Thus, whereas previously DA was divided into approximately 100 sectoral and 78 local associations, by the end of 1989 there was a total of only 51 member associations. Most importantly, on the initiative of the Metal Industry Employers, a merger was effectuated in 1989 between itself and the Association of General Industries, creating one large Industrial Employers' Association (later called Danish Industry or simply DI).

While expanding the bargaining area, the merger actually had a decentralizing effect on wage setting because all negotiations between this new association (whose members represent about half of DA's total pay bill) and the various unions and cartels (especially CO-Metal) now take place within the so-called minimum wage area where only minimum (rather than actual) wage rates are negotiated by the organizations. In response to these changes, a reorganization of unions into larger sectoral bargaining cartels has ensued. The changes have been most significant in the metalworking sector, where a new bargaining cartel, CO-Industri, was formed in 1992 to counterbalance the creation of the Association of Danish Industries.[36]

The changes have clearly affected the internal balance of power among both unions and employers. Whereas SID and its allies dominated the LO bureaucracy, in the new cartel system skilled workers are in the driver's seat with the chairperson of Metal acting as the chief negotiator. On the employer side, DI has clearly emerged as the center of employer power, partly because it has used its organizational grip on DA to ensure that it maintains its dominance in the decentralized bargaining system. DA affiliates must subject agreements to approval by the executive committee of DA, and until recently DI held a majority of votes in this committee (votes being allocated in proportion to the share of the total wage bill).[37]

For DI this exercise of power within DA is seen as an important mechanism by which to ensure that agreements in the exposed sector are pattern setting for the rest of industry. It is not clear, though, just how important this is for securing DI's basic interests. Employers in other bargaining areas do not necessarily want to jeopardize the competitiveness of Danish industry, and the early agreements concluded outside DI's area in 1995 were moderate despite being rejected by DA. In this context the Public Conciliator plays an important coordinating function. Because he can postpone conflicts and concatenate his own compromise proposals to other agreements, and then put them to a collective vote, it is easier for employers to follow a tough line without fear of a conflict in their own bargaining area. Sweden is lacking such a coordinating institution, and the situation in Denmark and Sweden is different from a country like Germany, where unions outside the metalworking sector are much weaker (see below). The issue of devising an effective coordination mechanism will continue to play a central role in the institutional evolution of the decentralized bargaining systems in Denmark and Sweden.

CONCLUSION

In both Sweden and Denmark the initiative to break with decades of centralized wage bargaining came from export-oriented engineering employers and from unions dominated by highly skilled and relatively well-paid workers in response to new international market conditions and growing sectoral divisions. Correspondingly, the decentralization of the system was associated with disintegration and loss of influence for the peak associations and for low-wage unions, but with a strengthening of the role played by unions and employers at the sectoral level, especially in the internationally oriented engineering sector. The shift was either delayed or facilitated by the government's macroeconomic policies depending on its willingness and capacity to commit to a Keynesian full-employment policy. Eventually, however, governments in both countries turned to monetarism, partly in response to growing international constraints on the capacity to pursue independent policies and partly in response to the pressures to decentralize themselves. In terms of the theory, these changes represent a sectoral realignment for monetarist decentralization.

THE DANISH AND SWEDISH EXPERIENCES IN COMPARATIVE PERSPECTIVE

As noted above, the institutional changes in the bargaining system that occurred in Denmark and Sweden were not matched in Austria and Norway despite obvious similarities in organizational structures and political institutions. In Austria the centralized system exhibited great stability throughout the 1980s, while in Norway attempts were made to *increase* centralization and cross-sectoral wage coordination. It would obviously greatly strengthen the explanation for decentralization in Denmark and Sweden if the divergent developments in Austria and Norway could be traced back to these countries' different positions on the theoretical variables. Subsequently, I compare the dynamics of the Scandinavian political economies to the monetarist decentralized equilibrium in Germany and ask whether the German system does indeed present a viable alternative for the future.

AUSTRIAN AND NORWEGIAN DIVERGENCE

Centralized wage setting institutions in Austria – in particular the Parity Commission for Prices and Wages (and its Sub-Committee on Wages), the Federal Economic Chamber (representing employers), and the ÖGB (the union confederation) – differ in one important respect from those in the other three countries: The distribution of wage increases has never been subject to centralized bargaining. Instead, adjustment of relative wages in response to changes in labor demand and supply is achieved through a complex system of plant- and sector-level negotiations (under the surveillance of the Sub-Committee on Wages and the ÖGB) whereby wage increases for particular groups of employees are approved by the Commission if they can be justified in terms of changes in relative labor scarcities. Subsequently, such wage increases trigger adjustments in the wage structure that form the basis for the demands in the following round of collective bargaining. Because lower level bargaining rights are delegated from the ÖGB, and because any agreement is subject to approval by the Commission, the peak level exerts an important influence over overall increases by signaling targets, but it does not attempt to influence the wage structure by setting different targets for different industries and occupational groups.

With a somewhat cumbersome expression, Marin (1983) calls the workings of the Austrian industrial relations system the "principle of centralism by decentralization." The core idea underpinning the bargaining process is that by allowing *relative* wages to be determined at the sectoral and firm level, negotiators at the peak level can focus on the achievement of appropriate adjustments in the economy-wide *level* of wages.[38] The centralized leadership thus acts more like a referee in a multiplayer game played at lower levels, rather than a player bargaining the outcome directly with employers. This system has allowed wage relativities to largely reflect relative labor scarcities, and, unlike the Danish and Swedish experiences, the wage structure in Austria has shown no signs of compression (Walterskirchen 1990: 54–7; Kindley 1992: 375–83; Rowthorn 1992).

The absence of solidaristic wage policies ensures that wage drift occurs only as a result of differential productivity gains, and unlike the Danish and Swedish cases, ÖGB and the Sub-Committee on Wages do not grant, and have not granted, compensation for drift to other groups of wage earners. Moreover, in the absence of solidaristic wage policies there is no need for the peak negotiators to anticipate the reverse distributive implications of subsequent drift and to "compensate" for this through higher bargained wages. This helps to explain the remarkable capacity of Austrian governments to combine full employment with low inflation. Thus, average unemployment during the 1980s was 3.3 percent – which was slightly higher than in Sweden (2.4 percent), but much lower than in Denmark (10.9 percent) – while prices increased at an annual rate of 3.9 percent, compared to 8.2 percent in Sweden and 6.0 percent in Denmark.

This is a crucial point because it helps us to understand why Austria has been able to combine a nonaccommodating policy regime with a relatively centralized bargaining system. Thus, in the absence of solidaristic wage policies it is possible to negotiate downward real-wage adjustments without currency devaluations during recessions, and without rises in unemployment. To my knowledge Austria is the *only* OECD country that satisfies these conditions. As a result, Austria has been able to maintain both full employment and price competitiveness without tampering with its DM hard currency policy. For example, after Austrian wage settlements in 1974 and 1975 had clearly exceeded what was compatible with maintenance of full employment and balance on the current account (much as had happened in the other cases), instead of devaluing the currency (as in Sweden) or embarking on a swift deflationary strategy (as in Germany), the Austrian government accepted a temporary current account deficit and relied fully on the ability of the social partners to recalibrate wages to a level compatible with full employment and balance on the external current account (Scharpf 1984).

The Austrian union federation (ÖGB) recognized this responsibility for restraint and accepted wage increases after 1976 that were substantially lower than in the previous years, and well below those in Denmark (until 1983) and in Sweden (see Figure 5.6). On the other hand, while nominal wage performance for Austrian workers was very modest, real wages rose faster than in all the other countries during the 1973–90 period. In fact, Austria has done as well as or better than comparable countries on nearly all performance measures. Thus, inflation has been kept at low German levels, and unemployment at low Swedish levels (until Swedish rates jumped in 1991) – without serious problems of trade imbalances. On the other hand, if wage equality is the standard against which to measure success, then Austria clearly failed. This is no coincidence. Rather, it reflects the importance of wage dispersion as a *precondition* for Austria's other economic accomplishments and has been a main reason for the comparative resilience of Austrian bargaining institutions through the 1980s.

Institutional stability in Austria comes at the expense of democratic control by unions over the political dispositions of the ÖGB leadership. Unlike the Scandinavian labor confederations, individual unions have little say in the formulation of ÖGB wage strategies. Rather, it is the ÖGB that controls its members. Thus, the confederation exercises very considerable authority over the financing and staffing of its affiliated unions, and it enjoys weighty influence over the formulation of wage strategies by individual unions (Katzenstein 1984. 47, 61). The ÖGB member unions have no legal personality apart from ÖGB itself, and the authority of the confederation is bolstered by legislation that ensures that centrally negotiated wage agreements cover practically all workers, regardless of whether or not they are members of unions affiliated with the ÖGB (Visser 1990: 156).[39] Individual unions can therefore not affect ÖGB wage policies by threatening to veto or defect from agreements that they find unsatisfactory, although they do exercise some (delegated) responsibility in the regulation of wages within their own bargaining area.

The unique design of the Austrian bargaining system conforms to a system of political organization that Arend Lijphart has dubbed "consociational" (1968). The defining characteristic of this system is intense elite cooperation in the context of potentially divisive conflicts between groups with opposed interests. The key to the success of the system is that elites enjoy a high degree of autonomy from followers so that "enlightened" accommodation for the sake of mutual gains substitutes for the destructive distributive conflicts that could otherwise ensue. The underlying assumption is that elites are fearful of a political deadlock and therefore exclude from the political agenda, so far as it is feasible, issues that may threaten such a deadlock.

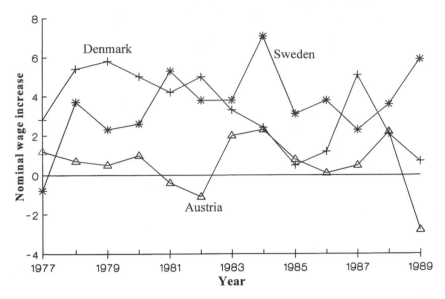

Source: OECD (1992c).

Figure 5.6. *Nominal wage increases in Austria, Denmark, and Sweden vis-à-vis Germany, 1977–89.*

This interpretation is echoed in historical accounts of the emergence of the corporatist Austrian wage bargaining institutions after World War II. Thus, Peter Katzenstein has argued that, unlike the Scandinavian countries, Austrian corporatism was born as a result of elite compromises in the context of sharp societal divisions (1984: 181–90). The loss of World War I, the outbreak of civil war in 1934, and the devastating experience of the Left during the Nazi occupation taught Austrian leaders the high costs of political conflict and instilled in these leaders a degree of political caution and risk aversion found in few other countries. As Katzenstein puts it: "In Austria, democratic corporatism is built on both a community of fate (*Astgemeinschaft*) and a community of fear (*Angstgemeinschaft*)" (1984: 189). After the war, such caution was virtually built into Austrian collective bargaining institutions through a combination of extreme elite dominance and depoliticization of potentially divisive distributive issues through delegation of bargaining power (Scharpf 1991: 178–80, 188–90, 193–4). In particular, Austrian leaders sought to avoid a politicization of wage differentials which would have deepened the divisions between Catholic and socialist unions (which had been on different sides in the civil war) and have jeopardized the goal of creating a united labor movement.

Austrian exceptionalism may also partly be attributed to organizational-structural factors. Thus, it has been suggested that the privileged position of the Metalworkers' Union in the Austrian nationalized economy and in the labor movement helps to account for the particular wage policy adhered to by the ÖGB (see Kindley 1992: 375–83). Because a large proportion of the members of the Metalworkers' Union are skilled and have relatively well-paying jobs, it has been difficult to form a consensus around a solidaristic wage policy. Another contributing explanation may be that because a nonaccommodating economic regime was in place before the formation of a centralized system, peak-level decision makers knew from the outset that solidaristic wage policies would run counter to monetary constraints (at least after the beginning of the first oil crisis), and therefore left distributive issues to be determined at lower levels in the bargaining hierarchy. For lack of detailed comparative and historical evidence, I leave these ideas as conjectures.

This brief account of the origins and nature of Austrian bargaining institutions helps to highlight those features of the Austrian system that make it different from the Scandinavian cases. Because Austrian institutions allow the control of wage costs to be dissociated from wage leveling, external pressures stemming from internationalization and technological change have been absorbed without generating a strong opposition to centralized bargaining the way it happened in Denmark and Sweden. Hence, although Austria faced similar challenges from the international economy, these could be addressed without a major restructuring of domestic institutions.

Norway, as we have seen, constitutes another exception to the trend toward pluralist bargaining, but for different reasons than in Austria. Thus, the "outlier" status of this case is related less to unique institutional features than to the political-economic consequences of the Norwegian oil boom from the early to mid-1970s. Because workers and employers in the oil sector and in industries benefiting from the forward and backward linkages of oil production – especially in energy-intensive petrochemical, electrometallurgical, and paper and pulp industries – were sheltered from normal competitive pressure, the linkage between wage push and competitiveness was severed (Midttun, 1990: 311). Thus, rising oil prices and the prospect of high profits in oligopolistic markets generated huge capital investments, drove up demand for labor, and empowered workers to push for higher wages without providing moderating incentives for restraint. Moreover, since workers in the oil industry were being organized largely by unions outside any of the traditional federations, they were not bound by the established Norwegian bargaining system (Elvander, 1990: 10). The oil industry, in other words, constituted a wage-spiraling combination of cost-insensitive employers and independent, militant unions.

As employees in other sectors sought to defend their relative wage positions, operating from the assumption that the oil revenues would improve the standard of living for *all* wage earners (OECD, 1987b), the economy-wide pressure on wages soared. In addition, the revenues from oil exports relaxed fiscal constraints on the state and empowered Norwegian governments to increase public sector employment (up 40 percent between 1973 and 1989) and to pursue expansionary Keynesian policies even during periods when the international economy was on the upswing (Calmfors, 1990: 26–8; Dølvik and Stokland 1992: 155). The consequences were extremely tight labor markets and intense inflationary pressure, which placed Norwegian wage-setting institutions under severe strain.

These problems were evident already in the 1974 bargaining round when negotiations, under pressure from radical left-wing member unions of LO, were decentralized for the first time in 13 years. Widespread strikes broke out, and the resulting wage increases were nearly three times higher than in the previous bargaining round (Flanagan, Soskice, and Ulman 1983: 168–9). The consequence was a rapid deterioration in the international competitiveness, causing the export of processed goods to drop by 8 percent between 1973 and 1979 (Mjøset 1986: 233).[40] Simultaneously, the increase in consumption benefited the more sheltered consumer and service sectors and caused a rapid growth in imports (Steigum 1984).

The 1974 wage explosion required a new approach to wage bargaining. Hence, when the government proposed a multilateral negotiation formula involving the main labor market organizations, the employers' association dropped its previous opposition to government involvement in collective bargaining, and LO seized the chance to restore its authority after the decentralized settlement in 1974. The tripartite bargaining approach agreed to in the following three bargaining rounds, however, and the mix between local and centralized forms of bargaining adopted between 1982 and 1988, produced only modest results in terms of containing wage costs (Flanagan et al. 1983: 184–91; Mjøset 1989: 330). The principal problems were that the centrally bargained wages covered only part of the labor market and that LO lacked the power to prevent local unions from engaging in inflationary wage competition during the contract period.

These problems became particularly acute during the rapid expansion of consumption under the bourgeois coalition government from 1982 to 1986. Thus, labor costs grew much faster in Norway than in the other three countries in our sample (see Figure 5.7), and competitiveness (measured in relative unit labor costs) deteriorated rapidly (Calmfors 1990: 15–22). The result was a relative decline of industrial production, growing imports, and a fall in non-oil exports (Midttun 1990: 313–21).

When oil prices suddenly dropped in 1986, the cushion effect of oil revenues on the Norwegian economy was removed, and the long decline in the competitiveness of Norwegian industry was manifested in a rapid deterioration of the external current account. Labor markets, however, remained tight and the decentralized bargaining formula adopted in the 1986 wage negotiation was poorly designed to shore up inflationary wage competition between unions in different sectors. On this background, the Social Democratic government (which

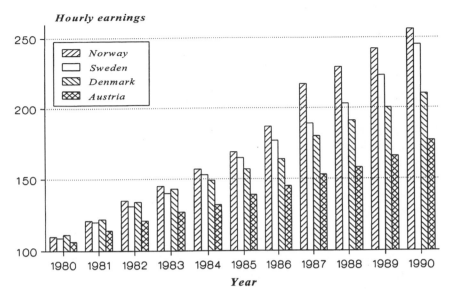

Source: OECD (1992c).

Figure 5.7. *Hourly earnings in manufacturing, 1980–90 (1979 = 100).*

came to power in 1986) declared 1987 a year of "emergency incomes policies" and agreed with LO and the Norwegian employers' association (NAF) that centrally negotiated limits on wage increases were absolutely essential for restoring the competitiveness of Norwegian industry. As a condition for accepting such limits, however, LO demanded that the government impose the terms of an agreement on the entire labor market, including the ground-rent sectors.

In the 1988 bargaining round this coalition for controlling wage costs generated a settlement in which the government, under protest from other unions, used legislation to extend an agreement negotiated by LO and the newly formed employers' association, NHO (created as a merger between NAF and a number of other employer organizations), to cover most other bargaining areas, and to ban local bargaining (Mjøset, 1989: 334; Calmfors, 1990: 33). A similar highly centralized formula, backed by legislative power, was adopted in 1990 followed by LO–NAF agreements in subsequent bargaining rounds. The consequences of these measures were immediately recorded in a deceleration of wage increases. Thus, the average yearly growth in manufacturing earnings of 5.7 percent during the period 1988–90 was only slightly above the figures in Austria and Denmark (5 and 5.3 percent, respectively), and far below those recorded for Sweden (9.1 percent) and other small European countries (7.2 percent).

The recentralization of Norwegian bargaining institutions was a natural consequence of the rapid growth of the oil industry, expansionary fiscal and monetary policies, and the wage-push inflation that this economic expansion generated. When the costs of the declining competitiveness of Norwegian industry were suddenly revealed with the collapse of oil prices in 1986, cost-sensitive employers and workers in the exposed sectors allied with an "activist" government to control the militancy of privileged "maverick" unions and to restore the competitiveness of Norwegian industry. This solution, of course, very much resembled the dynamic that gave rise to centralized bargaining institutions in the 1930s as described by Swenson (1991a).

The recentralization of the Norwegian bargaining system did not prevent unemployment from rising in the early 1990s, reaching a postwar high of 6 percent in 1992. It created an institutional framework, however, within which to address such problems, and the recommendations of a 1992 tripartite commission (the "Kleppe committee") to combine wage restraint and solidaristic wage policies with public sector employment expansion were essentially observed by the social partners between 1993 and 1997 and has led to a reduction in unemployment. But the success of centralization in the late 1980s and 1990s should not blind us to the underlying pressures for decentralization. As in Denmark and Sweden, capital market integration has increased considerably, and with credit market liberalization during the 1980s the degrees of freedom in economic policies have been reduced (Moses 1994; Dølvik and Stokland 1992). Likewise, the flexibilization of production and work organization has created pressures for greater wage dispersion (reflected in the introduction of new pay systems) that run up against the solidaristic wage policies of LO (Dølvik and Stokland 1992: 161).

In this context, employers have expressed criticism of the centralized bargaining system that they themselves helped to bring about. It is now the official goal of the employers' association (renamed NHO) to get rid of the guaranteed minimum wage – which is the cornerstone of the solidaristic wage policy in Norway – and there is talk about a definitive break with the centralized bargaining system as well as a withdrawal from corporatist public bodies. In fact, the bargaining system has exhibited subtle signs of decentralization throughout the early 1990s. Although the LO has consistently pursued solidaristic wage policies, an increasing portion of total increases (between 55 and 85 percent) has come in the form of wage drift that disproportionately benefits better paid workers in the private sector. Indeed, this helped make the centralized system more palatable to employers since it not only meant greater de facto wage flexibility but also undermined the relative wages of white-collar workers in especially the public sector who were subjected to the same "blueprint" agreements between LO and NHO yet gained little from wage drift.

Although it is too early to say whether fundamental change in Norwegian industrial relations along Danish or Swedish lines will occur, there are certainly signs to this effect, and it would be consistent with the theory. Thus, new legislation (supported by both LO and NHO) has been introduced to strip bargaining and strike rights from smaller unions, thereby solving the problem of militant oil sector unions once and for all. As a consequence, the largest affiliate of the oil workers' union (OFS) has decided to affiliate with the vocational union confederation (YS). Moreover, mirroring organizational developments in Denmark, two large bargaining cartels, LO–Industry and LO–Service, have been created in the private sector to take over responsibilities from the LO in a more sector-centered bargaining system.

GERMANY: FLEXIBLY COORDINATED WAGES

When comparing German wage bargaining institutions to those of the Scandinavian countries, one is struck by the comparative stability of the former. Apart from the experimentation with a weak form of macrolevel coordination from 1967 to 1977 (*Konzertierte Aktion*) German wage bargaining has been thoroughly dominated by large and well-organized industrial unions and employers' associations, with a particularly central role played by the metalworking sector.[41] Although the 17 industrial unions are organized into an overarching union confederation, DGB, all wage bargaining takes place at the industry level, with the industry organizations of employers and workers coordinating the bargaining process in individual *länder* (federal states). Similarly, macroeconomic policies are heavily influenced by an independent central bank whose policies have been consistently oriented toward the goal of maintaining price stability, even when this goal has occasionally come into conflict with other economic objectives.

Central bank commitment to restrictive monetary policies has created an economic context in which unions and employers can anticipate with a high degree of confidence the likely response of the Bundesbank to inflationary wage settlements. In turn, because unions and employer associations are sufficiently large that their negotiated settlements will influence the general price level in the economy, they are induced to take into account the policies of the Bundesbank and the effects these will have on profits and unemployment (Hall 1994). In general, since price increases are not being accommodated by lax monetary policies, employers have a strong incentive to resist excessive wage demands, and since unions can anticipate the adverse employment consequences of militant strategies, they have an incentive not to make such demands (Scharpf 1984; Hall 1994; Streeck 1994).

Under conditions like these, wage increases tend to be determined by the position of German industry in international markets (Soskice 1990b: 44–5). In particular, it has given the strong metalworkers' unions (IG Metall) and their employer counterpart (Gesamtmetall) – both with a concentration of members in the most dynamic, export-oriented firms – a wage-leading position vis-à-vis the rest of the German labor market.[42] A review of bargaining rounds since 1974 through 1994 reveals that in 15 out of 21 bargaining rounds the export-oriented metalworking sector set the norm for wage increases.[43] In four bargaining rounds (1975, 1986, 1989, and 1991) public sector unions were first to conclude agreements, but it is noteworthy that in every bargaining round where the public sector played a significant role, the demands of the unions were centered around "catching up" with the private sector.[44] Moreover, IG Metall has not been unsupportive of these claims, fearing that the alternative could be more radical demands for centralized wage-redistribution through the German labor confederation that would undermine its dominant role in the bargaining system (cf. Swenson 1991b). Hence, the occasional interruptions in IG Metall's wage-leading role are hardly expressive of any fundamental weakness. In political, if not in economic, terms the problem for IG Metall seems rather to be the weakness of other unions. This situation contrasts sharply with Denmark and Sweden, where the metalworkers' unions have fought a long battle to limit the power of other unions within the centralized bargaining framework, a battle that continues in the present more decentralized systems.

I am not implying that the German system is always working smoothly or that it is without inherent tensions, but I *am* implying that it is much more stable and attractive to employers than either the old centralized systems of Scandinavia or the more decentralized systems of the British–United States variety. Indeed, I will argue that the German model has considerable appeal to employers in Sweden and Denmark and that the latter countries have moved – in their own idiosyncratic ways, of course – closer to a monetarist decentralized system of the German type. How can this view be reconciled with the widespread notion that the German model is in deep crisis (cf. Silvia 1999; Mahnkopf 1993)?[45] To answer this question it is necessary to distinguish between equilibrium and off-equilibrium behavior within the system. Second, and related, it is necessary to distinguish between problems that are endogenous and exogenous to the system. Finally, it is necessary to distinguish between rhetoric and actual behavior.

On the first point, because wage restraint is premised on the credibility of a publicly announced threat, this threat must be carried out whenever the low-inflation target is being challenged. For example, in 1974 when widespread strikes broke out in the public sector and triggered large wage increases throughout the German economy, the Bundesbank responded by embarking on aggressive deflationary policies, causing a steep increase in unemployment (doubling during 1974, and then nearly doubling again in 1975) (Scharpf 1991: 128–30; Goodman 1992). This incident was not unprecedented, nor did the severe consequences for employment deter the bank in the future. In 1965 the bank had induced the first postwar recession by imposing a tight monetary policy on an overheated economy, and in 1979 just as the German government had given in to foreign pressure and embarked on a moderately expansionary policy (the "locomotive strategy"), the second oil shock and the severe tightening of the U.S. monetary policy triggered a strong response by the Bundesbank similar to that following the first oil crisis. In sharp contrast to monetary policies in Sweden, the bank was motivated by fears that rising American interest rates and the appreciation of the dollar would cause the DM to devalue and trigger unacceptable domestic inflation. Although such a devaluation made economic sense in the midst of a world recession and stagnating German exports, the bank did not wish to send any signals that could be interpreted as weakness on inflation (Scharpf 1991: 149). This time around the unions did not question the credibility of the bank's policy, and, unlike in 1974, wage negotiations proceeded smoothly in both 1981 and 1982.

These are examples of deviations from the equilibrium prediction that are temporary and correctable. We saw that this also happened in Denmark in 1987, and such deviations are inherent to a complex system operating in an uncertain world. It is therefore impossible to draw broader implications from the occasional breakdown of coordination. Of course, the combination of unification and the worst economic crisis in Germany since the 1930s has caused uniquely difficult problems for the industrial relations system, and coordination has failed in several consecutive years. It is important to recognize, however, that these problems are due to exogenous shocks and say nothing about the costs and benefits of the system itself. Let me be more specific by addressing different aspects of the current "crisis."[46]

In 1991 an agreement between Gesamtmetall and IG Metall established a time schedule for calibrating eastern and western wage rates, but when the agreement turned out to cause more difficulties for East German firms than anticipated, it was unilaterally revoked by Gesamtmetall. The renegotiated contract incorporated a "hardship clause" that permitted firms in particularly difficult economic situations to negotiate wages locally, creating a crack in the otherwise fully industry-based bargaining system. More tellingly, perhaps, the unions in the west have found it difficult to lower their wage expectations sufficiently to counteract the redundancies created in the east and by the ensuing economic crisis. Much of the blame for this must fall on the fiscal policies of the Kohl government. Thus, while deliberately downplaying the costs of unification, the government embarked upon a politically popular but economically irresponsible fiscal bonanza that prompted the Bundesbank to step on the brakes, drive up interest rates, and cause unemployment to rise. There were unique circumstances that triggered these policies, and they jeopardized the virtuous interplay between wage and monetary policies by decoupling unions' wage demands from economic outcomes.

It is noteworthy that the unions acted in a restrained the bargaining rounds immediately following unification. But since restrictive monetary policies eliminated any stimulus to the economy that wage restraint combined with fiscal expansionism could have achieved, unemployment kept growing while real wages fell. On this background unions were not inclined to make further sacrifices when the 1995 bargaining round commenced in Bavaria. After a series of strikes IG Metall won a major victory with settlements well above consumer inflation (the pilot agreement occurred in Bavaria and was later adopted in other regions and industries). In the context of a restrictive monetary policy, the settlement led to rising unemployment and thus came back to haunt the unions. By all indications, the lesson that unions drew from this experience was to recognize the need for moderation, and the 1996 two-year benchmark agreement in the metalworking sectors is an exemplary case of restraint. Evidently, once the linkage between wages and unemployment was reestablished, unions adjusted their behavior in a moderate direction. Even the General Secretary of IG Metall, Klaus Zwickel, has hailed the 1996 agreement as a vindication of the advantages of an industry-based bargaining system (*EIRR*, February 1997).

On the third issue (rhetoric versus behavior), it is obvious that the system is not without its critics. On the employer side, pressure for reforms in the collective bargaining system has come mainly from the *Mittelstand* of small and medium-sized employers who feel that the coordination of wages and employment conditions across firms, industries, and sectors (*Bundeseinheitstarif*) pays too little attention to the needs of smaller firms (Streeck 1984; *EIRR*, June, 1992; Silvia 1999).[47] This is especially the case in the area of working hours because small firms have been less capable than large firms of compensating for shorter work hours through shift work (Thelen 1999). For these employers greater flexibility is needed at the firm level, and this requires a devolution of bargaining authority from the industry level to the level of works councils.

If such a devolution of bargaining authority were to take place, it would indeed constitute a major transformation of the German bargaining system. In particular, the ban on works councils' engagement in collective bargaining would have to be repealed, and the associated peace clause would probably have to go with it. Both are essential components of the present system. Some German employers – in particular those represented by the Verband Mittelständiger Unternehmer (Association for Small and Medium-Sized Enterprises) – have pointed to the desirability of such a reform, emphasizing the long history of constructive relations with works councils that are legally independent from the unions (Thelen 1999). However, this view completely overlooks the possibility that the cooperative relations at the firm level are *premised* on the industry-based bargaining system, which prevents workers at the firm level from transforming gains from cooperation into higher wages. It is precisely because works councils cannot bargain wages that they are able to play such a constructive role in production issues (Thelen 1999).

The prospect of such local empowerment is frightening to most German employers, and the notion of radical decentralization has little serious following within the main employers' associations. Although Gesamtmetall's president was chosen in 1991 from the ranks of the *Mittelstand* (though since replaced), the chief executive has continuously worried about how to effectively control wage competition and has repeatedly confirmed the commitment of Gesamtm-etall to the industry-based system of bargaining: "Only in strong associations, based on trust and solidarity of the maximum number of firms within a branch, can [employers] mount successful resistance against exorbitant union demands" (cited in *EIRR*, May, 1993). This recognition was brought out very dramatically in the 1995 bargaining round when engineering employers took a hard-line position on initiative from *Mittelstand* employers. Gesamtmetall even refused to bargain on wages until unions had made concessions on issues of flexibility. Yet when IG Metall stood firm and strikes broke out, individual firms started to offer separate deals to the union and small and medium-sized employers soon regretted their hard-line position, urging Gesamtmetall to step in and settle (Thelen 1999). Unions are strong in Germany, and employers have no alternative but to deal with them at the industry level. Although this does not provide the kind of flexibility in wages and work time that many employers would like, without centrally imposed constraints on wages, German employers cannot control costs.

On the union side the most outspoken critics to the industry-based systems are found among low-wage unions (such as the Textile and Garment Workers' Union, GTB) or unions in the nontraded sectors (such as the Construction Workers' Union, IG Bau). But *unlike Mittelstand* employers, these unions support a stronger role for peak-level bargaining because they do not feel their interests are sufficiently attended to in a "decentralized" industry-based system. *Like* Gesamtmetall, however, IG Metall is squarely opposed to this idea (Swenson 1989: ch. 5), just as they are opposed to granting bargaining rights to works councils. And with calls for both greater decentralization and greater centralization, the support for industry-level bargaining among the most powerful unions and employer organizations would appear to make the system highly resilient to demands for reform.

The main threat to the system may instead come from the new European Central Bank. If European, and by implication German, monetary policies come to be determined by concerns that are unrelated to behavior in the German labor market, it would pose a real threat to the implicit coordination of wage and monetary policies.[48] As long as there is a distinct German labor market, unions will still have an incentive to pay attention to the macroeconomic effects of wage militancy, but the likelihood that ECB monetary policies will be geared more toward European than German conditions will inject a destabilizing element, making full employment more difficult to achieve.

Summarizing, the most notable change in the political economies of Northern Europe is not the shift of the German system toward a British or neo-liberal industrial relations system. For all its critics, the German system has actually worked quite well and continues to represent an institutional equilibrium. Rather, the most notable change in Northern Europe is a shift in Scandinavia toward macroeconomic regimes and wage bargaining institutions that resemble those found in Germany. Monetarist decentralization is replacing Keynesian centralization among the Organized Market Economies, whereas the distinction between Organized Market Economies and Liberal Market Economies persists.

CONCLUSIONS

Since the early 1980s Denmark and Sweden have experienced a cross-class realignment of economic interests in which the post–World War II centralized bargaining regime predicated on wage solidarism and full employment has given way to a more decentralized regime based on flexible wage structures and the threat of unemployment. These changes in the wage-formation process have been accompanied by a reordering of economic policy priorities away from full employment and expansion of the welfare state toward a commitment to price stability and balanced budgets.

The regime change follows shifts in the relative power of partisan governments and different sectors of workers and employers occasioned by (i) a growing internationalization of product and capital markets, (ii) the introduction of new technology and organizational forms, and (iii) declining bargaining power of public sector and low-skill unions due to tighter fiscal constraints and skill-biased shifts in labor demand. Under these conditions, Keynesian centralization became both a barrier to competitiveness (by inhibiting flexibility) and a vehicle for wage redistribution rather than wage restraint. The result was an alliance between workers with marketable skills and diversified quality producers to end peak-level wage setting. In Denmark this alliance was strengthened by a bourgeois government committed to a monetarist strategy, while in Sweden the Social Democratic continuation of full-employment policies challenged the dominance of the alliance.

The regime transformations in Denmark and Sweden should be contrasted to the continued support for centralization in Austria and Norway, and with the high degree of stability in the decentralized German system. In these cases crucial elements of the situation in Denmark and Sweden are missing. In Austria the redistributive goal of wage leveling has been subordinated to the goal of collective gain, whereas in Norway the inflationary pressure from the oil sector rekindled support for centralized institutions in the late 1980s. In Germany the wage-leading role of the engineering sector and the restraint induced by the central bank have served the pivotal actors in the system well, and neither fragmentation nor centralization have been serious alternatives to the current system.

The five cases support the general thesis that there exists an intimate relationship between the institutional design of wage bargaining institutions, macroeconomic policy regimes, and economic outcomes. Despite the emphasis on the similarities between these countries in the neo-corporatist literature, the analysis points to important differences. The five countries inherited different monetary institutions – with Germany and Austria on the independent extreme, Sweden and Norway on the dependent extreme, and Denmark in a middle position – and the design of bargaining institutions has varied in important respects: "democratic centralism" in the Scandinavian countries, "centralized decentralization" in Austria, and "flexible coordination" in Germany. As a result of these differences, institutional change has followed different trajectories in the five countries. Broadly speaking, however, it is appropriate to distinguish between a Scandinavian model and a German model, which roughly correspond to what I called Keynesian centralization and monetarist decentralization in Chapter 4. To the extent that institutional change has followed a systematic pattern, the movement has been from the former to the latter.

6

CONCLUSION

The Fork in the Road for Social Democracy

The social democratic model of equality and full employment was built on centralized wage bargaining and accommodating macroeconomic and social policies. Although inflationary in its consequences, the model secured full employment through an encompassing alliance behind solidaristic wage restraint and an employment-intensive welfare state. The closest alternative to this model was not free-market capitalism, as is often assumed, but a well-organized industry- or sector-based collective bargaining system mated to a credible nonaccommodating monetary regime. Whereas negotiated solidarity and full employment went hand in hand in the centralized Keynesian model, decentralized monetarism deliberately ignored the distributive and full-employment interests of unions. The two models thus operated according to very different political-economic micrologics.

Keynesian centralization and monetarist decentralization are both varieties of organized capitalism and are clearly distinguished from liberal market capitalism, where economic actors lack strategic capacity. Each offers distinct solutions to problems of collective action and shortsighted behavior and can in this sense be thought of as institutional equilibria. While there has been no general shift toward free-market capitalism, however, the foundation of Keynesian centralization has been eroded over time by new technology, internationalization of product and capital markets, and deindustrialization. This raises some difficult questions about what may constitute a viable left agenda as we enter the new century. Broadly speaking we can distinguish three strategic responses. The first reaffirms the traditional social democratic commitment to full employment, equality, and continued welfare state expansion on the assumption that employers and unions will eventually find their way back to the centralized bargaining table. The second strategy, which we may call monetarist egalitarianism, uses a strict monetary policy rule to deter wage militancy while simultaneously secur-

166

ing an egalitarian structure of employment and wages through labor market regulations and a generous social wage. The third response acknowledges the importance of a well-organized collective bargaining system, strong independent unions, and a continued role for the government especially in education, but simultaneously seeks to boost the employment effects of a nonaccommodating macroeconomic regime by allowing greater flexibility in the wage and employment structure. In this chapter I assess the economic and political viability of these responses.

NO RETURN TO THE STATUS QUO ANTE

One of the most adamant proponents of the first response is Geoffrey Garrett (1998a, b). Although he recognizes that macroeconomic policy autonomy carries an economic cost in the form of higher interest rates, he argues that this cost may be well worth paying in order to preserve a system that has so many other virtues. Social democratic corporatism – defined as a system where "powerful left-wing parties are allied with broad and centrally-organized labor movements" (1998a: 1) – "is not only politically desirable in terms of winning elections, but also consistent with strong macroeconomic performance" (130). Although provocative and refreshing in a debate where the tone is set by neo-liberal voices, I suspect that Garrett has gotten both the political and economic arithmetic wrong.

The first problem is Garrett's counterposing of free-market capitalism with social democratic corporatism. This bipolar view of the world accepts too much of the standard neo-liberal diagnosis by assuming that free-market capitalism will prevail wherever social democratic corporatism fails. The real issue for social democracy, or for any of the main actors in social democratic systems, is not whether to mount an all-out defense of old institutions and policies, or sacrifice them to the market. Rather, it is how to adapt a traditional left agenda of inclusionary and egalitarian labor markets to the main tenets of what I have called decentralized monetarism.

The monetarist variant of organized capitalism is afforded no place in Garrett's conceptual framework. Because intermediately centralized systems can accommodate neither a left nor a right economic policy agenda, they are doomed to always be "incoherent" and therefore undesirable (if not unviable).[1] Calmfors and Driffill's (1988) model has a very similar implication. In fact, however, several of these "incoherent" countries have performed as well or better in terms of unemployment and inflation compared to centralized corporatist countries, and my theoretical analysis explains why.[2] Decentralized monetarism simultaneously facilitates control over wage costs while permitting greater wage flexibility, and it does so without requiring buffers against the vagaries of international financial markets. It is against this alternative, not the neo-liberal one, that we should measure the advantages of social democratic corporatism, and it is here that Garrett's arithmetic does not add up.

In this book I have discussed three important reasons why Keynesian centralization has become progressively less attractive when compared to monetarist decentralization. One is the introduction of new flexible production technologies, which makes greater interoccupational wage flexibility more attractive to both employers and skilled workers in the exposed sectors of the economy. Garrett points instead to the cost advantages of encompassing bargaining, and uses Austria and Norway as examples of continued support for centralized corporatist institutions (Garrett 1998a: 136). But it is highly doubtful that centralized bargaining has ever been cost-superior to industry bargaining (more on this below), and the cases of Austria and Norway are not really supportive of the notion. Thus, Austrian wage bargaining was never centralized to the peak level, and in most respects it resembles the industry-based German system. Norway *did* experience a recentralization of bargaining institutions in the late 1980s, but the conditions under which this occurred were exceptional and linked to the oil economy. Such conditions are unlikely to be replicated elsewhere, and even Norwegian bargaining has become more decentralized in the 1990s.

The second reason is the constraining effects of more open capital markets on macroeconomic policy autonomy. Garrrett (1998a: ch. 6; 1998b) quite rightly argues that capital mobility is compatible with flexible exchange rates, but he wrongly equates exchange rate flexibility with monetary policy autonomy. The core issue, in my view, is not whether exchange rates are nominally fixed or not, but the extent to which capital mobility makes the exercise of policy autonomy costlier. Capital market integration compels governments to use interest rates to regulate the cross-border flows of financial assets, and these flows are affected by markets' expectations about the future inflation and exchange rate effects of monetary policies. Pegging of the exchange rate may help to anchor a credible commitment to a nonaccommodating policy rule, but the important point about capital mobility is that it increases the costs of pursuing flexible and accommodating policies irrespective of the exchange rate regime.

Deindustrialization is another important force of change because it is associated with the rise of a wide array of personal and social services that tend to lag manufacturing in terms of productivity. Table 6.1 illustrates the phenomenon using OECD's estimates of total factor productivity growth since 1970 (the earliest date for which this data is available). The productivity gap between industry and services is large and consistent across branches and time.[3] The implication is that if wages are compressed across sectors it slows down the expansion of services employment *unless* demand is highly price inelastic. For some services – such as producer, educational, and medical services – demand probably *is* very price inelastic, but for a broad variety of other services –

Table 6.1. *Average Annual Rates of Growth in Total Factor Productivity for 14 OECD Countries, 1970–94.*

	1970-74	1975-78	1979-82	1983-86	1987-90	1991-94	1970-94
AGRICULTURE[a]	**4.6**	**1.2**	**3.6**	**2.5**	**2.7**	**n.a.**	**3.7**
INDUSTRY	**2.0**	**1.5**	**-0.1**	**1.5**	**1.4**	**1.8**	**1.6**
Manufacturing	*2.8*	*1.8*	*0.1*	*1.6*	*1.3*	*2.7*	*2.1*
Textiles	3.2	0.8	0.3	1.3	0.2	2.2	1.7
Chemicals	3.8	3.7	0.6	0.7	1.4	4.1	2.6
Machinery and equipment	3.6	0.7	0.5	1.7	1.6	3.4	2.6
Electricity, gas, and water	*3.0*	*1.5*	*-1.3*	*1.0*	*0.6*	*0.5*	*1.8*
Transport, storage, and communication	*2.2*	*1.7*	*0.3*	*2.1*	*3.2*	*2.0*	*2.7*
Construction	*-1.2*	*0.0*	*-0.4*	*0.7*	*0.3*	*-0.4*	*-0.4*
SERVICES	**0.2**	**0.2**	**-0.5**	**0.4**	**-0.4**	**-0.5**	**-0.2**
Private services	*0.8*	*0.2*	*-0.6*	*0.7*	*-0.4*	*-0.5*	*0.4*
Wholesale, retail, restaurants, and hotels	1.8	0.5	-0.9	1.1	0.1	-0.5	0.9
Finance, insurance, and real estate	0.4	0.2	-0.4	0.9	-0.4	-0.2	0.0
Community, social, and personal services	0.4	0.1	-0.4	0.3	-0.7	-0.6	-0.2
GAP	**1.8**	**1.3**	**0.4**	**1.1**	**1.8**	**2.3**	**1.8**

[a] Based on estimated labor productivity; n.a.: data not available.

Source: OECD (1997c)

especially wholesale, retail trade, restaurants and hotels, community, social, and personal services – it is probably not.[4]

If the government therefore cares about employment in addition to equality, it is forced to expand the government provision of low-productivity service jobs (Esping-Andersen 1993; Iversen and Wren 1998). From the perspective of private industry, the problem is that such expansion has to be paid for through higher taxes or, if you will, through higher prices on services. Clearly, the solution is not to strengthen the coordination of wages across sectors, as suggested by Garrett, but to decouple wage setting across sectors. As documented in Chapter 5, governments in both Denmark and Sweden attempted such a decoupling and thereby facilitated, not only the reduction of relative wages and prices in public service production, but also a broader decentralization of the bargaining system.

If centralized bargaining and accommodating macroeconomic policies are no longer solutions to problems of wage pressure and unemployment, what could possibly compel different groups of employers and workers into a broad

class alliance behind a resumption of social democratic corporatism? Garrett
(1998a) seems to believe that the answer lies in an increasingly globalized and
insecure economy:

> Perhaps the most important immediate effect of globalization is to increase
> social dislocations and economic insecurity, as the distribution of incomes
> and jobs across firms and industries becomes increasingly unstable. The
> result is that increasing numbers of people have to spend evermore time
> and money trying to make their future more secure. (7)

He concludes that "globalization has provided new and fertile ground for the
social democratic agenda" (8). I think Garrett is right to link risks to demand
for welfare state protection, but the story neglects that globalization affects
people very differently. While it may be true that low-skilled blue-collar workers have been hurt by competition from newly industrializing countries, there
is no evidence that either trade or capital mobility has raised the general level
of labor market risks (Iversen and Cusack 1998). To the contrary, well-educated
segments of the labor force have probably benefited from the opportunities
afforded by participation in expanding global markets (Rodrik 1997: ch. 4).

On the other hand, the risks and uncertainties produced by the process of
deindustrialization undoubtedly have contributed to a broad popular base of
support for the welfare state. This does not necessarily mean support for the
redistributive social democratic variety of the welfare state, however, and it has
certainly not contributed to a strengthening of support for centralized and
solidaristic bargaining. Earnings equality and expansion of public services are
not likely to be viewed by either employers or better paid, better educated
groups, especially in the private sector, as a necessary quid pro quo for "well-
behaved" unions in the low-paid and sheltered sectors, especially in the public.
This is reflected both in a decline of class voting and in a simultaneous rise in
sectoral voting.[5] For example, in the early 1970s private sector employees in
both Denmark and Sweden were slightly more likely than public sector employees to vote for left parties, but by the 1990s public sector employees were
between 8 (Sweden) and 20 (Denmark) percent more likely to vote for left
parties, while private sector employees were between 7 (Sweden) and 20 (Denmark) percent more likely to vote for right parties.[6] These patterns are even
more pronounced if we differentiate between high and low income groups
within the two sectors.

Along with the erosion of the economic advantages of social democratic
corporatism, the distributive politics in these countries has thus intensified
along intraclass lines. Garrett is right that social democracy has historically
thrived on distributive conflict, but these new divisions are problematic because
they run through the traditional social democratic constituencies. For example,
low-skilled public sector workers and high-skilled exposed sector workers are
both traditional supporters of the Left. Social democrats thus face a difficult

choice between attending to different constituencies and conceptions of equality, and it is unrealistic to suppose that they could sell the old centralized corporatist model as a reasonable compromise between these constituencies. In the next section I discuss the main alternatives, and what is at stake for the left.

HARD CHOICES FOR SOCIAL DEMOCRACY

Only by accepting an industry- or sector-based bargaining system mated to a nonaccommodating macroeconomic regime can social democracy secure a firm institutional foundation on which to build a competitive and prosperous economy. Unlike Garrett, most mainstream social democrats have come to accept this proposition. The politically salient questions are how far and in what direction to revise other aspects of the traditional social democratic platform. In the context of the transition toward a service economy and in the absence of labor market institutions that facilitate wage restraint and equality, the government will find it both politically and economically harder to combine egalitarian wage policies with full employment. As Fritz Scharpf (1991: 272) noted some time ago, full employment has become a distributive problem.

It is not that the promotion of pay equality through public policies is impractical. Equal pay and minimum wage legislation, public sector wage policies, mandatory extension laws, as well as a whole range of welfare and regulatory provisions (including unemployment compensation and competition policy) can significantly influence the relative pay and bargaining power of low-wage groups. But because the government cannot depend on centralized bargaining institutions to sponsor and "subsidize" such policies by keeping the relative prices of high-skilled labor low, the entire burden of finding solutions to the "oversupply" of low-skilled workers falls on the government.

The problem is illustrated in Figure 6.1, which shows the relationship between earnings equality – measured as d1/d5 ratios – and the average annual increase in private services employment as a percentage of the working-age population. The association is strong and holds across time for a variety of definitions of the dependent variable, as well as after control for a number of potentially confounding factors (see Glyn 1997; Iversen and Wren 1998). Norway is an outlier in Figure 6.1 primarily because of the rapid growth in gross incomes, which is in turn related to the expansionary macroeconomic effects of the booming oil and petrochemical sectors.

The dynamics of employment expansion in the rising service economy turns the Rehn–Meidner model on its head. While solidaristic wage policies were compatible with, and possibly even facilitating, private sector employment growth when the potential for such growth was concentrated in the most dynamic branches of industry, such policies served as a brake on employment expansion from the end of the 1960s, when the greatest potential for job

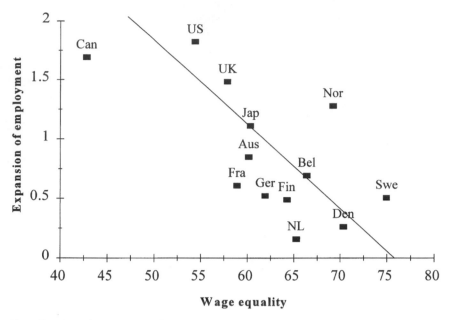

Notes: Equality of earnings is defined as d1/d5 ratios as in Figure 1.1. Private service sector expansion is the average annual increase in employment in all private services as a percentage of the working age population.

Sources: OECD (1991, 1996, 1997c).

Figure 6.1. *Wage equality and expansion of private service sector employment, 1970–92.*

expansion was in low-productivity services. Barring very high levels of wage restraint, which Rehn and Meidner never believed possible, the Rehn–Meidner model therefore cannot ensure full employment in the postindustrializing economy *except* if the government steps in and employs increasingly large numbers of low-skilled workers in public services (Esping-Andersen 1990; Appelbaum and Schettkat 1994; Iversen and Wren 1998).[7]

This is the route that was followed by social democratic governments in Scandinavia, as illustrated by the comparative service sector employment data in Table 6.2. In these countries, employment in private services has been stagnant or declining throughout the 1970–92 period, whereas public sector employment rose rapidly during the 1970s and early 1980s. By contrast, in countries such as the United States and Britain, where neo-liberal policies for privatization and deregulation held sway during the 1980s and early 1990s, employment in private services rose very fast while public sector employment was stagnant. Not surprisingly, these are also the countries with relatively

Table 6.2. *Public and Private Service Sector Employment in Six OECD Countries, 1970–92 (Percentage of Adult Population)*

	Denmark		Sweden		UK		US		Germany		Netherlands	
1970-3	14	20	17	19	13	20	10	26	8	17	7	21
1974-7	17	20	20	20	15	22	10	26	9	17	7	21
1978-81	20	20	24	20	15	23	11	29	10	18	8	21
1982-5	22	20	26	20	14	24	10	31	10	18	8	20
1986-9	22	21	26	22	14	28	11	35	10	19	7	22
1990-2	22	21	26	23	14	31	11	36	10	17	7	24
Change	*8*	*1*	*9*	*3*	*0*	*11*	*1*	*11*	*2*	*0*	*0*	*3*

Note: First column is total government employment as percent of the adult population; second column is total private sector service employment as percent of the adult population (excluding transport and communication).

Source: OECD (1997c).

*in*egalitarian wage structures (refer to Figure 6.1), and unlike the other countries in the table, Britain and the United States grew notably *more* inegalitarian during the 1980s.[8]

But there is clearly an alternative to the Scandinavian and neo-liberal models as exemplified by Germany and the Netherlands. In these countries services employment has been stagnant in *both* the public sector (as in the neo-liberal cases) *and* in the private sector (as in the social democratic countries), but compared to the liberal market economies wage compression is high, and unlike the Scandinavian countries government consumption has been kept down. The cost of these policies has instead come in the form of very low labor market participation rates, especially among women and older workers. This combination is at least partly a result of the strong influence over government policies of Christian democratic parties. In the case of the Netherlands, for example, a "consociational" political system has accorded equal weight to the Christian democratic concern for keeping the state in a subordinate role and the social democratic concern for class solidarity and equality (Van Kersbergen 1995: ch. 4). Correspondingly, wage equality in this country is close to Scandinavian levels.

If we assume that there is little or no scope for further public service expansion – politically as well as fiscally – the choice for social democracy thus pivots around limiting the supply of labor or accepting greater inequality in wage and employment contracts. The Dutch case is instructive in this respect because governments have made notable choices over this trade-off during the past two decades. One component of these changes has been a very effective macroeconomic adjustment achieved through negotiated wage restraint in the context of a strictly nonaccommodating macroeconomic policy regime. Since this strategy got underway in the early 1980s the effect has been an almost halving of unemployment from its peak in the early 1980s. In this respect the Dutch strategy is very similar to the Danish, and was even initiated at around the same time (1982) under similar economic and institutional conditions. But at the same time the Dutch macroeconomic strategy has been accompanied by a very substantial rise in part-time and temporary jobs, which often do not carry the same benefits and protection as full-time employment (Schmidt 1997). Moreover, there has been an increase in wage dispersion, even though the changes have been far more modest than in countries such as Britain and the United States (Visser and Hemerijck 1997: ch. 2). As a consequence, employment in private services has risen quite remarkably during the 1980s and 1990s, and participation rates have started to converge to those in Scandinavia.

The Dutch solution to employment problems thus combines restrictive macroeconomic policies and bargained wage restraint with an expansion of mostly part-time employment in private services. This then is the critical choice for social democracy (assuming that it accepts monetary decentralization): Either embark on a "Dutch" strategy of promoting private service sector employment through a graduated and controlled flexibilization of wages and employment contracts, or sacrifice employment to retain a smaller full-time work force characterized by highly egalitarian wages. Danish and Swedish social democrats have thus far been very reluctant to cut benefits and wages for the low skilled and have instead accepted very high unemployment levels among these groups. On the other hand, early retirement schemes and paid sabbaticals have been increasingly employed to encourage exit from the labor market. The result has been a reduction in the number of people in employment as a percentage of the working-age population from its peak of over 76 percent in 1986 to about 70 percent in 1994 in the case of Denmark, and from over 82 percent in 1989 to less than 72 percent in 1994 in the case of Sweden.[9]

Some attempts have also been made to loosen the egalitarian effects of the welfare state, most notably in the area of unemployment compensation and marginal tax rates. Still, the unemployment benefit reforms have only marginally affected replacement rates for the lowest paid, and although the tax reforms have increased the spread of net incomes, they have not necessarily helped to make low-income groups more employable. What is still missing from the Scandinavian experience is anything resembling a national agreement that would politically legitimize a flexibilization of the wage and employment structure. Thus far low-wage unions have effectively vetoed any reforms that would jeopardize their wages or social benefit position, and social democratic governments have been unwilling to press the issue by threatening strong unilateral action.

CONCLUSION

The success of social democracy has always been premised on the capacity of governments to combine an efficient and competitive economy with the pursuit of a fair distribution of income and life chances. The failure of the model resulted from a perpetuation of egalitarian ideals and a commitment to full-time employment for all, which went beyond what was compatible with sustained international competitiveness and ignored the shifting balance of power between different sectors of workers and employers. If social democracy wants to be electorally competitive in the future and vie for government power, it has to accept institutions and policies that are broadly in alignment with the underlying cross-class coalition structure and are therefore economically viable.

This means that there can be no way back in the foreseeable future to a class-based, centralized Keynesian equilibrium with an expansive and egalitarian welfare state. Any concerted attempt to regain control over macroeconomic policy instruments through extensive capital controls would be a recipe for economic disaster, and technological and sectoral changes have made employers in the most dynamic sectors of the economy opposed to such a strategy. If the principle of economic efficiency is going to be a cornerstone in the social democracy strategy, as it has in the past, then monetarism and sector- or industry-based wage bargaining must be accepted as the institutional foundations for the economy, *despite* their antithetical relationship to traditional socialist commitments to wage solidarity and full employment.

This has been a hard lesson for social democrats to learn, and one that in some cases has required long stints in opposition. But today it is almost universally accepted among party elites, an acceptance that has helped in the electoral revival of social democracy. Fritz Scharpf recognized that much almost a decade ago and recommended instead that social democrats should "hold firm to the solidaristic ideals of democratic socialism" and promote "socialism within one class" (1991: 275). Yet we need to go further than that and ask: Which of the competing ideals of solidarity, and which particular intraclass interests, should be accorded prominence? The difficult issue that now confronts social democrats is how to choose over the trade-off between wage equality and employment, or between the deepening of class distinctions and perpetuation of insider–outsider divisions. High pay for unskilled workers in the public sector combined with generous and collectively financed flat-rate unemployment benefits undermine expansion of private service sector employment and can interfere with the creation of a more rational wage incentive structure. Perhaps this is a price well worth paying, but it is one that has to be subjected to free and undogmatic debate. Such a debate may in turn yield new and innovative ideas about how to cushion the inequalizing effects of a more market-conforming wage structure. Negative income taxes, wage subsidies, state-guaranteed retraining opportunities, and even greater use of means testing are ideas that, for all their practical problems, exemplify such creative thinking.

A particularly important issue for both politicians and researchers concerns the extent and means by which the state can encourage national specialization in the production of high-quality and high-value-added services just as such specialization occurred in manufacturing in the past. Since division of labor is limited by the size of the market, one apparent precondition would be further liberalization of the international services trade. This in turn requires a rethinking of the traditional opposition on the left toward greater international competition in previously sheltered, and presumably therefore secure, services. Only if this happen may it be possible to reestablish a virtuous interplay between solidaristic wage policies and the expansion of employment. There would ultimately be no greater accomplishment for social democracy than to put the Rehn–Meidner model back on its feet.

NOTES

Chapter 1

1. Recently models have been proposed that assume that wage bargainers also have preferences over monetary variables (see Skott 1997; Cukierman and Lippi 1998). These models come close to assuming money illusion, and I wish to avoid this route. I do, however, share their concern for the real effects of monetary policies.

2. The index of central bank independence is an average (after standardization) of three widely used indices by Bade and Parkin (1982), Grilli, Masciandaro, and Tabellini (1991), and Cukierman (1992). The exchange rate index is based on OECD data for relative growth in nominal effective exchange rates.

3. The data consists of five four-year intervals between 1973 and 1993 for a total of 75 observations.

4. The data are discussed in detail in Chapter 3.

5. Decline in trade-union membership is sometimes argued to provide further evidence of decentralization (Katz 1993). However, the fall in density rates is often of little consequence for bargaining due to the widespread use of extension laws that legally obligate employers to follow collectively negotiated pay rates (OECD 1997a). Exceptions are Britain and the United States. Conversely, growing unionization, which has occurred in the Scandinavian countries, does not necessarily imply centralization since much of the membership growth has come outside the previously dominant blue-collar unions, causing deconcentration of union membership. This tendency is mirrored in the centralization data.

6. Bargaining over non-wage issues, especially work time, has increasingly taken place at the plant level in Germany and Austria (Thelen 1991, 1993; Traxler 1992).

7. The difficulty in detecting a universal trend is echoed in Hyman (1994), Wallerstein, Golden, and Lange (1997), and Kitschelt, Marks, Lange, and Stephens (1999).

8. In the case of Germany, Katzenstein does not offer a detailed comparison with the smaller states, but he *does* note that the country "comes closer than any other large state to the logic by which political life in the small European states is organized" (1985: 31).

9. The construction of the index is explained in detail in Chapter 3.

10. In a later piece, however, they are more cognizant of the possibility that intermediately centralized systems may exhibit good economic performance, and therefore also of the possibility that they will be stable. See Garrett and Lange (1995).

Chapter 2

1. A prominent example of this logic is Lucas's (1972) "signal-extraction model" in which firms raise output and employment in response only to relative price increases, not general economy-wide price increases. Since increases in aggregate demand necessarily result in general price increases, expansionary fiscal and monetary policies would be inefficient.

2. I discuss the central bank independence literature below.

3. This is a somewhat peculiar aspect of a rational expectations model since it would seem to imply that voters are not being rational when they vote for left parties. They may of course do so for other reasons, but then there would be no partisan incentive to adopt distinct macroeconomic policies. The only exception would be if inflation had lasting effects on income distribution. But if this were the case (and the evidence for this is weak), then Alesina's contention that a low-inflation commitment (especially through greater central bank independence) would be Pareto-improving is untenable (some would in fact be worse off).

4. I do, however, share a focus on the interaction between monetary policies and wage bargaining with Cubitt (1992), Skott (1997), and Cukierman (1997).

5. For expositions of the new Keynesian approach see Rowthorn (1977), Carlin and Soskice (1990), and Layard, Nickell, and Jackman (1991).

6. This sectoral division in the open economy version of the competing claims model is of great significance for the analysis of coalition behavior, and I will return to the idea below.

7. The main studies include Edgren, Faxén, and Odhner (1973), Lindbeck (1979), Swenson (1989), and Crouch (1990).

8. This logic is spelled out in detail in Soskice and Iversen (1999).

9. Technically speaking, it is a two-stage game with complete but imperfect information.

10. Traditional sheltered sectors such as construction and retail are not exempted from the logic. To the contrary, one can argue that these sectors are particularly sensitive to restrictive monetary policies since rising interest rates and falls in domestic consumption have very severe consequences. The story for the public sector is more complicated because the potential for cost-externalization depends on the ability of the government to raise taxes. With a commitment to

a restrictive monetary policy, the government is limited in terms of its ability to impose an inflation tax, but it can obviously still raise taxes directly. In this sense, expansion of the public economy can be viewed as a form of accommodation, and it will be discussed further below.

11. This logic follows very closely the idea of nonmyopic equilibria proposed by Steven Brams (1990, 1994). In this highly pertinent game-theoretic formulation (called the Theory of Moves), players ask themselves before they act whether a change in their own behavior is likely to trigger retaliation by others, possibly leaving them worse off than in status quo. If this is the case, then gains that could be realized only if others stayed put (such as defection in a PD-game) are effectively discounted. For this "nonmyopic" logic to work, individual players' actions must have significant effects on the welfare of other players.

12. This logic also applies to the state as a public employer since an increased wage bill can no longer be accommodated through monetary expansion, but has to be either covered through higher taxes (an unpopular option among private sector employees given the purpose), or will lead to deflationary central bank responses. For an excellent analysis along these lines, see Scharpf (1991). Commenting on the German experience in the early 1970s, Scharpf concludes that "regardless of all theoretical controversies . . . , there could be no doubt that a restrictive monetary policy could neutralize expansionary fiscal stimuli . . . and produce unemployment on its own" (1991: 137).

13. Strategic capacity presupposes that people possess what Elster (1983: 77) has termed "strategic rationality": players must anticipate the decisions of others and then make the choice that maximizes their own welfare. Strategic rationality, which applies to all game theory, assumes common knowledge of rationality. Andrew Graham has pointed out to me that common knowledge is not an innocuous assumption under conditions of institutional change because rational response patterns cannot be assumed by the players until a *history* of responses has been developed. In the transition to a new institutional outcome, such history is absent and may throw off the predictions of a model assuming common knowledge. I address this objection below.

14. Again, it is illuminating to recall Brams's (1990, 1994) theory of moves and how it contrasts with conventional game theory. If each player's behavior has negligible effects on other players' welfare and behavior, standard game theoretic solutions imply that the negative externalities of individual behavior are entirely discounted and that other players' actions can be assumed constant. Elster (1983) calls the logic underpinning such behavior "parametric" rationality, while Brams calls it "myopic." In contrast, when each player's behavior has nonnegligible effects on the welfare of others, it is prudent for players to take into account the effect of their own choices on other players' choices *before* deciding to act. Nonmyopic behavior of this type leads to different outcomes because of the deterrence effect that anticipated retaliation can have on any player's choices.

15. This argument contrasts to Scharpf (1991), who maintains that "a conservative-monetarist policy does not depend on the organizational power, solidarity, and discipline of large unions" (175). In fact, Scharpf maintains that under such a

policy regime ". . . it is reasonable to presume that small unions would be even quicker to make concessions in [wage] negotiations" (175). The problem with this argument is twofold. First, the real-wage behavior of small unions must be independent of the macroeconomic regime. Unless there exists a sustainable Phillips curve trade-off (which practically no modern economist believes), the behavior of small unions will simply be a function of the NAIRU level of unemployment. Second, the beneficial deterrence effects of monetarist policies on the real-wage behavior of large unions are discounted. It is *only* unions with strategic capacity that can be induced to observe wage restraint by the use of nonaccommodating monetary policies. This is a crucial point that is amply illustrated by Scharpf's empirical analysis, though (curiously enough) not by his theoretical analysis.

16. This approach is very different from explanations emphasizing the importance of distributive norms. Although I do not deny that norms play a role, normative explanations are often unsatisfactory. Jon Elster has pushed a normative explanation farther than any other scholar, and his work is an exemplar of the epistemological problems involved in such explanations. First he identifies a set of feasible wage norms, of which the norms of equal wages for different work (equality) and equal wages for equal work (equity) are the most important (1989: 224). He then argues that "usually . . . equality and . . . equity cannot be reconciled" (246), and goes on to note that the Swedish labor movement has oscillated in its adherence to these norms. But apart from an obscure reference to changes in public opinion, there is no attempt to account for these oscillations in terms of norms. How then are the explanandum (the wage strategies of LO) and the explanans (distributive norms) to be separated?

17. I would like to underscore that the relationship is *not* a result of centralized unions pursuing solidaristic wage policies with greater zeal than decentralized unions – a point that is for some reason often misunderstood.

18. On logical grounds – but not on empirical grounds, as I will show – it may be objected to this spillover logic that high-wage unions can dissipate nominal wage pressure by agreeing to more radical bargained redistribution (i.e., by choosing a $r_b > 1$). Yet the Nash solution is clearly more realistic. First, since wage drift is not contractually agreed to and since it occurs in the future, it represents a risky prospect for union members, whereas bargained increases are certain. Granting that most people are risk-averse when it comes to their personal income, the median union member would rationally prefer to maximize his or her share of the bargained increase. Second, since union members do not possess the same information and foresight as their leaders, they cannot easily assess the quality of their bargaining representatives *except* by their ability to secure the largest possible share of the collective wage gain. Either way, representative union leaders can be expected to try to maximize their share of the bargained increase from which the Nash solution follows. I am grateful to Peter Lange for helping me to clarify these issues.

19. Under these circumstances, labor faces a "trilemma" in the terminology proposed by Peter Swenson (1989): By squeezing profits and raising real wages it is possible to pursue solidaristic wage policies, but only at the expense of employment. If wages are kept down to a level that is compatible with full

employment, the goal of redistribution will be thwarted. Any "compromise" between these strategies – depending on the shape of the employment–wage indifference curves of different unions and the outcome of bargaining between these unions – will lead to higher unemployment with some element of redistribution.

20. The alternative to public sector employment expansion, while pursuing full employment and wage equality, is to discourage labor market entry (especially of women) and encourage labor market exit (especially of older workers). As discussed below, this is a strategy that has been followed in Austria, Germany, and some other countries dominated by Christian democracy. It is not a strategy that has been pursued by either social democratic governments or liberal governments (although this may be changing).

21. In game-theoretic jargon this is called a pooling equilibrium.

22. In game-theoretic terms, this is a separating equilibrium.

23. Even in the completely centralized case, the model predicts that type does matter since unions are always able to achieve their distributive objectives with lower employment sacrifices when monetary policies are accommodating, implying that some inflationary wage solidarism will be traded for less unemployment when the monetary regime turns in a nonaccommodating direction.

24. As shown by Calmfors and Driffill, it is possible to employ a bargaining model where wages are determined through negotiation between unions and organizations of employers, but the relationship between centralization and wage behavior is unaffected.

25. Barro and Gordon (1983). Strictly speaking, the present game is a two-stage game with complete but *imperfect* information since multiple players (unions) are making simultaneous moves in the first stage.

26. All references to wage increases are net of productivity increases.

27. To see this, note that when the relative price effect is π_i^r, the aggregate price effect is simply the sum of all relative price increases divided by the number of bargaining areas: $1/n\sum\pi_i^r$, which is equivalent to $c\pi_i^r + (1 - c)\pi_o^r$. Since $\pi_i^r = cw_i$ the aggregate effect can be written as $c^2w_i + (1 - c)\pi_o^r$. The marginal effect on the aggregate price level of a wage increase by union i is then $\delta\pi/\delta w_i = c^2w_i^1 + (1 - c)\pi_o^r = c^2$.

28. This result also follows from Rubinstein bargaining theory under reasonable assumptions (Osborne and Rubinstein 1991). In this conceptualization the solution depends on (i) who makes the first offer, and (ii) the relative time preferences of the two players. The player who makes the first offer and who is more patient (or more willing to risk a bargaining breakdown) has an advantage and will secure the greater share. Since there is no a priori reason to believe that unions will differ either in their time preferences or in their capacity to make the first offer, Rubinstein bargaining theory predicts that the collective gain will be divided equally.

29. Specific contracts are often more complicated because, among other reasons, they contain non-wage elements (such as work-time reductions and vacation) over which high- and low-wage unions have divergent preferences.

30. The reason is explained below.

31. The only requirement is that $w_i < \hat{w}_i + w_d$, which is the case for all examples

used below. In fact, the logic and the results would be retained if $\hat{w}_i$ were substituted with a constant.

32. Although it must be assumed that drift does not fully offset centralized wage increases, since otherwise bargaining structure would be irrelevant for outcomes (Moene et al. 1993: 100–5).

33. This follows the approach in Moene et al. (1993: 102–3). A more complicated formulation is presented in Hibbs and Locking (1996), but with very similar results in terms of the effects of wage drift on centrally negotiated wages.

34. The result was computed by hand and checked with the mathematical software program Maple V, Release 3 (Brooks/Cole Publishing Company).

35. If β is very high, nonaccommodation will always be associated with higher unemployment. Conversely, if wage drift (w_d) is very high nonaccommodation may never be associated with higher unemployment. The reason is that for very large values of w_d, the marginal effect of higher bargained wage increases on equality is so small compared to the effects of such increases on unemployment that unions will not find it worthwhile to try to affect wage relativities by bargaining higher wages. Since this result holds only when wage drift is much greater than bargained increases, this is not an issue in practice.

36. The easiest way to see this is to create an "organizational chart" with 16 unions organized from low to high income and amalgamating in adjacent pairs (until there is only a single confederation: $c = 1$). At each level, amalgamated unions get the same flat-rate increase, but increases vary across bargaining areas.

Chapter 3

1. A related issue concerns the effects of historically rooted cleavages among unions that run *through* industrial sectors and even companies. The distinction between labor unions that are organized along craft lines and unions organized along industry lines has attracted particular attention, but organizational separation between blue- and white-collar unions and between unions with different political or religious orientations has also been deemed important. The logic behind these distinctions is that wage competition is more likely within a firm or an industry if workers in that firm or industry, by virtue of belonging to different unions, can partially externalize the costs of militancy to members of other unions. It is questionable, however, if these distinctions add any insights that are not already captured in figures for the number and relative size of unions. Whether unions are divided along skill lines, occupation, or political affiliation, the key theoretical issue is the effect of fragmentation (the opposite of concentration) on wage competition.

2. In Visser (1990) coordination is a component in what he calls the horizontal dimension of bargaining institutions.

3. This distinction between behavioral and institutional (or structural) aspects of corporatism goes back to Schmitter's seminal 1981 article. Since then it has been customary to distinguish between corporatist intermediation – referring to the structural, or institutional, aspects of corporatism – and corporatist concertation – referring to the process or behavior that is exhibited in different institutional settings.

4. This critique does not apply to Crouch (1993), who *does* rate the organizational strength of business. However, Crouch does not develop a composite index of centralization.

5. Such an approach has also been proposed in the study of political parties. For a discussion, see Laver and Schofield (1991: ch. 2, esp. 30–2).

6. This is particularly important for the leadership relationship between exposed and sheltered sectors as I discuss below.

7. See Laakso and Taagepera (1979) for the original definition applied to parties.

8. It can also be shown that $1/N$ is the probability that two randomly picked union members are from the same union (see Visser 1990: 172).

9. For example, if there are 100 equally sized bargaining units at the lowest level ($n = 100$), and all bargaining power is concentrated at this level ($w_l = 1$), then $C = .01$.

10. For example, if $C = .1$, then the implied number of bargaining units is 10.

11. The sources are listed in Appendix A.

12. I discuss stability and change in the organization of employers in greater detail in the analysis of individual countries.

13. He also discusses staffing and finances, although their significance for power over the bargaining process is less clear. I will discuss these aspects where it seems warranted in specific national cases.

14. Admittedly (and unavoidably), there is an element of discretion in the assignment of weights, but most intercoder discrepancies would center around whether particular bargaining rounds should be reclassified to adjacent cells, *not* whether the general location of bargaining systems in the authority hierarchy is reasonable. The problem of intercoder reliability is further reduced when the index is used to detect intertemporal changes *within* countries. A minor change in the assignment of weights would have negligible effects on the overall picture that emerges from such an analysis.

15. It should be noted, however, that complete union data are not always available, especially for smaller unions. In those cases the size of the missing unions is assumed to be identical. The procedure makes little difference for the overall number.

16. I thank Michael Wallerstein for clarifying this for me.

17. Austria is discussed in greater detail in Chapter 5.

18. This argument holds with greater force in the case of the predecessor to the ERM, the European currency "snake," which allowed for frequent and often large currency realignments. But even in the ERM, Weber has detected a "strong" and a "weak" currency bloc (the former organized around the German DM, the latter around the French franc) (Weber 1991).

19. Specifically, the index was created by partitioning the 1973–93 period into three subperiods of varying length. The rule for the partitioning was that within-period variance in growth rates should be minimized, while between-period variance should be maximized. No country exhibited more than three distinct subperiods, and in some cases there is little variance between the periods.

20. Yet there is some disagreement about the coding of the Japanese central bank in terms of independence. For example, in the Bade and Parkin index, Japan shares the third most independent bank with the United States.

21. The cross-country correlation between the CBI index and the combined I index is 0.96. Most of the discrepancy is due to Japan which, according to the hard currency index and most observers, has followed a monetarist strategy since the mid-1970s, yet scores low on most central bank independence indices. For the institutional key to restrictive monetary policies see Hutchison, Ito, and Cargil (1997: ch. 8) and Lincoln (1988: 179).

22. The countries are (in alphabetical order): Austria, Belgium, Britain, Canada, Denmark, Finland, France, Germany, Italy, Japan, Netherlands, Norway, Sweden, Switzerland, and the United States. The time periods are four-year intervals, except for one five-year period (1989–93). The periodization was prompted partly by the high degree of temporal stability in the monetary regime variable, and partly the uncertainty about the lag structure between change in bargaining institutions and outcomes. As it turns out, the reported results are actually very similar for the annual data, but the lagged dependent variable is close to exhibiting unit roots.

23. The analysis was tried on data based exclusively on national definitions ("commonly used definitions"), but it has little effect on the results.

24. The unemployment and inflation data were corrected for differences in period averages so that changes in the distribution of cases across categories do not affect the results.

25. To see this, note that the slope of the function is: $\delta U/\delta C = b_1 + 2b_2 C$. If C is very small ($C \rightarrow 0$), the slope is positive, which requires b_1 to be positive; if C is high, the slope of the hump-shaped curve would be negative, which requires b_2 to be negative.

26. OECD (1997a).

27. For example, R_2 is .96 when I is regressed on C, C^2, CI, and C^2I simultaneously.

28. The curves are the estimated equilibrium levels of unemployment for different levels of centralization (restricted to the range of actually observed values).

29. See Golden (1993) for a review of this debate.

30. Although this assumes retaliation to unilateral trade restrictions (otherwise it would be possible for a country to reduce imports while benefiting from growing export markets).

31. The same is the case if the partisanship variable is used in a conditional form that depends on the centralization of the bargaining system (as suggested by Lange and Garrett 1985).

32. Two observations – Italy 1982–84, and Switzerland 1973–75 – turned out to be outliers with high leverage on the results (both failed a Welsch distance test). In the Swiss case, the fact that all central bank indices ranked the Swiss central bank as the most independent, combined with the fact that the Swiss currency appreciated more rapidly than that of any other country, created such low inflation "expectations" that even though Switzerland exhibits the second lowest rate of inflation (it is slightly lower in Germany), it is still "too high." In the Italian case, the model correctly predicts the highest rate of inflation for the entire sample (5 percent higher than in France, the second most inflationary country), but actual inflation is higher still (by several percentage points). The reason is not clear, but it is unlikely that any model would capture this outlier and still offer a good fit for the rest of the sample. These two observations (out of a total of 75) were consequently excluded from the analysis.

33. In Iversen (1999) I reproduce these results using a number of different central bank indexes.

34. This is entirely consistent with the theory since otherwise the implication would be that centralized bargainers would accept more unemployment for the same level of inflation and wage equality.

35. If this sounds counterintuitive, the reader should go back to the theoretical chapter and check that it follows directly from the theoretical model.

36. This conclusion suggests that wage bargainers are not very predisposed to relax wage solidarism *even when* it may imply higher unemployment. Whether such zeal in the pursuit of solidarism can be attributed entirely to the political costs for union representatives in giving up wage shares, or whether there is a normative element to the story, is very difficult to say. The reason is that even "selfish" union representatives have an incentive to try to "look good" by justifying their actions with reference to union ideals. My own sense is that much of the "rigidity" in wage structures is due to the fact that union representatives find it politically expedient – relative to constituents, and occasionally also political authorities – to work for their "fair share." Certainly the effect of norms seems to strongly depend on the institutional form of bargaining – a finding that is entirely consistent with a simple bargaining argument.

37. Italy is a borderline case, but none of the substantive results reported below are affected by the inclusion of Italy.

38. The easiest way to explain the predicted signs is to differentiate equation 7 with respect to C and I. Taking the partial derivative with respect to C yields the following slope of the unemployment function: $b_1 + b_3 I$. If the value of I close to zero (i.e., the monetary regime is accommodating), then the theoretical argument implies that increasing centralization reduces unemployment and hence that b_1 should be *negative*. If the value of I is high (i.e., the monetary regime is nonaccommodating), then centralization should raise unemployment, which implies that b_3 must be *positive*. Similarly, taking the partial derivative with respect to I yields the following slope for the unemployment function: $b_2 + b_3 I$. If C is close to zero (i.e., bargaining is decentralized), then the theory implies that nonaccommodation would reduce unemployment and hence that the value of b_2 must be *negative*. Finally, if C is high (i.e., bargaining is centralized), nonaccommodation should raise unemployment which, as before, requires b_3 to be positive.

39. For a more detailed discussion, refer back to the theoretical argument in Chapter 2.

40. The index has the same range as the hard currency index.

41. The data are biyearly and from the *OECD Database on Unemployment Benefit Entitlements and Replacement Rates* (1997b). The compensation rate for the first year of unemployment is weighted twice that of the second or third year since the compensation rates for the first year of unemployment are likely to influence union wage policies more than rates for the second and third year. Compensation rates beyond this three-year time horizon are assumed not to affect the wage behavior of unions. In one case, Sweden, the data were adjusted to take into account that unemployed in this country can re-earn rights to full compensation by accepting a guaranteed employment offer in a labor market program. The low legal compensation rates for the second and third years are otherwise highly misleading.

42. This problem has a long history in the Marxist literature, where the controversial concept is the "relative autonomy" of the state (see Jessop 1982 for an extensive review of this literature).

43. It has to be noted, however, that what is referred to here as a monetary regime varies considerably in degree and character of institutionalization, if by institutionalization we mean a set of constraints on government policies that are politically difficult or costly to alter. I discuss this variation in the individual cases.

44. Union membership figures in Belgium are not recorded in any official statistics. At the confederal level figures are available for some years and have been estimated by interpolation for others. Considering the relative stability of fragmentation at this level, this poses no serious problems. Figures at the industry/sector level are based on information about the number of affiliated unions and the membership in unions with more than 100,000 members in 1985 (Hutsebaut 1987). For unions with less than 100,000 members, it has been assumed that membership is evenly distributed.

Chapter 4

1. For example, Grilli, Masciandaro, and Tabellini (1991) have argued that ". . . having an independent central bank is almost like having a free lunch; there are benefits but no apparent costs in terms of economic performance."

2. In the absence of strategic competence – as in the case of a finite multiplayer PD-game – all players have a dominant strategy, and their choices are unaffected by the choices of others.

3. Systems in which all bargaining takes place at the firm or plant level fall into the Liberal Market Economy category. Perhaps it would therefore be more appropriate to speak of centralized and "semicentralized" bargaining systems, but as long as the definitions are kept in mind it should be possible to avoid this more cumbersome terminology.

4. The term "Keynesian" is used here in the sense that policies can be flexibly adjusted to economic conditions in pursuit of full employment. It does *not* mean that macroeconomic policies are necessarily expansionary (especially not fiscal policies). The concept is developed further in Appendix A.

5. I discuss this "division of labor" in the institution-building process in more detail in the following chapter.

6. Principal–agent models suggest that there are two main ways in which the behavior of agents, in this case workers, can be made to comply with the interests of principals, in this case employers: either through a system of monitoring combined with sanctions for noncompliance, or through an appropriately designed reward system that tailors the incentives of agents (workers) to the goals of principals (employers). However, the efficient combination of monitoring/sanctions and reward/incentives will vary with the type of production.

7. This argument is related to the theory of "contested exchange" proposed by Samuel Bowles and Herbert Gintis (1990). They argue that workers who enjoy

some autonomy over their work situation will be tempted to shirk their responsibilities *unless* the remuneration of their work is sufficiently high that the risk of job loss makes hard work worthwhile (178–80). The more difficult it is to monitor individual effort, the higher the wage rate must be for the employer to generate a satisfactory level of work effort. Efficient wage structures will therefore become more inegalitarian to the extent that growing work autonomy varies between occupational groups and between firms. Mainstream new organizational economics implies a similar association between the costs of monitoring, worker autonomy over shop floor decisions, and the use of efficiency wages, group bonuses, and profit sharing. See Milgrom and Roberts (1992) for an excellent review of the literature.

The argument is also related to the work by David Soskice on training systems (1990b, 1992). Soskice argues that diversified quality production is highly dependent on firm-level investments in training and upgrading of skills. For such investments to pay off, the retention rate of trainees must be high, requiring employees be given positive incentives to stay with the firm providing the training. Firms pursuing diversified quality product strategies must therefore be allowed to reward employees for seniority and for acquiring firm-specific skills.

8. It should be noted, however, that in Swenson's account there is no consideration of macroeconomic policies, whereas these are essential to the current argument. Such policies do show up in various guises in Swenson's analysis – especially in the form of tight labor markets and booming construction industries.

9. The logic is discussed more fully in Appendix A, and Chapter 5 offers several empirical examples.

10. In terms of the model presented in Appendix A, one refinement is required to ensure a payoff structure for workers that is compatible with that in Figure 4.3: When policies are accommodating, workers and employers in the exposed sector must prefer centralization to decentralization. The justification for this specification is that, when distribution of wages is subject to intraconfederal bargaining, low-wage unions should not demand compression beyond the point where high-wage unions would want to abandon the centralized system (since this would mean an end to solidaristic policies).

11. In turn, the increase in integration has been attributed to a complex set of factors – including changes in communication technology and the rise of the Euro-dollar market – which combine with widespread liberalization of financial markets (partly through the auspices of the European Community) to make it very difficult for individual countries to control cross-border capital flows (see for example Goodman and Pauly 1993; Frieden 1991).

12. Nor was the importance of barriers to capital mobility ever doubted by Keynes: "The whole management of the domestic economy depends upon being free to have the appropriate rate of interest without reference to the rates prevailing elsewhere in the world" (quoted in Heillener 1994: 34).

13. Of course, people are still getting something for their money (public services). The point is that many of these could be provided for less through the private market.

14. Bargaining systems are divided into those with a strong element of peak-level

bargaining, those where bargaining is predominantly industry based, and those where bargaining predominantly takes place at the plant or firm level. The time constraint was imposed because a small deviation in the level of bargaining for one or two years probably does not constitute a significant change in the bargaining system. The use of this "counting rule," however, is not important for the overall results.

Chapter 5

1. The composition of imports and exports in the years after World War II has been used to explain the countercyclical behavior of the Danish economy. Thus, when world demand for relatively income-elastic manufactures increased during booms, the positive effect would be limited by the small size of the industrial sector and by increasing raw material prices. On the other hand, during recessions the economy would be relatively sheltered (Andersen and Åkerholm 1982).

2. The policies under the center-right government later became the basis for the claim by Mogens Glistrup – the flamboyant founder of the Progress Party – that Denmark had four social democratic parties (SD, the Conservatives, the Liberals, and the Radical Liberals) and only one liberal party (his own). No doubt, this charge struck a chord in the electorate, and descriptively it was quite on target.

3. Although, as mentioned above, it became more difficult during the 1960s to maintain interest rates far below the international level as a result of growing internationalization of capital markets.

4. Over time there has been a shift in the meaning of wage leveling in Sweden. As noted, the solidaristic wage policy was introduced at the 1951 LO Congress and meant essentially "equal pay for equal work." This market-conforming (or even market-perfecting) form of wage leveling was superseded in the 1960s by a more radical market-nonconforming interpretation emphasizing interoccupational (and intrafirm) leveling (Elvander 1988: 30–6, 256–68). In Denmark, solidaristic wage policies always had an interoccupational form because that form reflected a compromise between the main unions in a craft-based organizational structure.

5. Because the methods of calculation vary, the relative size of these figures must be taken with a grain of salt. Yet the trend toward considerably more wage equality through the late 1970s/early 1980s is indisputable.

6. The somewhat aberrant pattern for Danish manual work may (partly) be an artifact of the available data. Thus the index compares the evolution of wages for skilled men and unskilled women. Since gender equality, which is not directly comparable to the issue of interoccupational leveling, enters into the index, the measure may be somewhat unreliable. Equally important, the wage data are very aggregated and may conceal important intragroup changes. In figures published by the Ministry of Finance (Finansredegørelse 1993: 195), which uses a methodology that is more similar to that used for Sweden, the rise in wage dispersion appears to be considerably higher (about 6–7 percent). Still

there is consensus that the increase in wage dispersion in the LO area has been modest. Apart from various aspects of the bargaining system, the reason for this stability has to do with the structure of the unemployment benefit system. See below.

7. Wood (1994) has forcefully argued that the growing "dualism" of labor markets in the advanced industrialized countries is the result of intensified competition from the Newly Industrialized Countries. Although the thesis is consistent with the data and argument presented here, most assessments of Wood's uni-causal explanation find it irreconcilable with the magnitude of the observed changes. See Freeman (1995). Most likely, the rise in wage inequality is a function of both skill-biased shifts in technology and growing NIC trade. The weight accorded to these causal factors need not concern us here.

8. Andersen and Risager (1990) could not find a significant effect of intergender wage compression on wage drift. Perhaps this is due to the fact that leveling between the sexes mostly reflects an approximation of equal pay for equal work, not the more radical (and market nonconforming) interoccupational type of leveling.

9. Distributive conflicts also developed *within* the public sector, despite a collective interest in maintaining parity with private sector wage increases. See Due and Madsen (1988) for a thorough documentation in the case of Denmark, and Elvander (1988) in the case of Sweden.

10. Figures are based on United Nations, *World Investment Directory*, Vol. 3, pp. 155, 411.

11. For an analysis of the growing polarization of public and private sector interests in Sweden, see Swenson (1991b: 379–99).

12. After leaving the "snake" in 1976, the value of the Swedish krona was again pegged to a basket of foreign currencies weighted by relative trade shares. The Swedish government sovereignly decided de- or revaluations.

13. Theoretically, current account improvements from devaluations occur whenever the sum of the price elasticity of exports and imports exceeds one (the so-called Marshall–Lerner condition). According to most studies, elasticities on *both* imports and exports in Scandinavia vary between .8 and 2.2, thus easily satisfying this condition (Gylfason 1990: 187).

14. The actual operation of the "green money rates" and the so-called monetary compensation amounts is a great deal more complicated than I have implied, but the basic tendency for the system to disadvantage weak currency countries is relatively straightforward and well-documented, and this determined the position of farm interests on the exchange rate issue. See McNamara (1993) for a discussion of the operation of the Common Agricultural Policy.

15. In its 1980 report, for example, the bank charged that fiscal policies had been persistently too expansionary from the mid-1960s to the late 1970s and that the only solution would be "several years of severe restraint on increases in nominal incomes and public sector activities" combined with a monetary policy aimed at "holding the rate of inflation low and the foreign exchange conditions stable" (quoted in Johansen 1987: 168).

16. However, when Belgium and Denmark asked for another devaluation in early 1982, they met strong opposition from the other members.

17. The confusion and disillusion of the Social Democrats could almost be read off the face of Prime Minister Jørgensen, who had gone through a physical transformation akin to the change in appearance of Jimmy Carter during his presidency.

18. The new policy was outlined in the government's inauguration speech in 1982, in which the hard currency policy was singled out as a centerpiece in the plan: "The new government is firmly determined to recreate the balance in the Danish economy. The government has no intentions of devaluing the krone. Confidence in the value of the Danish krone at home and abroad is a good start for a new economic policy" [Inauguration speech, September 10, 1982; printed in the finance ministry's Financial Report (Finansredegørelse, October 1982: 81–2); my translation].

19. Using rates on 10-year government bonds and the GDP deflator.

20. The savings ratio fell from 25 to 18 percent between 1982 and 1986 (Finansredegørelse 1987).

21. In some respects the situation was therefore similar to the sheltered sector wage pressure that had precipitated the adoption of a more centralized bargaining system earlier in this century (see Swenson 1991a).

22. Signaling the shift, a government-sponsored report (Ministry of Labor 1980) declared inflation to be the most pressing economic problem.

23. It was called the Third Way strategy because it was supposed to stake out a different economic policy path than in either France or Britain (Pontusson 1994: 34).

24. With this new devaluation the Swedish krona had been devalued by 52 percent since 1976, compared to 24 percent for the Danish krone. See Gylfason (1990: 186), Gros and Thygesen (1992: 17), Hansen, Kjærsgaard, and Rosted (1991: 148–9).

25. Despite sometimes considerable wage drift, the correlation (Pearson's r) between bargained and actual wage increases is .97. Between bargained wage increases and wage drift the correlation is .75 (after log-transforming wage drift), while the correlation between bargained wage increases and wage compression is .77. A very similar pattern holds for Denmark, but the picture is complicated by the effect of an automatic cost-of-living compensation mechanism.

26. Swedish unit labor cost in manufacturing grew by an average annual rate of 11.3 percent during 1973–79 compared to 9.4 percent in Denmark, 5.3 percent in Austria, 5 percent in Germany, and 8.8 percent in the entire OECD.

27. A perverse example is the 1988 bargaining round where an agreement was first reached in the baking [sic] sector, which awarded wage increases that were totally unacceptable to the exposed industries. Another example is the decentralized 1984 bargaining round when public sector wages broke the proposed 6 percent pay norm.

28. Unit labor costs rose much faster than in the rest of OECD, and in 8 of the 10 years since 1980, hourly earnings in manufacturing increased faster in Sweden than in Denmark.

29. The concerns of cost-sensitive employers were addressed in 1989 when SAF agreed to return to centralized bargaining with LO (while VF and Metall conducted separate negotiations). The resulting two-year SAF–LO agreement

became pattern-setting for other bargaining areas and it thus resembled the traditional centralized system.

30. This policy option was first officially advocated in the 1985 economic report from the SNS. Here a distinction was made between a "price stabilization norm" and an "employment norm," and it was argued that the benefits of the former now outweighed the latter. For a dissenting opinion see Agell and Vredin (1991).

31. Overnight lending rates at one point reached 500 percent, but to no avail.

32. A beneficiary had to have been employed for only 26 weeks, and maximum duration of benefits was as long as 130 weeks (Hagen 1992: 152).

33. See Pedersen and Søndergaard (1989) for a review of the evidence and the literature.

34. With the collapse of the EMS exchange rate system, and the resulting explosion of speculative capital movements, the basis for the proposals (which were premised on Social Democratic votes) fell through.

35. The cartel encompasses employees organized in Metall, the white-collar union SIF, and the civil engineering affiliate of the SACO/SR, the academic and professional union federation.

36. Structural changes have been on LO's agenda since the early 1960s when a proposal to form nine industrial unions was adopted. Yet only in the 1980s was this proposal revived, although not implemented. A proposal to form five bargaining cartels was first adopted and then revoked at the 1991 LO congress. However, the formal process has largely been irrelevant to the actual restructuring that has taken place.

37. The practice has generated considerable tension between DI and smaller employer associations who have seen their own agreements vetoed by DA on several occasions (three times in the 1995 bargaining round, for example).

38. The so-called Wage Quota (*Lohnqoute*) provides the benchmark for determining wage increases. Basically, wage increases are permitted if they do not bring the functional division of income between capital and labor out of synch with macroeconomic requirements (Kindley 1992: 202, 243, 354).

39. Since all companies are compulsory members of the Federal Economic Chamber, which negotiates wages on behalf of employers, virtually all employees are covered by collective agreements.

40. Denmark and Sweden experienced an increase of about 10 percent in the same period.

41. As an effective coordinating institution, *Konzertierte Aktion* was killed in the aftermath of the 1974 wage-bargaining round when widespread strikes in the public sector triggered a wage explosion throughout the German economy.

42. The pace-setting role of the metalworking sector has other institutional supports that I discuss below.

43. This is my own tally based on the monthly monitoring of bargaining rounds contained in the *European Industrial Relations Review*.

44. In one bargaining round (1987) there were few apparent linkages between the agreements concluded in the public and private sectors (the latter patterned after the IG Metall agreement). On another occasion (1983) a company agreement at Volkswagen was first, while IG Chemie exerted some impact on

collective agreements in both this round and in 1985 (primarily in the area of time reductions for older workers and early retirement).

45. The term "German model" has many different connotations. When I use it I exclusively refer to the combination of an industry-based bargaining system and a restrictive monetary regime.

46. I use quotation marks around "crisis" because though Germany is experiencing an economic crisis, it is not so clear that it is also a crisis of German institutions.

47. In the metalworking sector, for example, collective agreements cover 13 different industries with a wide range of companies in terms of size, technology, and efficiency.

48. On the other hand, a common European currency would eliminate the problem that restrictive monetary policies erode competitiveness through currency appreciation. The EMS, however, already addressed this problem quite effectively.

Chapter 6

1. The basic model was first presented in Lange and Garrett (1985) and later refined in Alvarez, Garrett, and Lange (1991).

2. Garrett's interpretation of Denmark in the 1980s is interesting because it contrasts so sharply with my own. Whereas I see the conservative governments in the 1980s as the midwives for a new institutional equilibrium with improved employment performance, Garrett (1998a) contends that "conservative governments (rendering the political economy more incoherent) allowed unemployment to increase substantially in the 1980s" (p. 20).

3. For similar results, see Gordon (1987).

4. I say "probably" because we really do not have any data on such elasticities and, therefore, have to make guesses based on the nature of services.

5. See, for example, Goul-Andersen (1989, 1992) for Denmark, and Swenson (1991b) for Sweden.

6. These figures are based on my own calculations from Danish and Swedish election studies.

7. The alternative to public sector employment expansion, while pursuing full employment and wage equality, is to discourage labor market entry (especially of women) and encourage labor market exit (especially older workers). As discussed below, this is a strategy that has been followed in the Netherlands, Germany, and some other countries dominated by Christian democracy.

8. According to the OECD wage data the d1/d5 ratios went from 60 to 55 in Britain, and from 55 to 48 in the United States during the 1980s (OECD 1996).

9. The magnitude of the figures is slightly reduced by subtracting cyclical unemployment, defined as the difference between the actual unemployment rate and OECD's estimate of the NAIRU rate of unemployment (OECD 1996).

BIBLIOGRAPHY

Agell, Jonas and Anders Vredin. 1991. "Normer eller Diskretion i Stabiliserings-politikken?" *Ekonomisk Debatt*, 5.

Albåge, Lars-Gunnar. 1986. "Recent Trends in Collective Bargaining in Sweden. An Employer's View." *International Labor Review*, 125: 98–122.

Ahrne, Göran and Wallace Clement. 1994. "A New Regime?" In Wallace Clement and Rianne Mahon (Eds.), *Swedish Social Democracy*: Pp. 223–244. Toronto: Canadian Scholars' Press.

Al-Marhubi, Fahim and Thomas D. Willett. 1995. "The Anti Inflationary Influence of Corporatist Structures and Central Bank Independence: The Importance of the Hump Shaped Hypothesis." *Public Choice* 84: 153–162.

Alesina, Alberto. 1987 "Macroeconomic Policy in a Two-Party System as a Repeated Game." *Quarterly Journal of Economics* 103 (August): 651–78.

Alesina, Alberto and Jeffrey Sachs. 1988. "Political Parties and the Business Cycle in the United States, 1948–1984." *Journal of Money, Credit, and Banking* 20: 63–82.

Alesina, Alberto. 1989. "Inflation, Unemployment and Politics in Industrialized Democracies." *Economic Policy* 8: 58–98.

Alesina, Alberto and Allan Drazen. 1991. "Why Are Stabilizations Delayed?" *The American Economic Review* 81 (December): 1170–1188.

Alesina, Alberto and Nouriel Roubini. 1992. "Political Cycles in OECD Econo-mies." *Review of Economic Studies* 59 (October): 663–688.

Alesina, Alberto, Gerald Cohen, and Nouriel Roubini. 1992. "Macroeconomic Pol-icy and Elections in OECD Democracies." *Economics and Politics* 4: 1–30.

Alesina, Alberto and Vittorio Grilli. 1993. "The European Central Bank: Reshaping Monetary Policy in Europe." In Matthew Canzoneri, Vittorio Grilli, and Paul Masson (Eds.), *Establishing a Central Bank: Issues in Europe and Lessons from the United States*: Pp. 49–77. Cambridge: Cambridge University Press.

Alesina, Alberto, Nouriel Roubini, and Gerald Cohen. 1997. *Political Cycles and the Macroeconomy*. Cambridge: Cambridge University Press.

Alesina, Alberto and Lawrence H. Summers. 1993. "Bank Independence and Macroeconomic Performance: Some Comparative Evidence." *Journal of Money, Credit, and Banking* 25 (2): 151–62.

Alogoskoufis, G. and A. Manning. 1988. "On the Persistence of Unemployment." *Economic Policy* 7: 427–69.

Alvarez, Michael, Geoffrey Garrett, and Peter Lange. 1991. "Government Partisanship, Labor Organization, and Macroeconomic Performance." *American Political Science Review* 85: 539–56.

Alt, James. 1985. "Political Parties, World Demand, and Unemployment: Domestic and International Sources of Economic Activity." *American Political Science Review* 79: 1016–40.

Andersen, Torben M. and Ole Risager. 1990. "Wage Formation in Denmark." In Lars Calmfors (Ed.), *Wage Formation and Macroeconomic Policy in the Nordic Countries*: Pp.137–88. Stockholm: SNS Forlag.

Andersen, Palle S. and Johny Åkerholm.1982. "Scandinavia." In Andrea Boltho (Ed.), *The European Economy. Growth and Crisis*: Pp. 610–644. Oxford: Oxford University Press.

Andrews, David M. 1994. "Capital Mobility and Monetary Adjustment in Western Europe, 1973–1991." *Policy Sciences* 27 (4): 425–55.

Appelbaum, Eileen and Ronald Schettkat. 1994. "The End of Full Employment? On Economic Development in Industrialized Countries." *Intereconomics*: 122–30.

Appelbaum, Eileen and Ronald Schettkat. 1995. "Employment and Productivity in Industrialized Countries." *International Labour Review*, 134 (4–5): 605–23.

Backus, David and John Driffill. 1985. "Inflation and Reputation." *American Economic Review*, 75: 530–8.

Bade, Robin and Michael Parkin. 1982. "Central Bank Laws and Inflation – A Comparative Analysis." University of Western Ontario. Typescript.

Baglioni, Guido and Colin Crouch (Eds.). 1991. *European Industrial Relations: The Challenge of Flexibility*. London: Sage Publications.

Barro, Robert and David Gordon. 1983. "Rules, Discretion and Reputation in a Model of Monetary Policy." *Journal of Monetary Economics* 12 (July): 101–22.

Baumol, William J. 1967. "The Macroeconomics of Unbalanced Growth." *American Economic Review* 57 (3): 415–26.

Baumol William J. and William G. Bowen. 1966. *Performing Arts: The Economic Dilemma*. New York: The Twentieth Century Fund.

Bayoumi, Tamin. 1990. "Savings-Investment Correlations: Immobile Capital, Government Policy or Endogenous Behavior?" *IMF Staff Papers* 37: 360–87.

Beck, Nathaniel and Jonathan Katz. 1995. "What to Do (And Not to Do) with Time-Series Cross-Section Data."*American Political Science Review* 89 (September): 634–48.

Berthet-Bondet, Claude, Derek Blades, and Annie Pin. 1988. "The OECD Compatible Trade and Production Data Base." *OECD Working Papers*. Paris: Economic Statistics and National Accounts Division.

Bislev, Sven and Rafael Lindquist. 1992. "Sick-Leave Regimes: The Private-Public

Mix in Sickness Provision." In Jon Eivind Kolberg (Ed.), *The Study of Welfare State Regimes*: Pp.169–98. New York: M. E. Sharpe, Inc.

Bleaney, Michael. 1996. "Central Bank Independence, Wage-Bargaining Structure, and Macroeconomic Performance in OECD Countries." *Oxford Economic Papers* 48 (January): 20–38.

Block, Fred. 1977. "The Ruling Class Does Not Rule: Notes on the Marxist Theory of the State." *Socialist Review* 33: 6–28.

Bockelmann, Horst. 1979. "Experience of the Deutsche Bundesbank with Monetary Targets." In John E. Wadsworth and François Leonard de Juvigny (Eds.), *New Approaches in Monetary Policy*. Alphen aan den Rijn: Sijthoff and Noordhoff.

Borre, Ole. 1984. "Critical Electoral Change in Scandinavia." In R. J. Dalton, S. C. Flanagan, and P. A. Beck (Eds.), *Electoral Change in Advanced Industrial Democracies. Realignment or Dealignment?* Princeton: Princeton University Press.

Bowles, Samuel and Herbert Gintis. 1990. "Contested Exchange: New Microfoundations for the Political Economy of Capitalism." *Politics and Society* 18 (2): 165–222.

Brams, Stephen. 1990. *Negotiation Games*. New York: Routledge Press.

Brams, Stephen. 1994. *Theory of Moves*. Cambridge: Cambridge University Press.

Bruno, Michael and Jeffrey Sachs. 1985. *The Economics of Worldwide Stagflation*. Cambridge: Harvard University Press.

Buchanan, James. 1984. "Politics without Romance. A Sketch of Positive Public Choice Theory and Its Normative Implications." In James M. Buchanan and Robert D. Tollison (Eds), *The Theory of Public Choice – II*: Pp. 11–22. Ann Arbor: University of Michigan Press.

Buchanan, James M. and Robert D. Tollison (Eds). 1984. *The Theory of Public Choice – II*. Ann Arbor: University of Michigan Press.

Bundesamt für Statistik. *Statistisches Jahrbuch der Schweiz* [various years].

Burdekin, Richard D. K. and Thomas. D. Willett (1991). "Central Bank Reform: The Federal Reserve in International Perspective." *Public Budgeting and Financial Management*.

Calmfors, Lars. 1990. "Wage Formation and Macroeconomic Policy in the Nordic Countries: A Summary." In Lars Calmfors (Ed.), *Wage Formation and Macroeconomic Policy in the Nordic Countries*: Pp. 11–60. Uppsala: SNS Forlag.

Calmfors, Lars. 1993. "Lessons from the Macroeconomic Experience of Sweden." *European Journal of Political Economy* 9 (March): 25–72.

Calmfors, Lars and John Driffill. 1988. "Centralization of Wage Bargaining." *Economic Policy* 6 (April): 14–61.

Calmfors, Lars and Ragnar Nymoen. 1990. "Real Wage Adjustment and Employment Policies in the Nordic Countries." *Economic Policy*, 11 (October): 398–447.

Cameron, David. 1978. "The Expansion of the Public Economy: A Comparative Analysis." *American Political Science Review*, 72: 1243–61.

Cameron, David. 1984. "Social Democracy, Corporatism, Labor Quiescence, and the Representation of Economic Interest in Advanced Capitalist Society." In

John H. Goldthorpe (Ed.), *Order and Conflict in Contemporary Capitalism*: Pp. 143–178. New York: Oxford University Press.

Card, David and Richard B. Freeman (Eds.). 1993. *Small Differences that Matter: Labor Markets and Income Maintenance in Canada and the United States.* Chicago: University of Chicago Press.

Carlin, Wendy and David Soskice. 1990. *Macroeconomics and the Wage Bargain. A Modern Approach to Employment, Inflation and the Exchange Rate.* Oxford: Oxford University Press.

Castles, Francis and Peter Mair. 1984. "Left-Right Political Scales: Some 'Expert' Judgments." *European Journal of Political Research* 12: 73–88.

Clark, Terry N. and Seymour M. Lipset. 1991. "Are Social Classes Dying?" *International Sociology* 6 (4): 397–410.

Clark, Terry N., Seymour M. Lipset, and Michael Rempel 1993. "The Declining Political Significance of Class." *International Sociology* 8 (3): 292–316.

Collins, Susan. 1988. "Inflation and the European Monetary System." In Francesco Giavazzi, Stefano Micossi, and Marcus Miller (Eds.), *The European Monetary System*: Pp. 112–33. Cambridge: Cambridge University Press.

Cohen, Stephen S. and John Zysman. 1987. *Manufacturing Matters*. New York: Basic Books.

Cox, Gary W. 1987. "Electoral Equilibrium under Alternative Voting Institutions." *American Journal of Political Science* 31: 82–108.

Cox, Gary W. 1990. "Centripetal and Centrifugal Incentives in Electoral Systems." *American Journal of Political Science* 34: 903–35.

Crouch, Colin. 1985. "Conditions for Trade Union Wage Restraint." In Leon N. Lindberg and Charles S. Mair (Eds.), *The Politics of Inflation and Economic Stagnation: Theoretical Approaches and International Case Studies*: Pp. 105–139. Washington: Brookings Institution.

Crouch, Colin. 1990. "Trade Unions in the Exposed Sector: Their Influence on Neo-Corporatist Behavior." In Renato Brunetta and Carlo Dell'Aringa (Eds.), *Labor Relations and Economic Performance*: Pp. 68–91. London: Macmillan.

Crouch, Colin. 1993. *Industrial Relations and European State Traditions*. Oxford: Clarendon Press.

Cubitt, Robin P. 1992. "Monetary Policy Games and Private Sector Pre-Commitment." *Oxford Economic Papers* 44 (3): 513–30.

Cubitt, Robin P. 1995. "Corporatism, Monetary Policy and Macroeconomic Performance: A Simple Game Theoretic Analysis." *Scandinavian Journal of Economics* 97 (2): 245–59.

Cukierman, Alex. 1992. *Central Bank Strategy, Credibility, and Independence.* Cambridge: MIT Press.

Cukierman, Alex. 1997. "Central Bank Independence, Coordination of Wage Bargaining, Inflation and Unemployment." Typescript.

Cukierman, Alex and Allan H. Meltzer. 1986. "A Theory of Ambiguity, Credibility and Inflation under Discretion and Asymmetric Information." *Econometrica* 54 (September): 1099–1128.

Cukierman, Alex, Steven B. Webb, and Bilin Neyapti. 1992. "Measuring the Independence of Central Banks." *The World Bank Economic Review* 6: 353–98.

Cukierman, Alex and Francesco Lippi. 1998. "Central Bank Independence, Centralization of Wage Bargaining, Inflation and Unemployment." Center for Economic Policy Research Discussion Paper No. 1847.

Cusack, Thomas. 1991. "The Changing Contours of Government." WZB Discussion Paper, P91–304, Wissenschaftszentrum Berlin für Sozialforschung.

Cusack, Thomas. 1997. "Partisan Politics and Public Finance: Changes in Public Spending in the Industrialized Democracies, 1955–1989." *Public Choice* 91 (June): 375–95.

Cusack, Thomas and Geoffrey Garrett. 1993. "International Economic Change and the Politics of Government Spending." Wissenschaftszentrum Berlin für Sozialforschung. Typescript.

Danish Election Studies [various years]. Odense: Dansk Data Arkiv.

Danmarks Statistik. *Statistiske efterretninger* [various years].

Danmarks Statistik. *Statistisk Årbog* [various years].

Dansk Arbejdsgiverforening. *Lønstatistikken* [various years].

Danthine, Jean-Pierre and Jennifer Hunt. 1994. "Wage Bargaining Structure, Employment and Economic Integration." *Economic Journal* 104: 528–41.

Dell'Aringa, Carlo. 1990. "Industrial Relations and the Role of the State in EEC Countries." In Commission des Communautés Européennes, DG V, and London School of Economics, *Salaires et intégration Européenne*. Brussels: European Commission.

Dornbusch, Rudiger. 1976. "Expectations and Exchange Rate Dynamics." *Journal of Political Economy* 84: 1161–76.

Douglas, Mary. 1986. *How Institutions Think*. Syracuse, N.Y.: Syracuse University Press.

Downs, Anthony. 1957. *An Economic Theory of Democracy*. New York: Harper and Row.

Due, Jesper and Jørgen Steen Madsen. 1988. *Når der slås søm i: Overenskomstforhandlinger og Organisationsstruktur*. Copenhagen: Jurist og Økonomforbundets Forlag.

Due, Jesper, Jørgen Steen Madsen, Carsten Strøby Jensen, and Lars Kjerulf Petersen. 1994. *The Survival of the Danish Model. A Historical Sociological Analysis of the Danish System of Collective Bargaining*. Copenhagen: Jurist og Økonomforbundets Forlag.

Dølvik, Jon E. and Dag Stokland. 1992. "Norway: The 'Norwegian Model' in Transition." In Anthony Ferner and Richard Hyman (Eds.), *Industrial Relations in the New Europe*: Pp. 143–167. Oxford: Basil Blackwell Ltd.

Edgren, Gösta, Karl-Otto Faxén, and Clas-Erik Odhner. 1973. *Wage Formation and the Economy*. London: Allen and Unwin.

Elster, Jon. 1983. *Explaining Technical Change*. Cambridge: Cambridge University Press.

Elster, Jon. 1989. *The Cement of Society. A Study of Social Order*. Cambridge: Cambridge University Press.

Elvander, Nils. 1988. *Den Svenske Modellen: Lönforhandlingar och inkomstpolitik 1982–1986*. Stockholm: Allmanna Forlaget.

Elvander, Nils. 1990. "Incomes Policies in the Nordic Countries." *International Labor Review* 129 (1): 1–21.

Erickson, Christopher and Andrea Ichino. 1995. "Wage Differentials in Italy." In Richard Freeman and Lawrence Katz (Eds.), *Differences and Changes in Wage Structures*: Pp. 265–306. Chicago: University of Chicago Press.

Erixon, Lennart. 1984. "Den Svenska Modellen in Motgång. En Analys av Dess Effekter och Forandrade Forutsätninger under Perioden 1974–1984." *Nordish Tidsskrift for Politisk Ekonomi*, 15/16.

Esping-Andersen, Gøsta. 1985. *Markets Against Politics. The Social Democratic Road to Power*. Princeton: Princeton University Press.

Esping-Andersen, Gøsta. 1990. *The Three Worlds of Welfare Capitalism*. Princeton: Princeton University Press.

Esping-Andersen, Gøsta. 1993. *Changing Classes: Stratification and Mobility in Postindustrial Societies*. London: Sage.

Esping-Andersen, Gøsta. 1994. "The Eclipse of the Democratic Class Struggle? European Class Structures at Fin de Siècle." Paper presented to the study groups on Citizenship and Social Policies and State and Capitalism, Center for European Studies, Harvard University.

European Industrial Relations Review [various years].

Feldstein, Martin and Charles Horioka. 1980. "Domestic Savings and International Capital Flows." *The Economic Journal* 90: 314–29.

Ferner, Anthony and Richard Hyman (Eds). 1992. *Industrial Relations in the New Europe*. Oxford: Basil Blackwell Ltd.

Finansredegørelse. [various years]. Copenhagen: Budgetdepardementet.

Finland's Statistical Bureau. Suomen Tilastollinen Vuosikirja [various years].

Fischer, Stanley. 1977. "Long-Term Contracts, Rational Expectations, and the Optimal Money Supply Rule." *Journal of Political Economy* 85: 191–205.

Fischer, Stanley. 1987. "International Economic Policy Coordination." NBER Working Paper No. 2344.

Flanagan, Robert J. 1990. "Centralized and Decentralized Pay Determination in Nordic Countries." In Lars Calmfors (Ed.), *Wage Formation and Macroeconomic Policy in the Nordic Countries*: Pp. 395–416. Stockholm: SNS Forlag.

Flanagan, Robert J., David Soskice, and Lloyd Ulman. 1983. *Unionism, Economic Stabilization, and Incomes Policies: European Experience*. Washington D.C.: The Brookings Institution.

Frankel, Jeffrey. 1991. "Quantifying International Capital Mobility in the 1980s". In B. Douglas Bernheim and John B. Stoven (Eds.), *National Savings and Economic Performance*. Chicago: University of Chicago Press.

Frankel, Jeffrey. 1992. "Measuring International Capital Mobility: A Review." *American Economic Association Papers and Proceedings* 82 (2): 197–202.

Franzese, Robert J. 1994. "Central Bank Independence, Sectoral Interests, and the Wage Bargain." Center for European Studies Working Paper Series #56.

Franzese, Robert J. 1996. "The Politics of Overcommitment." Ph.D. Dissertation, Harvard University.

Freeman, Richard B. 1988. "Labor Market Institutions and Economic Performance." *Economic Policy* 6 (April): 62–80.

Freeman, Richard B. 1995. "Are Your Wages Set in Beijing?" *Journal of Economic Perspectives* 9 (3): 15–32.

Friedman, Milton. 1962. *Capitalism and Freedom*. Chicago: University of Chicago Press.

Friedman, Milton. 1968. "The Role of Monetary Policy." *American Economic Review* 58: 1–17.

Frieden, Jeffry. 1991. "Invested Interests: The Politics of National Economic Policies in a World of Global Finance". *International Organization* 45: 425–51.

Galenson, Walter. 1952. *The Danish System of Labor Relations. A Study in Industrial Peace*. Cambridge: Harvard University Press.

Garrett, Geoffrey. 1993. "The Politics of Structural Change: Swedish Social Democracy and Thatcherism in Comparative Perspective." *Comparative Political Studies* 25 (4): 521–49.

Garrett, Geoffrey. 1995. "Capital Mobility, Trade and the Domestic Politics of Economic Policy." *International Organization* 49 (4): 657–87.

Garrett, Geoffrey. 1998a. *Partisan Politics in the Global Economy*. New York: Cambridge University Press.

Garrett, Geoffrey. 1998b. "Global Markets and National Politics: Collision Course or Virtuous Circle?" *International Organization* 52 (4): 787–824.

Garrett, Geoffrey and Peter Lange. 1986. "Performance in a Hostile World: Economic Growth in Capitalist Democracies, 1974–1982." *World Politics* 38: 517–45.

Garrett, Geoffrey and Peter Lange. 1989. "Government Partisanship and Economic Performance: When and How Does 'Who Governs' Matter?" *Journal of Politics* 51: 676–93.

Garrett, Geoffrey and Peter Lange. 1991. "Political Responses to Interdependence: What's Left for the Left?" *International Organization* 44 (4): 539–64.

Garrett, Geoffrey and Peter Lange. 1995. "Internationalization, Institutions and Political Change." *International Organization* 49 (4): 627–655.

Garrett, Geoffrey and Christopher Way. 1995. "Unions, Governments and Central Banks in Strategic Interaction." Paper presented at the 1995 Annual Meetings of the American Political Science Association.

Garrett, Geoffrey and Christopher Way. 1999. "Public Sector Unions, Corporatism and Wage Determination." In Torben Iversen, Jonas Pontusson and David Soskice (Eds.), *Unions, Employers and Central Banks: Macroeconomic Coordination and Institutional Change in Social Market Economies*. Cambridge. Cambridge University Press [forthcoming].

Giavazzi, Francesco and Alberto Giovannini. 1989. *Limiting Exchange Rate Flexibility: The European Monetary System*. Cambridge: MIT Press.

Gibbons, Robert. 1992. *Game Theory for Applied Economics*. Princeton: Princeton University Press.

Glyn, Andrew. 1993. "Stability, Inegalitarianism and Stagnation: An Overview of the Advanced Capitalist Countries in the 1980s." Paper prepared for the WIDER Project on Savings, Investment and Finance.

Glyn, Andrew. 1997. "Low Pay and the Volume of Work." Corpus Christi College, Oxford. Typescript.

Glyn, Andrew. 1995. "The Assessment – Unemployment and Inequality." *Oxford Review of Economic Policy* 11 (Spring): 1–25.

Golden, Miriam. 1993. "The Dynamics of Trade Unionism and National Economic Performance." *American Political Science Review* 87 (June): 439–54.

Golden, Miriam and Michael Wallerstein. 1995. "Unions, Employers, and Collective Bargaining: A Report on Data for 16 Countries from 1950 to 1990." Paper presented at the 1995 Annual Meeting of the Midwest Political Science Association, Chicago.

Goodman, John B. 1992. *Monetary Sovereignty. The Politics of Central Banking in Western Europe.* Ithaca: Cornell University Press.

Goodman, John B. and Louis W. Pauly. 1993. "The Obsolescence of Capital Controls? Economic Management in an Age of Global Markets." *World Politics*, 46: 50–83.

Gordon, Robert J. 1987. "Productivity, Wages and Prices Inside and Outside of Manufacturing in the U.S., Japan, and Europe." *European Economic Review* 31: 685–739,

Goul-Andersen, Jørgen. 1989. "Social Klasse og Parti." In Jørgen Elklit and Ole Tonsgaard (Eds.), *To Folketingsvalg,* Aarhus: Politica.

Goul-Andersen, Jørgen. 1992. "The Decline of Class Voting Revisited." In Peter Gundelach and Karen Siune (Eds. *From Voters to Participants*): Pp. 91–107. Copenhagen: Politica.

Gourevitch, Peter. 1978. "The Second Image Reversed." *International Organization* 32 (Autumn): 881–912.

Gourevitch, Peter. 1986. *Politics in Hard Times.* Ithaca: Cornell University Press.

Grauwe, Paul De and Wim Vanhaverbeke. 1990. "Exchange Rate Experiences of the Small EMS Countries: Belgium, Denmark and the Netherlands." In Victor Argy and Paul De Grauwe (Eds.), *Choosing an Exchange Rate Regime: The Challenge for Smaller Industrial Countries*: Pp. 135–55. Washington D.C.: IMF.

Grilli, Vittorio, Donato Masciandaro, and Guido Tabellini. 1991. "Political and Monetary Institutions and Public Financial Policies in the Industrialized Countries." *Economic Policy* 13: 42–92.

Gros, Daniel and Niels Thygesen. 1992. *European Monetary Integration: From the European System to European Monetary Union.* London: Longman.

Gylfason, Thorvaldur. 1990. "Exchange Rate Policy, Inflation, and Unemployment: The Nordic EFTA Countries." In Victor Argy and Paul De Grauwe (Eds.), *Choosing an Exchange Rate Regime: The Challenge for Smaller Industrial Countries*: Pp. 163–92. Washington D.C.: IMF.

Hagen, Kåre. 1992. "The Interaction of Welfare States and Labor Markets: The Institutional Level." In Jon Eivind Kolberg (Ed.), *The Study of Welfare State Regimes*: Pp. 124–68. New York: M. E. Sharpe, Inc.

Hall, Peter A. 1986. *Governing the Economy.* Oxford: Oxford University Press.

Hall, Peter A. 1993. "Policy Paradigms, Social Learning, and the State." *Comparative Politics* 25: 275–296.

Hall, Peter A. 1994. "Central Bank Independence and Coordinated Wage Bargaining: Their Interaction in Germany and Europe." *German Politics and Society* 30 (Autumn): 1–23.

Hall, Peter A. and Robert Franzese. 1998. "Central Bank Independence, Coordinated Wage-Bargaining, and European Monetary Union." *International Organization* 52 (Summer): 505–35.

Hansen, Sven Aage. 1983. *Økonomisk Vækst i Danmark*. Copenhagen: Universitetsforlaget.

Hansen, Erik D., Kaj Kjærsgaard, and Jørgen Rosted. 1991. *Dansk Økonomisk Politik. Teorier og Erfaringer*. Copenhagen: Nyt Nordisk Forlag.

Hardin, Russell.1982. *Collective Action*. Baltimore: Johns Hopkins Press.

Havrilevski, Thomas and James Granato. 1993. "Determinants of Inflationary Performance: Corporatist Structures Vs. Central Bank Autonomy." *Public Choice* 76: 249–61.

Helleiner, Eric. 1994. *States and the Reemergence of Global Finance: From Bretton Woods to the 1990s*. Ithaca: Cornell University Press.

Hibbs, Douglas. 1977. "Political Parties and Macroeconomic Policy." *American Political Science Review*, 71: 1467–87.

Hibbs, Douglas and Håkan Locking. 1991. "Löneutjamning och Löneökningstakt under den Solidariske Lönepolitiken." *Ekonomisk Debatt* 19, 8: 653–64.

Hibbs, Douglas and Håkan Locking. 1996. "Wage Compression, Wage Drift, and Wage Inflation in Sweden." *Labour Economics*, 3 (September): 109–41.

Holmberg, Søren and Mikael Gilljam. 1987. *Väljare och valg i Sverige*. Stockholm: Bonniers.

Hotz-Hart, Beat. 1992. "Switzerland: Still as Smooth as Clockwork?" In Anthony Ferner and Richard Hyman (Eds.), *Industrial Relations in the New Europe*: Pp. 298–322. Oxford: Basil Blackwell Ltd.

Howell, Chris. 1992. *Regulating Labor*. Princeton: Princeton University Press.

Huber, Evelyne and John Stephens. 1998. "Internationalization and the Social Democratic Model." *Comparative Political Studies* 31 (June): 353–97.

Hutsebaut, Martin. 1987. *The Trade Union Movement in Belgium*. Brussels: European Trade Union Institute.

Hutchison, Michael, Takatoshi Ito, and Tom Cargil. 1997. *Political Economy of Japanese Monetary Policy*. Cambridge: MIT Press.

Hyman, Richard 1994 "Industrial Relations in Western Europe." *Industrial Relations* 33: 1–24.

IA/CO-Metal. 1991. *90's Lønsystem*. Copenhagen.

Ibsen, Flemming. 1990. "DELTA Projektet om Decentral Lønfastsættelse – en Præsentation." DELTA-Projektets Skriftserie Nr. 1. Aalborg: AUC.

Ibsen, Flemming and Henning Jørgensen. 1979. *Fagbevægelse og Stat*. Copenhagen: Gyldendal.

Ibsen, Flemming and Jørgen Stamhus. 1993a. *Fra Central til Decentral Lønfastsættelse*. Copenhagen: Jurist-og Økonomforbundets Forlag.

Ibsen, Flemming and Jørgen Stamhus. 1993b. *Decentral Lønfastsættelse. En Virksomhedsundersøgelse*. Copenhagen: Jurist- og Økonomforbundets Forlag.

IMF. *International Financial Statistics Yearbook* [various years].

Inglehart, Ronald. 1977. *The Silent Revolution: Changing Values and Political Styles among Western Publics*. Princeton: Princeton University Press

Inglehart, Donald. 1987. "Value Change in Industrial Society." *American Political Science Review* 81: 1289–1303.

Inglehart, Donald. 1990. *Culture Shift in Advanced Industrial Society*. Princeton: Princeton University Press.

Iversen, Torben. 1996. "Power, Flexibility and the Breakdown of Centralized Wage Bargaining: The Cases of Denmark and Sweden in Comparative Perspective." *Comparative Politics* 28 (July): 399–436.

Iversen, Torben. 1994. "Political Leadership and Representation in West European Democracies: A Test of Three Models of Voting." *American Journal of Political Science* 38: 45–74.

Iversen, Torben. 1999. "The Political Economy of Inflation: Bargaining Structure or Central Bank Independence." *Public Choice* [forthcoming].

Iversen, Torben and Thomas Cusack. 1998. "The Causes of Welfare State Expansion: Deindustrialization or Trade Openness?" Paper presented at the 1998 Annual Meetings of the American Political Science Association, Sheraton Boston (September 3–6).

Iversen, Torben and Anne Wren. 1998. "Equality, Employment, and Budgetary Restraint: The Trilemma of the Service Economy." *World Politics* 50 (July): 507–46.

Iversen, Torben, Jonas Pontusson and David Soskice. 1999. *Unions, Employers and Central Banks: Wage Bargaining and Macroeconomic Regimes in an Integrating Europe*. Cambridge University Press [forthcoming].

Jaccard, James, Robert Turrisi, and Choi Wan. 1990. *Interaction Effects in Multiple Regression*. London: Sage.

Jackman, Robert. 1986. "Elections and the Democratic Class Struggle." *World Politics* 39: 122–46.

Jackman, Robert. 1987. "The Politics of Economic Growth in Industrialized Democracies, 1974–1980." *Journal of Politics* 49: 242–56.

Jackman, Robert. 1989. "The Politics of Economic Growth, Once Again." *Journal of Politics* 51: 646–61.

Japan Labor Bulletin. Tokyo: Japan Institute of Labour.

Judge, G., W. E. Griffiths, H. Lutkepohl, and T. Lee. 1982. *On the Theory and Practice of Econometrics*. New York: John Wiley.

Jessop, Bob. 1982. *The Capitalist State*. Oxford: Martin Robertson.

Johansen, Hans Christian. 1987. *Danish Economy in the Twentieth Century*. London: Croom Helm.

Judge, George G., William E. Griffiths, Helmut Lutkepohl, and T. C. Lee. 1982. *Introduction to the Theory and Practice of Econometrics*. New York: John Wiley.

Kangas, Olli and Joakim Palme. 1992. "The Private-Public Mix in Pension Policy." In Jon Eivind Kolberg (Ed.), *The Study of Welfare State Regimes*: Pp. 199–238. New York: M. E. Sharpe, Inc.

Katz, Harry. 1993. "The Decentralization of Collective Bargaining." *Industrial and Labor Relations Review* 47: 3–22.

Katzenstein, Peter. 1984. *Corporatism and Change: Austria, Switzerland, and the Politics of Industry*. Ithaca: Cornell University Press.

Katzenstein, Peter. 1985. *Small States in World Markets*. Ithaca: Cornell University Press.

Kindley, Randall. 1992. "Rational Organization: Labor's Role in the Emergence and Reproduction of Austrian Neo-Corporatism." Ph.D. Dissertation, Department of Political Science, Duke University.

Kitschelt, Herbert. 1988. "Left Libertarian Parties. Explaining Innovation in Competitive Party Systems." *World Politics* 40: 194–234.

Kitschelt, Herbert. 1989. *The Logics of Party Formation*. Ithaca: Cornell University Press.

Kitschelt, Herbert. 1994. *The Transformation of European Social Democracy*. Cambridge: Cambridge University Press.

Kitschelt, Herbert. 1995. *The Radical Right in Western Europe*. Ann Arbor: Michigan University Press.

Herbert Kitschelt, Gary Marks, Peter Lange, and John Stephens (Eds.). 1999. *Continuity and Change in Contemporary Capitalism*. New York: Cambridge University Press.

Kjellberg, Anders. 1992. "Sweden: Can the Model Survive?" In Anthony Ferner and Richard Hyman (Eds.), *Industrial Relations in the New Europe*: Pp. 88–142. Oxford: Basil Blackwell Ltd.

Kjellberg, Anders. 1983. *Facklig Organisering i Tolv Lander*. Lund: Arkiv forlag.

Kloosterman, Robert C. 1994. "Three Worlds of Welfare Capitalism? The Welfare State and the Post-Industrial Trajectory in the Netherlands after 1980." *West European Politics* 17, 4.

Knight, Jack. 1992. *Institutions and Social Conflict*. Cambridge: Cambridge University Press.

Kogut, Bruce, Gordon Walker and Jaideep Anand. 1996. "Agency and Institutions: Organizational Form and National Divergences in Diversification Behavior." Typescript.

Kolberg, Jon E. and Gøsta Esping-Andersen. 1992. "Welfare States and Employment Regimes." In Jon Eivind Kolberg (Ed.), *The Study of Welfare State Regimes*: Pp. 3–36. New York: M. E. Sharpe, Inc.

Korpi, Walter. 1978. *The Working Class in Welfare Capitalism: Work, Unions and Politics in Sweden*. London: Routledge and Kegan Paul.

Korpi, Walter. 1983. *The Democratic Class Struggle*. London: Routledge & Kegan Paul.

Korpi, Walter and Michael Shalev. 1979. "Strikes, Industrial Relations and Class Conflict in Capitalist Societies." *British Journal of Sociology* 30: 164–87.

Kristensen, Ole P. 1982. *Væksten i de Offentlige Udgifter*. Copenhagen: Økonom og Juristforbundets forlag.

Kristiansen, Michael, Thomas Larsen, and Michael Ulveman. 1992. *Poul Schlüter, En Biografi*. Copenhagen: Spektrum.

Kydland, Finn E. and Edward C. Prescott. 1977. "Rules Rather than Discretion: The Inconsistency of Optimal Plans." *Journal of Political Economy* 85 (June): 473–86.

Laakso, Markku and Rein Taagapera. 1979. "Effective Number of Parties: A Measure with Application to West Europe." *Comparative Political Studies* 12: 3–29.

Lange, Peter. 1984. "Unions, Workers, and Wage Regulation: The Rational Bases of Consent." In John Goldthorpe (Ed.), *Order and Conflict in Contemporary Capitalism*: Pp. 98–123. Oxford: Clarendon Press.

Lange, Peter and Geoffrey Garrett. 1985. "The Politics of Growth: Strategic Interaction and Economic Performance in the Advanced Industrial Democracies, 1974–1980." *Journal of Politics* 47: 792–827.

Lange, Peter and Geoffrey Garrett. 1987. "The Politics of Growth Reconsidered." *Journal of Politics* 49: 257–74.

Lange, Peter, Michael Wallerstein, and Miriam Golden. 1995. "The End of Corporatism?" In Sanford Jacoby (Ed.), *The Workers of Nations: Industrial Relations in a Global Economy*: Pp. 76–100. New York: Oxford University Press.

Laver, Michael and Norman Schofield. 1991. *Multiparty Government. The Politics of Coalition in Europe*. Oxford: Oxford University Press.

Layard, Richard, Stephen Nickell, and Richard Jackman. 1991. *Unemployment. Macroeconomic Performance and the Labour Market.* Oxford: Oxford University Press.

Leamer, Edward E. 1996. "A Trade Economist's View of U.S. Wages and 'Globalization'." Paper presented at the Political Economy of European Integration Study Group Meeting, University of California at Berkeley, January 1996.

Lewis-Beck, Michael S. 1988. *Economics and Elections: The Major Western Democracies*. Ann Arbor: University of Michigan Press.

Lijphart, Arend. 1968. *The Politics of Accommodation*. Berkeley: University of California Press.

Lincoln, Edward. 1988. *Japan Facing Economic Maturity*. Washington D.C.: Brookings Institution.

Lindbeck, Assar. 1979. *Inflation. Global, International and National Aspects*. Louvain: Presses Universitaires de Louvain.

Lipset, S. M. & S. Rokkan. 1967. "Cleavage Structures, Party Systems, and Voter Alignments: An Introduction." In Lipset and Rokkan (Eds.), *Party Systems and Voter Alignments*: Pp. 1–64. New York: Free Press.

Lohmann, Susanne. 1992. "Optimal of Commitment in Monetary Policy: Credibility versus Flexibility." *The American Economic Review* 82 (March): 273–86.

Lucas, Robert E. 1972. "Expectations and the Neutrality of Money." *Journal of Economic Theory*, 4 (April): 103–24.

Lucas, Robert E. 1976. "Econometric Policy Evaluation: A Critique." In Karl Brunner and Allan H. Meltzer (Eds.), *The Phillips Curve and Labor Markets*: Pp. 19–46. Amsterdam: North-Holland.

Mahnkopf, Birgit. 1993. "The Impact of Unification on the German System of Industrial Relations." WZB Discussion Paper, FS-1–102, Wissenschaftszentrum Berlin für Sozialforschung.

Mahon, Rianne. 1991. "From Solidaristic Wages to Solidaristic Work: A Post-Fordist Historical Compromise for Sweden?" *Economic and Industrial Democracy* 12: 295–325.

Mankiw, Gregory N.. 1990. "A Quick Refresher Course in Macroeconomics." *Journal of Economic Literature*, 28 (December): 1645–60.

Marin, B. 1983. "Organising Interests by Interest Associations: Organizational Prerequisites of Co-Operation in Austria." *International Political Science Review*, 4: 197–216.

Markovits, Andrei S. 1986. *The Politics of West German Trade Unions*. Cambridge: Cambridge University Press.

Marks, Gary. 1986. "Neocorporatism and Incomes Policy in Western Europe and North America." *Comparative Politics* 18 (April): 253–77.

Martin, Andrew. 1979. "The Dynamics of Change in a Keynesian Political Economy: The Swedish Case and Its Implications." In Colin Crouch (Ed.), *State and Economy in Contemporary Capitalism*: Pp. 88–121. New York: St. Martin's Press.

Martin, Andrew. 1984. "Trade Unions in Sweden: Strategic Responses to Change and Crisis". In Peter Gourevitch, Andrew Martin, George Ross, Christopher Allen, Stephen Bornstein, and Andrei Markovits, *Unions and Economic Crisis: Britain, West Germany, and Sweden*: Pp. 190–359. London: Allen and Unwin.

Martin, Andrew. 1985. "Wages, Profits, and Investments in Sweden." In Leon N. Lindberg and Charles S. Mair (Eds.), *The Politics of Inflation and Economic Stagnation*: Pp. 403–466. Washington D.C.: The Brookings Institution.

McNamara, Kathleen. 1993. "Systems Effects and the European Community." In Robert Jervis and Jack Snyder (Eds.), *Coping with Complexity in the International System*: Pp. 303–327. Boulder: Westview Press.

Melitz, Jacques. 1988. "Monetary Discipline and Cooperation in the EMS: A Synthesis." In Francesco Giavazzi, Stefano Micossi, and Marcus Miller (Eds.)., *The European Monetary System*: Pp. 51–79. Cambridge: Cambridge University Press.

Metall. 1985. *Det Goda Arbetet*. Stockholm: Metall.

Metall. 1989. *Solidarisk Arbetspolitik for det goda arbetet*. Stockholm: Metall.

Midttun, Atle. 1990. "Norway in the 1980s: Competitive Adaptation or Structural Crisis? A Comment on Katzenstein's Small-State/ Flexible-Adjustment Thesis." *Scandinavian Political Studies* 13 (4): 307–26.

Milgrom, Paul R. and John Roberts. 1992. *Economics, Organization, and Management*. Englewood Cliffs: Prentice Hall.

Ministry of Labor. 1980. *Langtidsutredningen*. Copenhagen.

Mjøset, Lars. 1986. *Norden Dagen Derpå*. Oslo: Universitetsforlaget.

Mjøset, Lars. 1989. "Norway's Full-Employment Oil Economy – Flexible Adjustment or Paralysing Rigidities?" *Scandinavian Political Studies* 12 (4): 313–41.

Moene, Karl O., Michael Wallerstein (and Michael Hoel). 1993. "Bargaining Structure and Economic Performance." In Robert Flanagan, Karl O. Moene, and Michael Wallerstein (Eds.), *Trade Union Behavior, Pay-Bargaining, and Economic Performance*: Pp. 63–131. Oxford: Clarendon Press.

Moses, Jonathan. 1994. "Abdication from National Policy Autonomy: What's Left to Leave?" *Politics and Society* 22: 125–48.

Nannestad, Peter. 1991. *Danish Design or British Decease? Danish Economic Crisis Policy in Comparative Perspective*. Århus: Aarhus University Press.

Nickell, Stephen. 1997. "Unemployment and Labor Market Rigidities: Europe versus North America." *Journal of Economic Perspectives* 11 (3): 55–74.

Nielsen, Klaus and Ove K. Pedersen. "Is Small Still Flexible? – An Evaluation of Recent Trends in Danish Politics." *Scandinavian Political Studies* 12 (4): 343–71.

Nordhaus, William D. 1975. "The Political Business Cycle." *Review of Economic Studies* 42: 169–90.

Notersman, Ton. 1992. "The Abdication from National Policy Autonomy. Why the Macroeconomic Policy Regime Has Become So Unfavorable to Labor." *Politics and Society*, 21: 133–67.

Nørby Johansen, L. 1986. "Denmark." In Peter Flora (Ed.), *Growth to Limits*, Vol. 1: Pp. 293–381. New York: de Gruyter.

OECD. *OECD Economic Outlook*. Paris (various years).

OECD. 1979. *OECD Economic Surveys: Denmark*. Paris.

OECD. 1987. *OECD Economic Surveys: Austria*. Paris.

OECD. 1987b. *OECD Economic Surveys: Norway*. Paris.

OECD. 1988. *OECD Compatible Trade and Production Data Base*.

OECD. 1991. *OECD Employment Outlook*. Paris: OECD.

OECD. 1992. *OECD Economic Surveys: Sweden*. Paris.

OECD. 1992b. *OECD Economic Surveys: Norway*. Paris.

OECD. 1992c. *OECD Economic Outlook: Historical Statistics*. Paris.

OECD. 1992d. *From Higher Education to Employment*. Paris.

OECD. 1993. *The OECD International Sectoral Data Base*. Paris: OECD.

OECD. 1994. *The OECD Jobs Study: Evidence and Explanations*. Paris: OECD.

OECD. 1996. *OECD Employment Outlook*. Paris: OECD.

OECD. 1997. "Economic Performance and the Structure of Collective Bargaining." *OECD Employment Outlook*. Paris: OECD.

OECD. 1997b. *The OECD Database on Unemployment Benefit Entitlements and Replacement Rates*. Paris: OECD.

OECD. 1997b. *International Sectoral Data Base*. Paris: OECD.

OECD. 1998. *OECD Economic Outlook*. Paris: OECD.

Olson, Mancur. 1965. *The Logic of Collective Action*. Cambridge: Harvard University Press.

Olson, Mancur. 1982. *The Rise and Decline of Nations*. New Haven: Yale University Press.

Osborne, Martin and Ariel Rubinstein. 1991. *Bargaining and Markets*. Boston: Academic Press.

ÖGB. *Tatigkeitsbericht* [various years].

Paloheimo, Heikki.1984. "Pluralism, Corporatism and the Distributive Conflict in Developed Capitalist Countries." *Scandinavian Political Studies* 9: 65–80.

Panitch, Leo. 1979. "The Development of Corporatism in Liberal Democracies." In Philippe Schmitter and Gerhard Lehmbruch (Eds.), *Trend Toward Corporatist Intermediation*: Pp. 119–146. Beverly Hills: Sage.

Panitch, Leo. 1981. "Trade Unions and the Capitalist State." *New Left Review* 125: 21–43.

Pedersen, Ove K. 1992. "Stabilitet og Forandring i Overenskomstsystemet på det Private Arbejdsmarked 1985–1991." *Økonomi og Politik* 65: 30–41.

Pedersen, Peder J. and Jørgen Søndergaard. 1989. "Det inflationære danske arbejdsmarked." *Nationaløkonomisk Tidsskrift*, 1, 1–20.

Pempel, T. J. 1982. *Policy and Politics in Japan: Creative Conservatism*. Philadelphia: Temple University Press.

Phelps, Edmund S. 1970. "Money-Wage Dynamics and Labour Market Equilibrium." In Edmund S. Phelps et al. (Eds.), *Microeconomic Foundations of Employment and Inflation Theory*: Pp. 124–166. New York: W. W. Norton.

Pierson, Paul. 1996. "The New Politics of the Welfare State." *World Politics* 48 (2): 143–179.

Pierson, Paul. 1996. "The Path to European Integration: A Historical Institutionalist Analysis." *Comparative Political Studies* 29 (2): 123–63.

Piore, Michael. 1986. "Perspectives on Labor Market Flexibility." *Industrial Relations* 25: 146–67.

Piore, Michael J. and Charles F. Sabel. 1984. *The Second Industrial Divide, Possibilities for Prosperity*. New York: Basic Books.

Pontusson, Jonas. 1992a. *The Limits of Social Democracy*. Ithaca: Cornell University Press.

Pontusson, Jonas. 1992b. "At the End of the Third Road: Swedish Social Democracy in Crisis." *Politics and Society* 20 (3): 305–332.

Pontusson, Jonas. 1994. "Trade Unions and the Representation of Worker Interests in Corporatist Political Economies." Paper presented to the Annual Meeting of the American Political Science Association, New York, September 1994.

Pontusson, Jonas. 1999. "Labor Market Institutions and Wage Distribution in Sweden and Austria." In Torben Iversen, Jonas Pontusson, and David Soskice (Eds.), *Unions, Employers and Central Banks: Macroeconomic Coordination and Institutional Change in Social Market Economies*. Cambridge: Cambridge University Press [forthcoming].

Pontusson, Jonas and Peter Swenson. 1996. "Labor Markets, Production Strategies, and Wage Bargaining Institutions: The Swedish Employer Offensive in Comparative Perspective." *Comparative Political Studies* 29 (April): 223–50.

Porter, Michael E. 1990. *The Competitive Advantage of Nations*. New York: The Free Press.

Posen, Adam. 1995. "Declarations Are Not Enough. Financial Sector Sources of Central Bank Independence." *NBER Macroeconomics Annual*: 253–74.

Przeworski, Adam and Michael Wallerstein. 1982. "The Structure of Class Conflict in Democratic Capitalist Societies." *American Political Science Review* 76: 215–38.

Przeworski, Adam and John Sprague. 1986. *Paper Stones*. Chicago: University of Chicago Press.

Purcell, John. 1995. "Ideology and the End of Institutional Industrial Relations." In Franz Traxler and Colin Crouch (Eds.), *Organized Industrial Relations in Europe*: Pp. 101–120. Aldershot: Avebury.

Rabinowitz, George and Stuart E. Macdonald. 1989. "A Directional Theory of Issue Voting." *American Political Science Review* 83: 93–121.

Rae, Douglas. 1967. *The Political Consequences of Electoral Laws*. New Haven: Yale University Press.

Ragin, Charles. 1987. *The Comparative Method: Moving Beyond Qualitative and Quantitative Strategies*. Berkeley: University of California Press.

Rama, Martin. 1994. "Bargaining Structure and Economic Performance in the Open Economy." *European Economic Review* 38: 403–15.

Regeringens Budgetförslag. [various years]. Stockholm: Budgetdepartementet

Regini, Marino. 1984. "The Conditions for Political Exchange: How Concertation Emerged and Collapsed in Italy and Great Britain." In John Goldthorpe

(Ed.), *Order and Conflict in Contemporary Capitalism*: Pp. 124– 42. Oxford: Clarendon Press.

Rehn, Gösta. 1985. "Swedish Active Labor Market Policy: Retrospect and Prospect." *Industrial Relations* 24: 62–89.

Robertson, John. 1990. "Transaction-Cost Economics and Cross-National Patterns of Industrial Conflict: A Comparative Institutional Analysis." *American Journal of Political Science* 34: 153–90.

Rodrik, Dani. 1997. *Has Globalization Gone Too Far?* Washington D.C.: Institute for International Economics.

Rogoff, Kenneth. 1985. "The Optimal Degree of Commitment to an Intermediate Monetary Target." *Quarterly Journal of Economics* 100: 1169–89.

Rogoff, Kenneth. 1990. "Equilibrium Political Budget Cycles." *American Economic Review* 25: 21–36.

Rogoff, Kenneth and Anne Sibert. 1988. "Equilibrium Political Business Cycles." *Review of Economic Studies* 55 (January): 1–16.

Rothstein, Bo. 1992. "Labor-Market Institutions and Working-Class Strength." In Sven Steinmo, Kathleen Thelen, and Frank Longstreth (Eds.), *Structuring Politics*: Pp. 33–56. New York: Cambridge University Press.

Rowthorn, Robert. 1977. "Conflict, Inflation and Money." *Cambridge Journal of Economics* 1: 215–39.

Rowthorn, Robert. 1992. "Corporatism and Labour Market Performance." In Jukka Pekkarinen, Matti Pohjola, and Bob Rowthorn (Eds.), *Social Corporatism*: Pp. 44–81. Oxford: Clarendon Press.

Rueda, David and Jonas Pontusson. 1997. "Wage Inequality and Varieties of Capitalism." Institute for European Studies Working Paper, Cornell University.

Sabel, Charles. 1989. "Flexible Specialization and the Re-emergence of Regional Economies." In Paul Hist and Jonathon Zeitlin (Eds.), *Reversing Industrial Decline*. Oxford: Berg.

Sabel, Charles. 1991. "Moebius-Strip Organizations and Open Labor Markets: Some Consequences of the Reintegration of Conception and Execution in a Volatile Economy." In Pierre Bourdieu and James Coleman (Eds.), *Social Theory for a Changing Society*: Pp. 23–54. Boulder: Westview.

Sabel, Charles. 1993. "Learning by Monitoring: The Institutions of Economic Development." In Neil Smelser and Richard Swedberg (Eds), *Handbook of Economic Sociology*. Princeton: Princeton University Press.

Salter, W. E. G. 1960. *Productivity and Technical Change*. Cambridge: Cambridge University Press.

Sargent, Thomas and Neil Wallace. 1975. " 'Rational Expectations,' the Optimal Monetary Instrument, and the Optimal Money Supply Rule." *Journal of Political Economy* 83 (April): 241–54.

Sartori, Giovanni. 1970. "Concept Misformation in Comparative Politics." *American Political Science Review* 64: 1033–53.

Scharpf, Fritz. 1984. "Economic and Institutional Constraints on Full-Employment Strategies: Sweden, Austria and West Germany (1973–82)." In John H. Goldthorpe (Ed.), *Order and Conflict in Contemporary Capitalism*: Pp. 257–90. New York: Oxford University Press.

Scharpf, Fritz. 1991. *Crisis and Choice in European Social Democracy*. Ithaca: Cornell University Press.

Scheuer, Steen. 1990. "Struktur og Forhandling. Aspekter af Fagbevægelsens Strukturudvikling i Efterkrigstiden: Ektern Struktur, Medlemstal Samt Strukturen i de Kollektive Overenskomstforhandlinger." In Svend Aage Andersen (Ed.), *Årbog for Abejderbevægelsens Historie, 20*: Pp. 17–79. Copenhagen: Selskabet for Abejderbevægelsens Historie.

Scheuer, Steen. 1991. "Leaders and Laggards: Who Goes First in Bargaining Rounds?" Leverhulme Public Lecture, University of Warwick.

Scheuer, Steen. 1992. "Denmark: Return to Decentralization." In Anthony Ferner and Richard Hyman (Eds.), *Industrial Relations in the New Europe*: Pp. 298–322. Oxford: Basil Blackwell Ltd.

Schmid, Gunther. 1997. "The Dutch Employment Miracle? A Comparison of Employment Systems in the Netherlands and Germany." *Wissenschaftszentrum Berlin Working Paper Series 202*.

Schmidt, Manfred G. 1982. "Does Corporatism Matter? Economic Crisis, Politics and Rates of Unemployment in Capitalist Democracies in the 1970s." In Gerhard Lehmbruch and Philippe C. Schmitter (Eds.), *Patterns of Corporatist Policy-Making*: Pp. 237–258. London: Sage.

Schmidt, Manfred G. 1983. "The Welfare State and the Economy in Periods of Economic Crisis: A Comparative Study of Twenty-Three OECD Nations." *European Journal of Political Research* 11: 1–26.

Schmitter, Philippe. 1974. "Still a Century of Corporatism?" *Review of Politics* 36 (1): 85–131.

Schmitter, Philippe. 1981. "Interest Intermediation and Regime Governability in Contemporary Western Europe and North America." In Suzanne Berger (Ed.), *Organizing Interests in Western Europe: Pluralism, Corporatism, and the Transformation of Politics*: Pp. 287–327. Cambridge: Cambridge University Press.

Schmitter, Philippe. 1985. "Neo-corporatism and the State." In Wyn Grant (Ed.), *The Political Economy of Corporatism*: Pp. 32–62. Macmillan.

Schwartz, Herman. 1994. "Small States in Big Trouble: State Reorganization in Australia, Denmark, New Zealand, and Sweden in the 1980s." *World Politics* 46: 527–555..

Schwerin, Don S. 1980. "The Limits of Organization as a Response to Wage-Price Problems." In Richard Rose (Ed.), *Challenge to Governance: Studies in Overloaded Polities*: Pp. 73–106. Beverly Hills : Sage Publications.

Shepsle, Kenneth A. and R. N. Cohen. 1990. "Multiparty Competition, Entry, and Entry Deterrence in Spatial Models of Elections." In James M. Enelow and Melvin J. Hinich (Eds.), *Advances in the Spatial Theory of Voting*: Pp. 12–45. Cambridge: Cambridge University Press.

Shirai, Taishiro. 1987. "Japan." In John P. Windmuller, *Collective Bargaining in Industrialized Market Economies: A Reappraisal*: Pp. 242–52. Geneva: ILO.

Silvia, Stephen. 1999. "Between Pattern and Participation: German Industrial Relations since 1980." In Andrew Martin and, George Ross (Eds.), *The Brave*

New World of European Labor: European Trade Unions at the Millennium. New York and Oxford: Berghahn Books [forthcoming].

Simmons, Beth. 1999. "The Internationalization of Capital." In Herbert Kitschelt, Peter Lange, Gary Marks, and John Stephens (Eds.), *Continuity and Change in Contemporary Capitalism*: Pp. 36–69. Cambridge: Cambridge University Press.

Skott, Peter. 1997. "Stagflationary Consequences of Prudent Monetary Policy in a Unionized Economy." *Oxford Economic Papers* 49: 607–22.

Smith, Nina and Niels Westergård-Nielsen. 1988. "Udviklingen i Lønforskelle Mellem den Offentlige og Private Sektor." *Nationaløkonomisk Tidsskift*, 1: 13–30.

Sociale Maandstatistiek. [Various years].

Sociaal-economische Maandstatistiek. [Various years].

Solow, Robert M. and John B. Taylor (Eds.). 1998. *Inflation, Unemployment and Monetary Policy*. Cambridge, MA: MIT Press.

Soskice, David. 1990a. "Wage Determination: The Changing Role of Institutions in Advanced Industrialized Countries." *Oxford Review of Economic Policy* 6: 36–61.

Soskice, David. 1990b. "The Institutional Infrastructure for International Competitiveness: A Comparative Analysis of the UK and Germany." Paper presented at the International Economic Association Conference on the New Europe.

Soskice, David. 1992. "The German Apprenticeship System: Reconciling Markets and Institutions." In Lisa Lynch (Ed.), *International Comparisons of Private Sector Training*. NBER Conference Volume. Chicago: University of Chicago Press.

Soskice, David. 1994. "Innovation Strategies of Companies: A Comparative Institutional Explanation of Cross-Country Differences." Typescript.

Soskice, David. 1999. "Macroeconomic Analysis and the Political Economy of Unemployment." In Torben Iversen, Jonas Pontusson, and David Soskice (Eds.), *Unions, Employers and Central Banks: Macroeconomic Coordination and Institutional Change in Social Market Economies*. Cambridge: Cambridge University Press [forthcoming].

Soskice, David and Torben Iversen. 1998. "Multiple Wage Bargaining systems in the Single European Currency Area." *Oxford Review of Economic Policy* 14 (3): 110–124.

Soskice, David and Torben Iversen. 1999. "The Non Neutrality of Monetary Policy with Large Price or Wage Setters." *Quarterly Journal of Economics*, forthcoming.

Standing, Guy. 1988. *Unemployment and Labour Market Flexibility: Sweden*. Geneva: International Labour Office.

Statistisches Bundesamt. Statistisches Jahrbuck für die Bundesrepublik Deutschland [various years].

Statistiska Centralbyrån. *Statistisk Årsbok i Sverige* [various years].

Statistiska Centralbyrån. 1987. "Løneutvecklingen 1973–1985." *Information om Arbetsmarknaden*. Stockholm: SCB.

Statistiska Centralbyrån. 1987. *Løner i Sverige 1982–1989*. Stockholm: SCB.

Statistisk Sentralbyrå. *Statistisk Årbok* (Norway) [various years].

Steigum, Erling. 1984. "Oljan och den Norska Ekonomin." *Economisk Debatt* 6: 375–85.

Stephens, John D. 1979. *The Transition from Capitalism to Socialism*. London: Macmillan Press Ltd.

Stephens, John D. 1994. "The Scandinavian Welfare States: Development and Crisis." Paper prepared for delivery at the World Congress of Sociology, Bielefeld, Germany, July 18–23.

Stimson, James A. 1985. "Regression in Space and Time: A Statistical Essay." *American Journal of Political Science* 29 (November): 914–47.

Streeck, Wolfgang. 1984. "Neo-Corporatist Industrial Relations and the Economic Crisis in West Germany." In John H. Goldthorpe (Ed.), *Order and Conflict in Contemporary Capitalism*: Pp. 291–314. Oxford: Clarendon Press.

Streeck, Wolfgang. 1991. "On the Institutional Conditions of Diversified Quality Production." In Egon Matzner and Wolfgang Streeck (Eds.), *Beoynd Keynesianism: The Socio-Economics of Production and Full Employment*: Pp. 2-61. Aldershot: Edward Elgar.

Streeck, Wolfgang. 1994. "Pay Restraint Without Incomes Policy: Institutionalized Monetarism and Industrial Unionism in Germany." In Ronald Dore, Robert Boyer and Zoe Mars, *The Return of Incomes Policy*. London: Pinter Publishers.

Streeck, Wolfgang.1997. "German Capitalism: Does It Exist ? Can It Survive ?" in Colin Crouch and Wolfgang Streeck (Eds.), *Political Economy and Modern Capitalism: Mapping Convergence and Diversity*. London: Sage

Suomen tilastollinen vuosikirja (Statistical Yearbook of Finland). Helsinki: Tilastokeskus.

Svensson, Lars E. O. 1996. "Optimum Inflation Targets, 'Conservative' Central Banks, and Linear Inflation Contracts." National Bureau of Economic Research, Working Paper No. 5251.

Swedish Election Studies [various years]. Göteborg: Dataarkiv I.

Swenson, Peter 1989. *Fair Shares: Unions, Pay, and Politics in Sweden and Germany*. Cornell: Cornell University Press.

Swenson, Peter. 1991a. "Bringing Capital Back In, or Social Democracy Reconsidered: Employer Power, Cross Class Alliances, and Centralization of Industrial Relations in Denmark and Sweden." *World Politics* 43 (4): 513–44.

Swenson, Peter, 1991b. "Labor and the Limits of the Welfare State." *Comparative Politics* 23 (4): 379–99.

Thelen, Kathleen. 1991. *Union of Parts*. Ithaca: Cornell University Press.

Thelen, Kathleen. 1993. "West European Labor in Transition." *World Politics* 46: 23–49.

Thelen, Kathleen. 1999. "Why German Employers Cannot Bring Themselves to Abandon the German Model." In Torben Iversen, Jonas Pontusson, and David Soskice (Eds.), *Unions, Employers and Central Banks: Macroeconomic Coordination and Institutional Change in Social Market Economies*. Cambridge: Cambridge University Press [forthcoming].

Thygesen, Niels. 1979. "Exchange-rate Experiences and Policies of Small Countries:

Some European Examples of the 1970s." Princeton Essays in International Finance, 136, International Finance Section, Princeton.

Traxler, Franz. 1992. "Austria." In Anthony Ferner and Richard Hyman (Eds.), *Industrial Relations in the New Europe*: Pp. 270–97. Oxford: Basil Blackwell.

Tsebelis, George. 1990. *Nested Games. Rational Choice in Comparative Politics*. Berkeley: University of California Press.

United Nations. 1993. *World Investment Directory*, Vol. 3. New York: United Nations.

Uusitalo, Paavo. 1984. "Monetarism, Keynesianism and the Institutional Status of Central Banks." *Acta Sociologica* 27.

van Kersbergen, Kees. 1995. *Social Capitalism: A Study of Christian Democracy and the Welfare State*. London: Routledge.

Vesterø Jensen, Carsten. 1985. *Det Tvedelte Pensionssystem*. Roskilde: Forlaget Samfundsøkonomi og Planlægning.

Visser, Jelle. 1989. *European Trade Unions in Figures*. Deventer/Netherlands: Kluwer Law and Taxation Publishers.

Visser, Jelle. 1990. *In Search of Inclusive Unionism*. Boston: Kluwer Law and Taxation Publishers.

Visser, Jelle. 1996. "Unionization Trends Revisited. University of Amsterdam." Typescript.

Visser, Jelle and Hemerijck, Anton. 1997. *A Dutch Miracle. Job Growth, Welfare Reform and Corporatism in The Netherlands*. Amsterdam: Amsterdam University Press.

Wallerstein, Michael. 1990. "Centralized Bargaining and Wage Restraint." *American Journal of Political Science* 34: 982–1004.

Wallerstein, Michael, Miriam Golden, and Peter Lange. 1997. "Unions, Employers' Associations, and Wage-Setting Institutions in Northern and Central Europe, 1950–1992." *Industrial Labor Relations Review* 50 (3): 379–401.

Walterskirchen, Edwald. 1990. *Unemployment and Labour Market Flexibility: Austria*. Geneva: International Labour Office.

Weber, Axel. 1991. "European Economic and Monetary Union and Asymmetries and Adjustment Problems in the European Monetary System: Some Empirical Evidence." *European Economy* (Special Edition):187–207.

Wildavsky, Aaron B. 1986. *Budgeting: A Comparative Theory of Budgetary Processes*. New Brunswick: Transaction Books.

Williamson, Oliver E. 1985. *The Economic Institutions of Capitalism: Firms, Markets, Relational Contracting*. New York: Free Press.

Windmuller, John P. 1981. "Concentration Trends in Union Structure: An International Comparison." *Industrial and Labour Relations Review* 35.

Windmuller, John P. 1987. *Collective Bargaining in Industrialized Market Economies: A Reappraisal*. Geneva: ILO.

Windolf, Paul. 1989. "Productivity Coalitions and the Future of European Corporatism." *Industrial Relations* 28: 1–20.

Wood, Andrian.1994. *North-South Trade, Employment and Inequality: Changing Fortunes in a Skill-Driven World*. Oxford: Oxford University Press.

Woolley, John T. 1984. *Monetary Politics. The Federal Reserve and the Politics of Monetary Policy*. Cambridge: Cambridge University Press.

Zetterberg, Johnny. 1988. "Lønstruktur i Privat og Offentlig Sektor." Forsknings-
    rapport Nr. 26. Stockholm: FIEF.
Zysman, John. 1983. *Governments, Markets and Growth: Financial Systems and the Politics
    of Industrial Change*. Ithaca: Cornell University Press.

INDEX

Alesina, Alberto, 20, 57–8, 79
Austria: absence of wage solidarism, 152–4; centralization of bargaining (1960–1995), 8–10; elite autonomy in, 153; inflation and unemployment in, 152; wage inequality in, 72

Bade, Robin, 56–8
bargaining: under accommodating and nonaccommodating monetary rules, 2–5; centralization in OECD countries (1973–1993), 6–8; concatenation rule in Denmark, 122; decentralization under EMU, 82; decentralized bargaining in model of, 24–8; effective number of units for, 53; EFO model implications, 26; intraorganizational, 29; levels of, 48; Nash bargaining theory, 29; potential coordination under EMU, 82; Rubinstein's theory, 181n28; union-monetary authority two-stage game, 39–46; with unions of unequal size, 52–3; weighting in construction of centralization index, 54–5, 83–5 See also bargaining institutions; bargaining system; individual countries
bargaining institutions: centralization of authority, 48–51; evolution in OECD countries (1973–1993), 8–10; interaction with monetary regime and economic performance, 2–5, 23–38; measuring decentralization of authority, 50–

1; in neo-corporatist theory, 23–4 See also individual countries
bargaining institutions, centralized: association with accommodating monetary policy, 77–8, 81, 100–103, 106–8; in Austria, 8–10, 151–5; in bargaining effects model, 67–74; in Denmark, 121–2, 124, 126, 138–9; employment performance with, 47; institutional design with, 93; in neo-corporatism, 24; in Norway, 156–9; relation to unemployment, 32–8, 67–9; in Sweden, 123–4, 126, 142–3; union strategies under, 28–32, 47
bargaining institutions, decentralized: in bargaining effects model, 67–74; under EMU, 82; monetary policy under, 47; relation to unemployment, 67–9; union strategies under, 24–6, 47
bargaining institutions, intermediately centralized: association with nonaccommodating monetary policy, 77–8, 81, 100–3; in bargaining effects model, 67, 71–2; in Germany, 8–10, 159–64; in neo-corporatism, 24; union strategies under, 26–8, 47
bargaining system: in bargaining effects model, 60–74; centralized system as coalition, 29; choice for social democracy, 171; decentralized system in economic policies-wage strategies model, 111–15; of LMEs, 74; social wage in,